Clive Oxenden   *Paul Seligson*
Christina Latham-Koenig

English File

student's book

2

OXFORD UNIVERSITY PRESS

Paul Seligson and Clive Oxenden are the original co-authors of
English File 1 (pub. 1996) and *English File 2* (pub. 1997).

Verbs and tenses

1 Verb *be* (present)

+   −

I'm	I'm **not**		
You**'re**	You **aren't**		
He She It	**'s**	He She It	**isn't**	American. very old.
We You They	**'re**	We You They	**aren't**	

Are you tired?
Yes, **I am**.

?   ✓✗ Short answers

Am I **Are** you **Is** it	French?	Yes, I **am**. / No, I'm **not**. Yes, we **are**. / No, we **aren't**. Yes, it **is**. / No, it **isn't**.

Contractions 'm = am   're = are   's = is
                 aren't = are not   isn't = is not

☐ *you* (singular) and *you* (plural) are the same.
☐ Put the verb before the subject in ⟨?⟩.
   She's Japanese. → **Is she** Japanese?
☐ Don't use contractions in ⟨+⟩ short answers.
   Are you tired? Yes, I **am**. NOT ~~Yes, I'm.~~
☐ Remember:
   you **aren't** / he **isn't**, etc. OR you**'re** not / he**'s** not, etc.
☐ Use *be* to say your age.
   How old **are** you? I**'m** 29 (years old). NOT ~~I have 29.~~

2 Verb *be* (past)

+   −

I He She It	**was**	**wasn't**	
You We They	**were**	**weren't**	at home yesterday.

Where **were** you yesterday?
I **was** ill.

?   ✓✗

Was **Were**	he you	at work yesterday?	Yes, he **was**. / No, he **wasn't**. Yes, we **were**. / No, we **weren't**.

Contractions wasn't = was not   weren't = were not

☐ Present to past:
   am / is → **was** are → **were**

3 Present continuous

+   −

I'm	I'm **not**		
You**'re**	You **aren't**		
He She It	**'s**	He She It	**isn't**	studying. working.
We They	**'re**	We They	**aren't**	

I'm studying for an exam.

?   ✓✗

Am **Are** **Is**	I they she	studying?	Yes, I **am**. / No, I'm **not**. Yes, they **are**. / No, they **aren't**. Yes, she **is**. / No, she **isn't**.

☐ Use the present continuous (*be* + (verb)-*ing*) for things happening now / at the moment.
☐ Remember the spelling rules for -*ing*.

Infinitive	(Verb)-*ing*	Spelling
cook try	cook**ing** try**ing**	+ ing
danc*e*	danc**ing**	*e̸* + ing
swim	swim**ming**	1 vowel + 1 consonant → double consonant

4 Present simple

+   −

I You We They	work.	I You We They	don't	
He She It	work**s**.	He She It	doesn't	work.

?   ✓✗

Do you work?	Yes, I **do**. / No, I **don't**.
Does he work?	Yes, he **does**. / No, he **doesn't**.

Contractions don't = do not   doesn't = does not

☐ Use the present simple for things you do every day / week / year.
☐ Remember the *s* for ⟨+⟩ *he / she / it*.
☐ Use the auxiliary in short answers.
   Yes, I **do**. NOT ~~Yes, I work.~~

+ he / she / it			Spelling
He	reads	*The Times.*	+ s
The film	finish**es**	at 9.00.	+ es
She	stud**ies**	biology.	consonant + y → ies

☐ The spelling rules for third person singular are the same as for plural nouns. ⓖ ◀◀ 18 *p.6*

Pronunciation: *-s / -es* ending

voiced	/z/	play**s**, live**s**
unvoiced	/s/	cook**s**, like**s**
es after ch, sh, s, x, z	/ɪz/	watch**es**, miss**es**

☐ Remember the pronunciation of the *s / es* ending for *he / she / it.*

Word order in questions

Question	**A**uxiliary	**S**ubject	**I**nfinitive
	Do	**you**	**smoke?**
	Does	she	speak English?
Where	**do**	**they**	**live?**
What time	does	David	finish work?

☐ Remember word order **ASI** and **QASI**.
☐ Compare the present simple with the present continuous.

I usually **work** in an office but today **I'm working** at home.
= simple (every day)   = continuous (now)

5 Imperatives

Don't open the door!

Infinitive	+ **Imperative**	− **Imperative**
open	**Open** the door.	**Don't open** the door.

☐ There are only two forms, one + and one −. Singular and plural are the same.

6 Past simple

+

Regular verbs		
I You He She It We They	**lived** in Turkey in 1980. **worked** for IBM. **stopped** working at 12.00. **studied** law.	+ d + ed y̶ → ied
Irregular verbs		
I You He She It We They	**went** to Greece in 1995. **had** a meeting yesterday. **saw** a film last night.	

☐ Use the past simple to talk about finished actions in the past.
☐ The past simple is the same for all persons.
☐ Learn the past simple of irregular verbs *p.141*. Remember, verbs are only irregular in +.

−	I You He etc.	**didn't**	live in the USA. go to New York. see the film.
?	**Did**	you	live in the USA?
✓✗	Yes, I **did**. / No, I **didn't**.		

Contraction didn't = did not

☐ Use *did* + infinitive in ? and *didn't* + infinitive in −. NOT ~~Did you saw the film? / I didn't went.~~
☐ Present to past:
   do / does → **did**
☐ Remember word order **ASI** and **QASI** is the same as the present simple. ⓖ ◀◀ 4 *p.3*

What **did** you **do** last night?
I **went** to an all-night party.

Pronunciation: regular verbs

voiced	/d/	play**ed**, live**d**
unvoiced	/t/	cook**ed**, like**d**
ending in t and d	/ɪd/	wait**ed**, land**ed**

☐ Remember the pronunciation of the *ed* ending.

3

7 Future: (be) going to ...

+		-			
I'm		I'm not			
You're		You aren't			
He She It	's	He She It	isn't	going to	buy a fax next week.
We They	're	We They	aren't		

?				✓ ✗
Am Are Is	I you he	going to	buy a car?	Yes, I am. / No, I'm not. Yes, we are. / No, we aren't. Yes, he is. / No, he isn't.

Plan

We**'re going to buy** a house.

Prediction

It**'s going to** snow.

☐ Use *be going to* + infinitive to talk about future plans and predictions.

8 Time expressions (past and future)

He went to Hungary	**yesterday.** **last** night / week / month / year. two years **ago.**
She's going to buy a flat	**today / tonight / tomorrow.** **next** week / month / year.

☐ Time expressions go at the beginning / end of a sentence.
Yesterday he went to Hungary.

☐ Don't use *the*. NOT ~~the last year / the next week~~

9 can / can't (ability, requests, and permission)

Help! I **can't** swim.

+ and -			?			✓ ✗		
I You He etc.	**can can't**	swim.	**Can**	I you he etc.	swim?	Yes, No,	I you he etc.	**can. can't.**

Contraction can't = cannot

☐ Use *can* for:

ability	**Can** you drive? / I **can't** cook.
requests	**Can** you open the window, please?
asking permission	**Can** I use your pen?

☐ *can / can't* is the same for all persons.

☐ Use *can / can't* + infinitive. NOT ~~I can to swim.~~

10 have (got) and have

We **haven't got** a car or a house, but we**'ve got** each other.

have got (possession)

+			-			
I You We They	've	got a car.	I You We They	haven't got	a fax.
He She It	's		He She It	hasn't got	

?		✓ ✗
Have you **got** any children? **Has** he **got** a flat?		Yes, I **have**. / No, I **haven't**. Yes, he **has**. / No, he **hasn't**.

Contractions 've = have haven't = have not
's = has   hasn't = has not

☐ Use *have got* for possession.

☐ Always contract *have / has not* in + and -.

☐ Don't use *do / does* with *have got*. NOT ~~Do you have got a car?~~

have (possession and activities)

I **have** a fax. He **doesn't have** a video. **Do** you **have** any children? **Does** he **have** a flat?	Yes, I **do**. / No, I **don't**. Yes, he **does**. / No, he **doesn't**.

☐ Use *have* for possession too.

☐ Don't contract *have* without *got*. NOT ~~I've a car.~~

☐ Use *do / don't* and *does / doesn't* in ? and -.

I **have** a shower every day. **Do** you usually **have** breakfast?

☐ Use *have* NOT *have got* for activities.
NOT ~~I've got a shower every day.~~
BUT in the past tense, you use *had / didn't have* for possessions and activities.
  + I **had** breakfast / a car.
  - I **didn't have** breakfast / a car.
  ? **Did** you **have** breakfast / a car?
Remember, NOT ~~I had got a car.~~

G
◄◄

11 *There is / are* and *There was / were*

Singular			Plural	
Present				
+	There's	an apple. a banana.	There **are**	some sweets.
−	There **isn't**		There **aren't**	any biscuits.
?	**Is** there		**Are** there	
✓✗	Yes, there **is**. No, there **isn't**.		Yes, there **are**. No, there **aren't**.	
Past				
+	There **was**	an apple. a banana.	There **were**	some sweets.
−	There **wasn't**		There **weren't**	any biscuits.
?	**Was** there		**Were** there	
✓✗	Yes, there **was**. No, there **wasn't**.		Yes, there **were**. No, there **weren't**.	

- ☐ Present to past: There is / are … → There **was** / **were** …
- ☐ Remember how to use *some* / *any*. Ⓖ◀◀18 *p.6*

12 *like / love / hate* + (verb)-*ing*

I **hate** cook**ing**.
Do you **like** fly**ing**?
She **loves** danc**ing**.

I hate fly**ing**.

- ☐ Use verb + *-ing* after *like*, *love*, and *hate*.
- ☐ Remember the spelling rules for *-ing*. Ⓖ◀◀3 *p.2*
- ☐ Use *it / them*, etc. in place of a noun after *like / love / hate*.
  What do you think of opera?
  I like **it**. NOT ~~I like.~~

Adjectives, adverbs, etc.

13 Adjectives

Singular	It's She's	a **new** car. **French**.
Plural	They're We're	**new** cars. **French**.

This is my **new** car.

- ☐ Adjectives go before nouns.
  NOT ~~It's a car new.~~
- ☐ Adjectives don't change.
  NOT ~~They're news cars. / We're Frenchs.~~
- ☐ Use an adjective to describe a noun.
- ☐ Use *very / quite / not very* with adjectives.

I'm	**very** **quite** **not very**	hungry.

Possessive adjectives

This is **our** house.

Pronoun	Adjective	
I	**my**	**My** name's James.
you	**your**	What's **your** address?
he	**his**	**His** wife is Chinese.
she	**her**	**Her** name's Ana.
it	**its**	London is famous for **its** parks.
we	**our**	This is a photo of **our** children.
they	**their**	**Their** names are Jim and Alice.

- ☐ Use *his* for a man, *her* for a woman.
  John's a teacher. **His** wife's a teacher too.
  NOT ~~Her wife …~~
- ☐ Possessive adjectives don't change.
  our children NOT ~~ours children~~

Comparative adjectives

	Adjective	Comparative	Spelling
1	cheap	cheap**er**	1 syllable: + er
2	big	big**ger**	1 vowel +1 consonant: double consonant
3	easy	eas**ier**	consonant + y: *y* → ier
4	expensive	**more** expensive	2 or more syllables: more / less + adjective
5	good bad	**better** **worse**	irregular

- ☐ Use comparative adjectives + *than* to compare things and people.

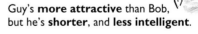

Guy's **more attractive** than Bob, but he's **shorter**, and **less intelligent**.

14 Adverbs
Adverbs of manner

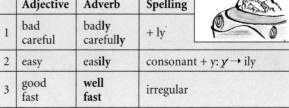

She drives very **slowly**.

	Adjective	Adverb	Spelling
1	bad careful	bad**ly** careful**ly**	+ ly
2	easy	eas**ily**	consonant + y: *y* → ily
3	good fast	**well** **fast**	irregular

- ☐ Use an adverb to describe a verb.
- ☐ Adverbs usually go after the verb / verb + noun.
  I speak Portuguese **quite well**.

Adverbs of frequency

I **never** have breakfast and I'm **always** tired.

I You We They	always usually / normally often sometimes	have	breakfast.
He She	hardly ever never	has	

☐ Adverbs of frequency go before the main verb but after the verb *be*. NOT <s>I always am tired.</s>

☐ Don't use a — verb with *never*.
I **never** have breakfast. NOT <s>I don't never have breakfast.</s>

Expressions of frequency

How often do you go to the cinema?			
I go to the cinema	(about)	once twice three times four times	a
			day. week. month. year.
		every	

☐ Expressions of frequency usually go at the end of a sentence.

15 Articles
a / an (indefinite article)

It's	a	credit card.
	an	umbrella.

☐ Use *an* before vowels (a, e, i, o, u).
☐ Use *a / an* + a singular noun.
☐ Use *a / an* to say what something is.
☐ Use *a / an* + jobs.
I'm **an** architect. NOT <s>I'm architect.</s>
☐ Remember:
When 'u' = /juː/ use *a*: **a** university
When 'h' is silent, use *an*: **an** hour.

the (definite article)

Open **the** door! We never go to **the** theatre.

What time does **the** film start?

☐ Use *the* to talk about specific things and places.
☐ Remember, before vowels, *the* /ðə/ = /ðiː/.
the /ðiː/ eighth

Zero article

I like music, cats, football, Italian food, and swimming. Life is wonderful.

☐ Don't use *the* when you talk about things in general.
NOT <s>I like the music and the cats.</s>

☐ Don't use *the* with:
time expressions
next week, **last** year, etc. NOT <s>the last week</s>
have + meals
We **have lunch** at 1.00. NOT <s>the lunch</s>
go + home
I **go home** at 5.30. NOT <s>the home</s>
go / get + *to school / work / bed*
Go **to bed**. NOT <s>the bed</s>
start / finish + *work / school*
She **starts work** at 9.00. NOT <s>the work</s>.

16 Capital letters

I'm **A**ndres.   I'm **M**exican.   I speak **S**panish and **E**nglish. **P**aris   **B**razil   **T**uesday   **D**ecember

☐ Use CAPITAL letters for the pronoun *I*, names, nationalities, languages, cities, countries, days, and months.

17 it

What time is **it**? **It**'s 5.00. **It**'s late. **It**'s 11th June. **It**'s Friday. **It**'s very hot today. **It** rained last night.

☐ Use *it* for times, dates, and the weather.

18 Nouns
Singular and plural

Singular	Plural	Spelling
a book a key	books keys	+ s
a watch a fax	watches faxes	+es (after ch, sh, s, x, z)
a city a shelf	cities shelves	consonant + y: ~~y~~ → ies f / fe → ves

☐ Add *s*, *es*, or *ies* to make plural nouns. ⓖ◀◀4 *p.3*
☐ Learn irregular plural nouns.
child   child**ren**
man   men
woman   women
person   pe**ople**

Countable and uncountable nouns

☐ There are two kinds of nouns in English, countable (**C**) and uncountable (**U**).
C = things you can count:
an apple, two apples
U = things you can't count:
rice, butter

How much …? / How many …?

How **much**	milk money	do you want?
How **many**	eggs stamps	

- ☐ Use *How much …?* + **U** nouns.
- ☐ Use *How many …?* + **C** plural nouns.

a / an / some / any

+	I need	**an** onion. (**C**) **a** tomato. (**C**)	
−	I don't need		
?	Do you need		
+	We need	some	potatoes. (**C**) bread. (**U**)
−	We don't need	any	oranges. (**C**) butter. (**U**)
?	Do you need		

- ☐ Use *a / an* + **C** singular nouns.
- ☐ Use *some* + **C** plural nouns and **U** nouns in + sentences.
- ☐ *some* = not an exact number / quantity.
- ☐ Use *any* + **C** plural nouns and **U** nouns in − and ? .

Would you like **some** more coffee?

- ☐ You can use *some* in ? to offer / ask for things.
  Would you like **some** vegetables?
  Can I have **some** water, please?

19 Object pronouns

I	**me**	Can you help **me**?
you	**you**	I love **you**.
he	**him**	I don't like **him**.
she	**her**	Do you know **her**?
it	**it**	We enjoyed **it**.
we	**us**	Wait for **us**.
they	**them**	I hate **them**.

- ☐ Use an object pronoun in place of a noun.
  I know **Richard**. OR I know **him**.
- ☐ Object pronouns go after a verb / verb + preposition.
  I hate **you**. NOT ~~I you hate.~~

20 Possessive *'s*

My brother**'s** wife. My parents**'** car. The capital **of** Italy.

- ☐ Use *'s* with people. NOT ~~the wife of my brother.~~
- ☐ Use *s'* with plural nouns. NOT ~~my parent's car.~~
- ☐ Use *of* with things. NOT ~~Italy's capital.~~

21 The time

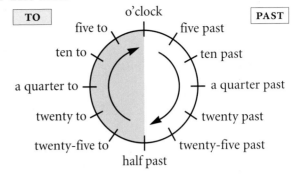

| TO | | | | | PAST |
| o'clock |
five to					five past
ten to					ten past
a quarter to					a quarter past
twenty to					twenty past
twenty-five to					twenty-five past
	half past	

What's the time?	(It's)	three o'clock. half past seven. a quarter to eleven.

- ☐ Use *it's* + time.
- ☐ Use minutes for numbers which are not 5 / 10 / 15, etc.
  It's **two minutes** to six.
- ☐ You can also say:
  six twenty-five (= 6.25 / twenty-five past), etc.
  BUT remember, six oh five (= 6.05 / five past)

Prepositions of time

in	on	at
the morning the afternoon the evening January 1995 the summer	Monday (morning) 1st May	six o'clock midnight / midday lunchtime Christmas / Easter night the weekend

- ☐ Use *in* for parts of the day, months, years, and seasons.
- ☐ Use *on* for specific days and dates.
- ☐ Use *at* for times of the day and festivals.
- ☐ Remember:
  at night / **at** the weekend

22 *this / that / these / those*

What's **this**?   What are **these**?

What's **that**?   What are **those**?

- ☐ Use *this / that* + a singular noun.
- ☐ Use *these / those* + plural nouns.
- ☐ *this / that / these / those* can be pronouns or adjectives.
  This is my bike.
  This car is expensive.

7

Progress chart

☑ = **I remember this**

Key to symbols

🛅 = Travel with English Travel phrasebook

◁▷ = Revision and extension

🔍 = Focus on …

Ⓥ = Vocabulary file

Ⓖ = Grammar file

▶◀ = Communication

⬝⬝ = Listening

✏ = Word bank

Ⓡ / Ⓡ = Revision (grammar / vocabulary)

🎲 = Game

Ⓖ◀◀ = Level 1 Grammar review

Contents   *Grammar*   *Vocabulary*

Introduction

> *Why are you learning English?*
> *I need it for my job.*

1 **a** Look at the **Student profile**.
Complete questions 1 to 10 below.

Questions

1 What's *your* first name?
   What's _____ surname?

2 Where _____ _____ live?

3 Where _____ _____ _____?

4 What _____ you _____?

5 Where _____ you _____?

6 What languages _____ _____
   _____?

7 _____ _____ you learning
   English?

8 _____ _____ study English last year?
   Where?

9 _____ you going _____ travel
   abroad next summer?
   Where _____ _____ _____
   _____ go?

10 What _____ _____ like _____
   in your free time?

Student profile

❶ **First name** _____
    Surname _____

❷ **City / Town** _____

❸ **Nationality** _____

❹ **Occupation** _____

❺ **Place of birth** _____

❻ **Languages** _____
   _____

❼ **Reason for** _____
    learning English

❽ **Previous study**   Yes ☐   No ☐
   _____

❾ **Travel plans**   Yes ☐   No ☐
   _____
   _____
   _____

❿ **Interests** _____
   _____
   _____

---

b ◦ **1** ◦ Listen and check. Underline the
important words in questions 1 to 10.
What's your first name?

Stress   **V**
surname = word stress
What do you do? = sentence stress

2 Interview a partner. Write the answers on the
Student profile form. Ask him / her to spell
surnames, street names, etc.

Classroom language   **V**
How do you say … in English?
How do you spell it?
Sorry? / Pardon?

PRONUNCIATION
The alphabet

❶ ❷ ❸ ❹ ❺ ❻ ❼

A	B	F				
	C					
	D					
	E					

Spelling ⓥ
B = <u>c</u>apital b
b = small b
bb = <u>double</u> b

a · 2 · Look at the chart above. What are pictures 1 to 7 in English? What are the sounds? Listen and check.

b · 3 · Write letters G to Z in the chart. Listen and repeat. Which letters are difficult for you?

c · 4 · Listen and write the names they spell. What are they?

1 _____
2 _____
3 _____

3 **a** Read the text. Find ten more mistakes (grammar, spelling, or capital letters). Correct them.

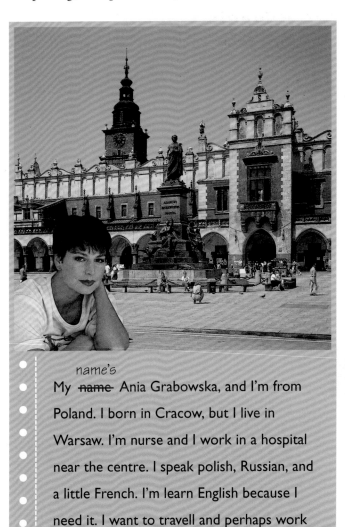

My ~~name~~ name's Ania Grabowska, and I'm from Poland. I born in Cracow, but I live in Warsaw. I'm nurse and I work in a hospital near the centre. I speak polish, Russian, and a little French. I'm learn English because I need it. I want to travell and perhaps work abroad in the future so English is very important. The last year I studyed English at home because I didn't had time to go to classes. Next july I going to study English in Bristol for a month.

b Cover the text. **A** Tell your partner what you remember about Ania. **B** Listen and check.

A *Her name's Ania Grabowska. She's Polish. She lives in Warsaw.*

4 **a** Write a paragraph about you. Use the **Student profile** to help you.

b Check your paragraph for mistakes. Then give it to a partner to check. Finally, give it to the teacher.

5 ✒ **Classroom language A** *p.143* Use the phrases in class. How do you say them in your language?

Summer in Siberia

What's the weather like in Moscow?
Lovely! It's 22° and sunny.

1 Match the seasons and photos A to D. Name the cities.

(the) spring ☐		(the) <u>su</u>mmer ☐	
(the) <u>au</u>tumn ☐		(the) <u>wi</u>nter ☐	

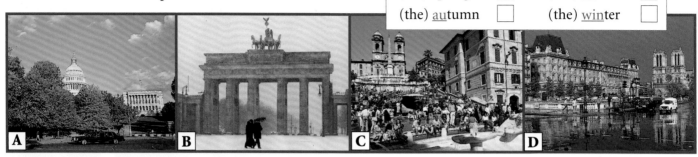

A   **B**   **C**   **D**

2 **a** Complete the expressions in the chart.

Weather		Temperature	
<u>fo</u>ggy	<u>clou</u>dy	hot	~~boiling~~
<u>rai</u>ning	<u>snow</u>ing	~~freezing~~	warm
<u>su</u>nny	<u>wi</u>ndy	cool	cold

What's the weather like?

1   It's _____.

2   It's _____.

3   It's _____.

4   It's _____.

5   It's _____.

6   It's _____.

What's the temperature?

7	40°.		It's *boiling.*
8	30°.		It's _____.
9	20°.		It's _____.
10	10°.		It's _____.
11	5°.		It's _____.
12	0°.		It's *freezing.*

It's

Temperature ⓥ
temperature /ˈtemprətʃə/
° = degrees /dɪˈgriːz/
0° = zero /ˈzɪərəʊ/
−5° = It's minus /ˈmaɪnəs/ five (degrees).

b Use the chart. Cover the words. Test a partner. *What's the weather like? What's the temperature?*

c ∘5∘ Listen to two extracts from Vivaldi's *Four Seasons.* Which seasons are they?

PRONUNCIATION

∘6∘ (Circle) the word with a different pronunciation of 'w'. Listen and check.

1 west   weather   winter   warm   wrong
2 why   where   what   who   when
3 always   snow   new   saw   how

GRAMMAR FOCUS 1

What's the weather like? It's …

What's the weather like **today**?	It's warm.
What was it like **yesterday**?	It was freezing.

a Use *What + (be) + the weather / it + like?* to ask about weather.

b Use *it* to talk about weather and temperature. **It** was 35° yesterday. **It** was really hot.

PRACTICE 1

a Ask a partner with photos A to D above.
A *What's the weather like in Rome?*
B *It's hot and sunny.*

b Ask about your weather and temperature today, yesterday, last weekend / month / Christmas, etc.
A *What was the weather like yesterday?*
B *It was hot and sunny.*

3 ◦7◦ Listen to the TV report. Complete the chart.

	Weather	Temperature
London	*cold, grey, raining*	*7°*
Moscow	_____	____
Budapest	_____	____
Milan	_____	____
Athens	_____	____

4 **a** Look at the photo of Siberia. What's the weather like? Would you like to live there? Why (not)?

b ◦8◦ Read the text and answer.

1 How many months is there snow in Siberia?
2 What happens when it's minus 35°?
3 How do people keep warm?
4 What do they close in winter and open in spring?
5 Is it often sunny?
6 Was it warmer or colder before Chernobyl?

Siberia
Svetlana Bogdanova

❄ Here in Siberia, the winter is always very long and it's freezing! It starts to snow in November and the snow doesn't normally disappear until May. The temperature is usually about −25° centigrade, but it's sometimes much colder. When it's −35° children can't go to school, but adults still go to work! We wear a lot of warm clothes: socks and boots, sweaters, hats, and fur coats. All the houses have central heating so it's never cold inside. In the winter, we close all the windows to stop the wind from getting in, and we don't open them again until spring.

In spring and summer it rains a lot, and we hardly ever see the sun. In the summer it's often about 25°, but the weather's very changeable. One day it's 25° and the next day it's 10°. People say that the weather was even colder in the past. They think it changed after Chernobyl. ❄

GRAMMAR FOCUS 2
Revision of adverbs of frequency

a Highlight the adverbs of frequency in the text. Complete the rules with 'before' or 'after'.

1 Adverbs of frequency go _____ the verb *be*.
2 Adverbs of frequency go _____ other main verbs.

b Complete the examples with 'usually' or 'now'.

Oh look! It**'s** rain**ing**. = _____

It **doesn't rain** much. = _____
Does it often **snow**?

PRACTICE 2

Put the adverbs in the sentences.

1 In Buenos Aires it's cloudy in autumn. (often)
In Buenos Aires it's often cloudy in autumn.
2 Summer evenings are warm. (usually)
3 It snows in Buenos Aires. (hardly ever)
4 It doesn't rain in the summer. (normally)
5 The temperature goes below 0°. (never)
6 December is very hot. (usually)

5 *Talk about ... the weather*

Talk in groups.

What's the weather like in your city / town in each season?
In autumn, it's sometimes foggy and it's cool.

What's the weather like in the north, south, east, and west of your country?

What do you do in winter / summer?

What's your favourite time of year? Why?

1

A

A typical Hollywood star?

> *What does he usually do before breakfast?*
> *He goes jogging.*

1 **a** 🖊 Activities A *p.134*

b Tell a partner about your typical day. Make ⊞ and ⊟ sentences. Use connectors.
I usually get up at eight o'clock and then I have a shower. I don't often have breakfast …

2 **a** Read the introduction to the article about Anthony Hopkins. Imagine his lifestyle.

b A read **Part 1**, B read **Part 2** for two minutes. Tell your partner at least five things about his day.
A *He gets up very early, at 6.30 …*

3 **a** Read both parts. Find words which mean:

1 _____ trousers and a jacket or sweater people wear for sport
2 _____ a large, yellow fruit
3 _____ the text of a film or TV programme
4 _____ a coloured pen you use to mark important information
5 _____ always moving, never quiet
6 _____ trousers and a jacket that go together
7 _____ a machine which takes phone messages

b In pairs, write true (T) or false (F). Correct the false ones.

1 He lives in Hollywood. | F
  He lives in Chelsea.
2 He's divorced and he has three children. | ☐
3 He worries about his health. | ☐
4 He doesn't usually work in the morning. | ☐
5 He's always interested in the news. | ☐
6 He has a sleep every afternoon. | ☐
7 He doesn't like buying clothes. | ☐
8 He hardly ever watches TV. | ☐
9 He has a busy social life. | ☐
10 He sleeps well. | ☐

c Do you think he's a typical Hollywood star? Why (not)?

1

B

Sir Anthony Hopkins

■ The actor Sir Anthony Hopkins was born in Wales on December 31st, 1937. He won an Oscar in 1988 for **The Silence of the Lambs**. He lives in Chelsea, London, with his wife Jenni. They don't have any children.

Part 1

■ Every day I get up at about 6.30 a.m., and I put on a tracksuit and go jogging for a couple of miles in the park. I go back home for breakfast. I have a grapefruit and an orange. I never use public transport in London, and I walk for miles, to meetings, to the dentist's – everywhere.

In the mornings, even when I'm not making a film, I always do something. I usually spend at least 90 minutes learning the script for my next film. I use a highlighter pen to mark each line. It helps me remember the words. I never read a newspaper or listen to the radio because it's all bad news.

I usually have a sandwich for lunch. I eat very fast – I don't really enjoy any meals because I'm always restless. I'm not good at relaxing. The only time I rest during the day is at about 3.00 every afternoon, when I have a 15-minute sleep.

Part 2

■ After my sleep I read the new scripts that people send me. I usually know after ten pages if they're good or not. Sometimes I do some shopping. We have a little Renault car, but I prefer walking. I like buying clothes, especially suits, by Armani or Cerruti.

My wife Jenni cooks in the evening, just a light dinner. I'm a terrible cook. We go out perhaps once or twice a week. We usually meet a friend and his wife. We hardly ever watch TV. I have a small television but it's in a cupboard. When we don't go out I play the piano after dinner, or I listen to messages on my answerphone and call people back.

I go to bed at about 10.30 p.m. and go to sleep quickly. But I often wake up at 4.00 in the morning, and listen to the noise of London and think about the next day.

GRAMMAR FOCUS

Revision of the present simple

a Look at the examples. Complete the rules.

Rules	Examples
+ Add __ for *he* / *she* / *it*. Remember the spelling changes: lives, watches, studies	I live in New York. He lives in London.
− Use _____ or _____ + infinitive.	They don't have a car. He doesn't go by bus.
? Use _____ or _____ + infinitive.	Do you read the papers? Does he make films?
✓✗	Yes, he does. No, I don't.

b Remember the word order in questions (**ASI** and **QASI**).

Question	**A**uxiliary	**S**ubject	**I**nfinitive
	Do	you	understand?
Where	does	she	work?

PRACTICE

a Make the sentences negative.

1 Anthony Hopkins has lunch in a restaurant.
   He doesn't have lunch in a restaurant.
2 He uses public transport.
3 They go out a lot.
4 His wife cooks at lunchtime.
5 They have a big car.

b Complete the questions and answers.

1 Where *does he live?*   He *lives* in London.

2 What time _____ _____ _____ up?
   He _____ _____ at about 6.30.

3 What _____ _____ _____ before breakfast?
   He _____ jogging.

4 What _____ _____ _____ for breakfast?
   He _____ a grapefruit and an orange.

5 How often _____ _____ _____ public transport?
   Never. He _____ everywhere.

6 What _____ _____ _____ _____
   _____ mornings?
   He _____ film scripts.

7 Why _____ _____ read the paper?
   Because _____ all bad news.

PRONUNCIATION

a ◦ **9** ◦ Listen and repeat.

He plays the piano.
He lives in London.
He wears a tracksuit.

He eats very fast.
He walks a lot.
He makes films.

/ɪz/

He never watches TV.
He relaxes after lunch.
He practises his lines.

b How do you say the *he* / *she* form of these verbs?

wash   run   read   cook
buy   go   use

4 ►◄ **Lifestyles A** *p.120* **B** *p.123*

NOTE After Anthony Hopkins gave this interview, he separated from his wife and moved to Hollywood!

1

B

15

An unforgettable holiday

> *Did you enjoy it?*
> *No, it was awful.*

1

C

A GOOD HOLIDAY? A BAD HOLIDAY?
THERE'S ALWAYS ONE YOU CAN'T FORGET!

Bruce Williams,
fashion designer

Maureen Lipman,
actress

Last Easter, I flew to New York for ten days with my friend Julia. We stayed in a hotel near Broadway. It was freezing but we didn't mind because we went shopping every day and saw a different show every night. We had some delicious meals at all kinds of restaurants. We never stopped! We forgot we were over forty and lived like teenagers again. It was incredible.

1 **a** ✎ **Activities B** *p.134*

b *Did you go …?* (*yesterday, last week / summer,* etc.) Ask a partner with ✎ **Activities B**. If your answer is yes, give more information.
A *Did you go shopping yesterday?*
B *No, I didn't. / Yes, I did. I bought a new CD.*

2 **a** You're going to hear an interview with Bruce Williams about his holiday. In pairs, look at the chart below and write the interviewer's questions, 1 to 10. Remember **QASI**.
1 *Where did you go?*

	Bruce	Maureen
1 Where /?	*the Caribbean*	_____
2 / have a good time?	_____	_____
3 When /?	_____	_____
4 Who / with?	_____	_____
5 How / get there?	_____	_____
6 Where / stay?	_____	_____
7 What / the weather /?	_____	_____
8 What / the food /?	_____	_____
9 What / do?	_____	_____
10 How long / stay?	_____	_____

b ◦**10**◦ Listen and check. Which words are stressed in each question?
1 *Where did you go?*

c Listen again. Complete the chart for Bruce.

3 **a** Look at the article. Read about Maureen's holiday. Complete the chart.

b **A** You're Bruce. **B** Interview Bruce with questions 1 to 10. Swap roles. **B** You're Maureen.

GRAMMAR FOCUS

Revision of the past simple

a Look at the text.

1 Find three ⊕ regular past simple verbs.
   What are their infinitives? Which one doubles the
   final consonant in the past simple?
2 Find six irregular verbs. What are their infinitives?

b Complete the examples.

⊕ He went to Cairo.

⊖ _____ to Cairo.

? _____ to Cairo?

PRACTICE

a Quickly read Inès's story. Did she enjoy it?

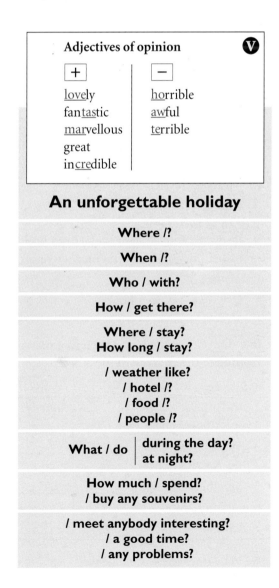

Inès de la Fressange, model

When I was a child my
parents ¹*sent* me to England
every August to learn English. I ²_____ in a
boarding school. There ³_____ a swimming
pool, a tennis court, and horses. But I ⁴_____
a terrible time: the water in the pool ⁵_____
freezing, I ⁶_____ tennis, and I ⁷_____
afraid of horses. I ⁸_____ _____
anybody and I ⁹_____ talk to the other
children because they only ¹⁰_____ Spanish,
Polish, or Turkish. The food ¹¹_____ awful.
I was really homesick. I ¹²_____ all the
time and ¹³_____ long letters to my parents
because I ¹⁴_____ them so much.
I ¹⁵_____ seven summers there because my
family really ¹⁶_____ me to learn English.

send
stay
be
have
be
hate be
not know
can't
speak
be
cry
write
miss
spend
want

b Complete with the verbs in the past simple.

c Write negative sentences about Inès.

1 She went to the USA.
  She didn't go to the USA.
2 She stayed in a hotel.
3 She wrote to her boyfriend.
4 She could speak Spanish.
5 She was very happy.
6 She had a good time.

PRONUNCIATION

Regular verbs

 We stayed in a hotel.
He travelled alone.
They enjoyed it a lot.

 We never stopped.
He missed his family.
I liked it too.

/ɪd/ We rented a car.
He needed a holiday.
She hated it.

a ∘**11**∘ Listen and repeat the verbs.
How do you pronounce *-ed*?

b ∘**12**∘ Listen and repeat the sentences.

4 *Talk about … holidays*

Ask questions about a partner's holiday.
Start with *Where /?* and ask more
questions too.

Adjectives of opinion	ⓥ
+	**−**
lovely	horrible
fantastic	awful
marvellous	terrible
great	
incredible	

An unforgettable holiday

Where /?
When /?
Who / with?
How / get there?
Where / stay? **How long / stay?**
/ weather like? **/ hotel /?** **/ food /?** **/ people /?**

What / do	**during the day?** **at night?**

How much / spend? **/ buy any souvenirs?**
/ meet anybody interesting? **/ a good time?** **/ any problems?**

What a bore!

> *Have you been to China?*
> *Yes, I have. It's incredible.*

1
D

A Ah, hello. I don't think I know you, do I? My name's Anthony – but call me Tony – and you are …?

B I'm B–

A Nice to meet you. Don't you think the music's terrible? Have you ¹*heard* the new Whitney Houston CD?

B No, I …

A Oh. It's brilliant. I've ²_____ Whitney twice. She's very nice, very nice. Could I have some more of that wine? Thanks. And have you ³_____ the new Steven Spielberg film?

B No, I haven't.

A It's marvellous! Have you ⁴_____ his biography? It's very interesting. I haven't ⁵_____ him personally but a friend of my brother's has ⁶_____ with him. Oh, I've ⁷_____ a lot, I've ⁸_____ to Egypt, Brazil, Japan … I love Japanese food. Have you ⁹_____ it?

B Yes, I have. It's …

A It's delicious. In fact, I've ¹⁰_____ to twenty-three countries. I've ¹¹_____ some wonderful holidays. Have you ¹²_____ to China?

B No, I haven't but …

A It's incredible! Have a look at my holiday photos of Beijing – just a moment, they're in my jacket – oh, she's ¹³_____! But you haven't ¹⁴_____ at my photos …

1 **a** ∘**13**∘ Cover the text. Listen to a man at a party. Complete the chart with the adjectives he uses.

		Adjectives
1	the music	*terrible*
2	the Whitney Houston CD	_____
3	Whitney Houston	_____
4	the Spielberg film	_____
5	Spielberg's biography	_____
6	Japanese food	_____
7	China	_____

b Why does the woman leave?

2 **a** Look at these past participles from the text.
1 What are their infinitives?
2 Complete the text with the past participles.

Regular	**Irregular**	
travelled	heard	been (× 3)
tried	had	gone
worked	met (× 2)	seen
looked	read	

b Listen again and check.

c 1 Which countries has he been to? When?
   2 Which famous person has he met? When?

GRAMMAR FOCUS

The present perfect

a Complete the rule and contractions.

Form the present perfect with:
the auxiliary verb _____ + past participle.

+			−		
I You We They	've	been to Brazil.	I You We They	haven't	been to Japan.
He She It	's		He She It	hasn't	
?			✓✗		
Have Has	you he	been to Kenya?	Yes, I have. / No, I haven't. Yes, he has. / No, he hasn't.		
Contractions	've = _have_		haven't = _____ _____		
	's = _____		hasn't = _____ _____		

b Use the present perfect to talk generally about your experiences. With this tense, you don't say 'when'.
I**'ve been** to Egypt.
I **haven't met** Steven Spielberg.

Past participles

a Irregular verbs A _p.141_

b Look at the past participles in ex.2a. Why are they in three groups?

been or _gone_?

been is the past participle of _be_.
Compare:

He's **gone to** the bank.
  = He isn't here. He's at the bank.
He's **been to** the bank.
  = He's here. He went to the bank and now he's come back.

PRACTICE

Write sentences.

1 we (see) that film twice
   We've seen that film twice.
2 he (not be) to Indonesia
3 you (hear) any Arab music?
4 she (met) his girlfriend?
5 they (work) in ten countries
6 I (not study) this before

3 **a** Ask the teacher _Have you been to ...?_ + local places (restaurants, shops, etc.).

b Now ask a partner. Find places that you've both been to. Compare opinions. Do you agree?

> **A** Have you been to Pizza Hut?
> **B** Yes, I have.   **B** No, I haven't.
> **A** What do you think of it?

PRONUNCIATION

a `14` Listen and write five sentences.

b `15` Listen and repeat.

have heard home happy
highlight horrible

verb voice leave never
favourite marvellous

c `16` Listen and repeat some irregular verbs. Is this a good way to learn them?

4 Use the pictures. Interview a partner.

> **A** Have you heard _Carmen_?
> **B** Yes, I have.   **B** No, I haven't.
> **A** Me, too.   **A** Me, neither.
> **B** Did you like it?

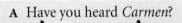

Morocco

Indian food

1

D

Getting there

Checking in

BAGGAGE SECURITY	
Is this your baggage?	✓
_____ you pack it yourself?	☐
_____ you carrying anything for anyone else?	☐
_____ you had it with you at all times?	☐
_____ you know what's in it?	☐
_____ it contain any electrical items?	☐

1 ·17· Complete the questions on the **Baggage Security** sign. Listen and check. Tick ✓ if he answers 'yes', cross ✗ if he answers 'no'.

2 **a** ·18· Listen and complete the boarding pass.

Flight	Destination	Time	Gate	Seat	aisle / window
					☐▭▭ / ☐☐✗

A _____ _____ _____ _____
hand-luggage?

B _____ _____ bag.

A That's fine. _____ _____ _____
smoking or non-smoking?

B Non-smoking. _____ _____ _____
a window seat, please?

A Let me see …

B I'm _____. _____ you _____ that?

A Yes …

B Sorry, which _____ is it?

A _____ number _____.

b Complete the dialogue. Listen again and check.

c Practise the dialogue. **A** You work at British Airways check-in. **B** You're travelling to London.

3 ·19· Listen to the announcement. Note the changes to the flight.

Arriving

4 **a** ·20· Listen to the passenger arriving at Gatwick. Is he on holiday?

b In pairs, remember and practise the dialogue. Listen again and check.

Losing your luggage

BA lost luggage report
BA flight no. BA 617
from Jakarta **to** London Gatwick
Date 22nd Sept.
Colour .... **Size** ....
Contents ....
Name ....
Home address ....
....
Temporary address ....
....
Tel. ....
Staying until ....

5 **a** ·21· Listen and complete the form.

b Listen again. What questions does she ask?

c Roleplay the dialogue. **A** Use the form to ask questions. **B** Answer. Swap roles.

B *Excuse me. One of my cases hasn't arrived.*
A *Can I see your ticket, please? …*

6 🛄 Travel phrasebook 1 *p.132*

Past, present, and future

1 Look at ✎ **Activities A** *p.134*. In pairs, **A** tell **B** what you did yesterday. **B** tell **A** what you're going to do tomorrow / at the weekend.

2 [a] Match the sentences and tenses.

1	He lives near here.	a	future (*going to*)	☐
2	She's been to the USA.	b	past simple	☐
3	We're going to buy a car soon.	c	past simple (*be*)	☐
4	He's looking for a job.	d	present continuous	☐
5	They're often late for class.	e	present perfect	☐
6	I went to the cinema last Friday.	f	present simple	1
7	She was tired last night.	g	present simple (*be*)	☐

[b] Write the ☐─ forms of sentences 1 to 7.
1 *He doesn't live near here.*

3 Interview a partner with the questionnaire below. Which of you has more contact with English?

4 *Talk about ... you*

In groups, each choose a different topic. Think about what you're going to say. Then talk for one minute about your topic.

my plans for the weekend
my family
last summer
the weather in my country
my typical day
places I've been to
in my free time
what my family are doing now

How much contact do you have with English?

❶ Did you ...?
☐ study English last year? What book / use?
☐ go abroad for your last holiday? Where?
☐ speak English on holiday? Who with?

❷ Have you ...?
☐ been to an English-speaking country? Which one(s)?
☐ had an English pen-friend?
☐ spoken on the phone in English?
☐ read any books in English?

❸ Do you ...?
☐ sometimes speak English outside class? Who to?
☐ read or write in English at work / school?
☐ listen to English outside class? What / listen to?

❹ Are you ...?
☐ using the 'Listen and speak' cassette?
☐ learning another language at the moment? Which one?
☐ studying any other subject(s)? What?

❺ Are you going to ...?
☐ practise English outside class? Who with?
☐ use English in your job / studies?
☐ go to Britain or the USA in the future?

❻ Have you got ...?
☐ any English-speaking friends?
☐ a bi-lingual dictionary? Which one?
☐ a ring file for your notes?
☐ a highlighter pen?

Focus on pronunciation

Good pronunciation helps you to communicate better.
You can easily improve your pronunciation.

Sounds

Tip 1 Concentrate on English sounds which you don't have in your language. Try to recognize phonetic symbols. Then you can check the pronunciation of words in a dictionary.

1 English has forty-four sounds.

a 🔊 **English sounds** *p.142* Look at **Vowels**. In pairs, try to remember the twenty words.

b Look at the symbols inside the pictures and say the sounds. What do the two dots (:) mean?

c 🔊 **English sounds** *p.142* Look at **Consonants**. In pairs, try to remember the twenty-four words.

d Look at the symbols inside the pictures and say the sounds. Which seven symbols are not 'letters'?

Tip 2 Many letters often have more than one pronunciation. Try to see spelling and pronunciation rules. Many combinations of letters always make the same sounds.

2 **a** ∘22∘ How do you pronounce 'a' in these words? Write the sound words above the right column.

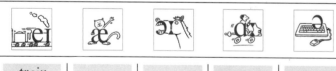

train				
cake	stamp	wall	party	arrive
rain	actor	awful	glasses	umbrella
day	fantastic	talk	father	central

b 🎵 *Every breath you take*, The Police

Write the words in three groups.

~~break~~ ~~day~~ ~~face~~ make play embrace
replace say stay take (× 2) trace aches

/eɪ/	/eɪs/	/eɪk/
day	*face*	*break*

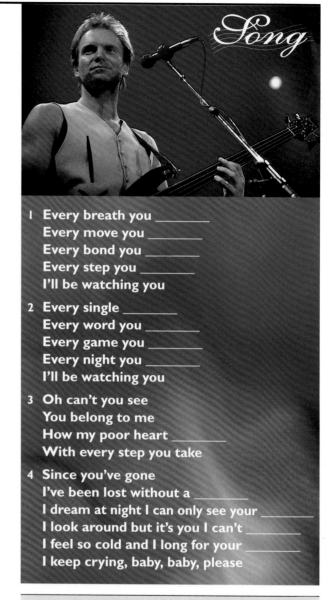

1 **Every breath you** _____
   Every move you _____
   Every bond you _____
   Every step you _____
   I'll be watching you

2 **Every single** _____
   Every word you _____
   Every game you _____
   Every night you _____
   I'll be watching you

3 **Oh can't you see**
   You belong to me
   How my poor heart _____
   With every step you take

4 **Since you've gone**
   I've been lost without a _____
   I dream at night I can only see your _____
   I look around but it's you I can't _____
   I feel so cold and I long for your _____
   I keep crying, baby, baby, please

Glossary

breath *n.* =   **face** *n.* =

bond *n.* = agreement   **replace** *v.* = find another the same

step *n.* =   **long for** *v.* = want very much

embrace *n.* = kiss

belong to *v.* = be the possession of   **keep crying** *v.* = not stop crying

heart *n.* =

ache *v.* = hurt
lost *v.* **without a trace** = totally lost
dream *v.* = to see pictures when you're asleep

c ∘23∘ Listen and complete the song.

Word stress

To communicate, correct word stress is important. A dictionary tells you where the stress is in a word.

stress   pronunciation

remember /rɪˈmembə/ *v.* ricordare

> **Tip 3** When you pronounce a word try to exAGGerate the stressed syllable. Always underline the stressed syllable on a new word.

3 ◦24◦ Underline the stress. Listen and repeat.

tomato	seventy	interesting
picture	important	begin
beautiful	yesterday	angry
nationality	Friday	engineer
sixteen	July	police

Sentence stress

To speak English well, you need the right rhythm in each sentence. In sentences we stress the words that carry the important information.

I'd <u>like</u> a <u>cup</u> of <u>coffee</u>, please.

We don't usually stress pronouns, articles, and prepositions. We only stress auxiliary verbs (e.g. *do, can*) in negatives ☐− and short answers ☐✓✗.

I <u>don't</u> want to <u>go</u>. / <u>Yes</u>, I <u>do</u>.

> **Tip 4** Pronounce strongly the stressed words or syllables. Say the other words quickly without stress. Try to get the right rhythm in each sentence you say.

4 a ◦25◦ Listen and underline the stressed words.

1	<u>What</u> <u>type</u> of <u>music</u> do you <u>like</u>?	I <u>love</u> <u>rock</u> <u>music</u>.
2	What type of music don't you like?	I don't like opera.
3	Where do your parents live?	They live in Brazil.
4	Have you got any brothers or sisters?	I've got two sisters.
5	Have you been to Switzerland?	Yes, I have.
6	What did you do last night?	I went to a concert.

b In pairs, ask and answer questions 1 to 6. Try to stress the important words.

Intonation

When we speak our voices go up and down, for example, when we're interested or surprised. This is called intonation. English intonation goes up and down a lot.

> **Tip 5** If you use the wrong intonation, people can think you are bored or unfriendly. Try to sound interested and friendly.

5 a ◦26◦ Listen. Which person sounds friendly, **A** or **B**?

b In pairs, turn to 1▭ *p.132.* **A** Say a phrase. Be friendly or unfriendly. **B** Listen and say 'friendly' or 'unfriendly'. Then swap.

> **Tip 6** Practise your pronunciation outside class. You can:
> 1 use a dictionary to help you to pronounce new words.
> 2 use the 'Listen and speak' cassette.
> 3 read aloud (and record yourself on a cassette).
> 4 listen to spoken English as much as possible, e.g. songs, films.

Vocabulary file 1

☐ How can I learn vocabulary?

People often say they have a 'bad' memory, but in fact, everybody has a good memory if they can learn how to use it. You can easily remember a large number of words if you:

– organize your vocabulary learning.
– revise regularly.

■ **Learn words in groups, e.g. 'weather'. Use the Word bank to learn new groups and revise old ones.**

1 Remembering words

a Look at 🖉 **Activities B** *p.134.* Test your memory.

b 🖉 **Prepositions A** *p.135*

2 Word groups   Add three words. Underline the stress.

Months: <u>Ja</u>nuary …
Seasons: spring …
Weather: <u>su</u>nny …
Adjectives of opinion: fan<u>tas</u>tic …
Compass: north …

3 Grammar words   Match the grammar words and examples.

1	nouns	*e*	a	does, did
2	<u>ad</u>jectives		b	co ffee
3	<u>ad</u>verbs		c	in, for
4	(main) verbs		d	a, e, i, o, u
5	au<u>xi</u>liary verbs		e	chair, money
6	prepo<u>si</u>tions		f	go, work
7	<u>vow</u>els		g	b, c, d, f
8	<u>con</u>sonants		h	big, cheap
9	<u>sy</u>llables		i	quickly, sometimes

4 Prepositions   Complete the text.

after   at   before   for   ~~in~~   in
of   on   to   until   with   near

¹*In* August last year I went ²_____ Greece ³_____ two weeks ⁴_____ a group ⁵_____ friends. We stayed at a small hotel ⁶_____ the sea. ⁷_____ the mornings we sunbathed ⁸_____ the beach. We had lunch ⁹_____ 2.00 and then we slept ¹⁰_____ 6.00. We went for a walk ¹¹_____ dinner and ¹²_____ dinner we went dancing.

5 Key words   Match the questions and answers. Translate them.

like
_____

1 What's China **like**?
2 Is she a good tennis player?
3 What do you **like** doing?
4 I'd **like** a cup of coffee, please.

☐ Reading and swimming.
1 It's incredible.
☐ Milk and sugar?
☐ Yes, she plays **like** Monica Seles.

6 Word-building   Write the noun.

sunny	*sun*	snowing	_____
foggy	_____	cloudy	_____
raining	_____	windy	_____

Organize your vocabulary learning
....

■ **Write new words and phrases in a vocabulary section in your file, or in a notebook.**

You can organize your vocabulary lists lesson by lesson, or in groups.

Travel with English 1   *10th October*

○ <u>THE AIRPORT</u>
pack (v.)   *faire la valise*
Did you pack it your<u>self</u>? *Vous l'avez faite vous-même?*
luggage

a Write the word or phrase (in a group when possible).

b Underline the stress.

c Write a translation, or example sentence, or draw a picture. Write in two columns, word on one side, translation, etc. on the other, so you can cover one column and test yourself.

Try it!

■ Find six new 'airport' words from **1**⬚ *p.20* (and the **1**⬚ listening scripts *p.126*). Follow steps **a** to **c**.
....

Grammar file 1

1 What ... like?

Present	What	's are	the weather the people	like?	It's cold and cloudy. They're friendly.
Past		was were	the weather the people		It was freezing. They were very nice.

What's the weather **like**? **It's** awful.

☐ Use *What* + (*be*) + noun + *like?* to ask for a description.

☐ Remember the difference between (*be*) *like* and the verb *like*.

What's your flat **like**? It's old and cheap. BUT **Do** you **like** your flat? Yes, very much.

2 it (weather)

It's very hot today.

What was the temperature yesterday? **It** was 28°.

☐ Use *it* to talk about weather and temperature.

3 Tense revision

☐ **Present simple** Ⓖ◄◄4 *p.2*

☐ **Present continuous** Ⓖ◄◄3 *p.2*

☐ **Past simple** Ⓖ◄◄6 *p.3*

☐ **Future: (be) going to ...** Ⓖ◄◄7 *p.4*

4 The present perfect

I've been to 15 countries!

+			−		
I You We They	've	worked in France. been to the USA.	I You We They	haven't	worked in Italy. been to Canada.
He She It	's		He She It	hasn't	

?			✓✗	
Have Has	you he	worked in Britain? been to Spain?	Yes, I **have**. / No, I **haven't**. Yes, he **has**. / No, he **hasn't**.	

Contractions 've = have 's = has
haven't = have not hasn't = has not

my experiences

I was born ——— now

present perfect

☐ Form the present perfect with *have* + past participle.

☐ Use the present perfect to talk generally about past experiences in your life. You don't say exactly when they happened.

I've been to America.

NOT ~~I've been to America last year.~~

To say when it happened, use the past simple.

I **went** to America last year.

Past participles

☐ For regular verbs, the past participle ends in *ed*. It's the same as the past simple form.

I work**ed** in Spain. / I've work**ed** in Spain.

☐ For irregular verbs, the past participle is sometimes different from the past simple.

☐ Learn ⬛ **Irregular verbs** *p.141*.

▶ **Progress chart** File 1 *p.8*   ▶ Workbook *p.15* Do **Grammar check 1**.

25

Classical experiences

> *Have you ever broken a bone?*
> *Yes, I broke my leg last year.*

1 🎵 Irregular verbs B *p.141*

CLASSICAL EXPERIENCES

🎵*Jan Latham-Koenig* was born in London on 15th December, 1953 and started playing the piano and the violin at the age of four. After working as a professional pianist, he became a conductor in 1974. He has conducted orchestras all around the world, but especially in Austria, where he often conducts the Vienna Opera. He's married, and lives in London, although he doesn't spend much time there because he travels for ten months a year. 🎵

PRONUNCIATION

◦ 1 ◦ Match two past participles to each sound. Listen and check.

done	~~broken~~	drunk	driven
read	said	spoken	written

broken			

2 Read the introduction to the interview.

1 What was Jan's first job?
2 What does he do now?
3 Which country has he worked in a lot?
4 How often is he in London?

3 **a** Read extracts 1 to 4 from the interview. Match each one to a picture, A to D.

A ☐   B ☐   C ☐   D ☐

❶

Q ⁱ Have you ever hitch-hiked?
A Yes, I have. When I was a student I hitch-hiked a lot.
Q Where did you go?
A Well, once I hitch-hiked from England to Poland with a friend. I was only sixteen at the time.
Q *What was it like?*
A Incredible. We had all kinds of experiences, some good, some bad, some dangerous. I remember we climbed the Carpathian mountains wearing only jeans and T-shirts.

❷

Q ⁱⁱ _____
A No, I haven't. I think that only happens in operas!

❸

Q ⁱⁱⁱ _____
A Yes, once. About six months ago when I was in Brussels I fell in the street and broke my ankle. I was in hospital for two weeks. The day I left hospital I flew to Canada and I conducted *La Traviata* on crutches.
Q _____
A They were very surprised!

❹

Q ⁱᵛ _____
A Yes, I have. All of them.
Q _____
A That's a difficult question. Probably *The Six Napoleons*. It's a perfect example of logic. Did you know that KGB agents had to read all the Sherlock Holmes stories as part of their training?

2
A

b Complete the extracts with the questions.

~~What was it like?~~
Have you ever broken a bone?
Which one did you like best?
Have you ever fallen in love at first sight?
Have you ever read any Sherlock Holmes stories?
What did the audience think?

4 a Cover the extracts. Look at pictures A to D.
Remember questions **i** to **iv**.

b Ask the teacher and other students the questions.

GRAMMAR FOCUS

Present perfect or past simple?

a Look at the extracts.

1 What tense is the first question in each one?
2 When the answer is 'yes', what tense is the second question?

b Read the rules. Is your language similar?

1 Use the present perfect to talk generally about past experiences. You don't say / ask 'when'.
I've been abroad a lot. / **Have** you **been** to Rome?

2 Use the past simple to talk about 'when'.
I **saw** your sister yesterday. / When **did** she **arrive**?

PRACTICE

a Write true sentences.

1 I've been to ... (country / city).
2 I've seen ... (a famous film).
3 I've read ... (a famous book).

Now write second sentences. Say when for each one.

1 *I've been to Turkey. I went there ten years ago.*

b Complete with the past simple or present perfect.

A [1]*Have* you ever _____ to an opera? (be)

B Yes, I [2]_____ to one last year. (go)

A [3]_____ _____ _____ it? (enjoy)

B No, it [4]_____ awful! (be)

A [5]*Have* you _____ the Picasso exhibition? (see)

B No, I haven't. Have you?

A Yes, I [6]_____ it last week. My daughter
[7]_____ me. (see, take)

B What [8]_____ it like? (be)

A Brilliant. We both [9]_____ it. (love)

---

ever / never
Have you **ever** broken a bone?
No, I've **never** broken a bone.
ever = at any time in your life

5 a List three countries / cities you've been to and three you haven't been to. Mix the order and give the list to a partner.

b Ask about the places on the list. Ask follow-up questions too.

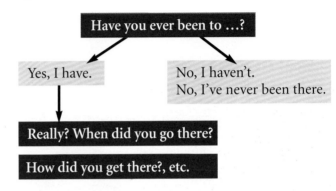

6 〈2〉 Listen to Jan. Choose the right answer. What happened in the end?

1 Jan lost his ...
   a watch
   b credit card
   c passport

2 He was at ...
   a an airport
   b a port
   c a bus station

3 He told the ...
   a police
   b ferry captain
   c taxi-driver

4 They didn't want to give it back to him because of his ...
   a intonation
   b photo
   c clothes

5 He showed them his ...
   a wallet
   b birth certificate
   c driving licence

7 ▶◀ **Have you ever ...?** A *p.120* B *p.123*

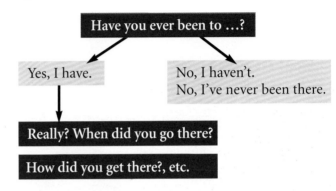

27

What's your job really like?

> *I don't have to get up very early.*

What's your job really like?

First this week we talked to Carla, a _____ from Birmingham. Then Jack Kelly, who lives in Brussels, gives us a husband's view of his wife's job. Danielle is an _____.

Carla says …

I don't like the uniform but it's a good job. I enjoy it. People think it's boring but it isn't. We have to concentrate all day. At least I don't have to work in an office. I get the chance to travel around and see what's happening. We change routes each week so I see a lot of the city. It's quite tiring. I have to work long hours and I'm quite badly-paid. But sometimes it's fun and I meet a lot of people. It's an important job but we don't carry much money so it isn't really dangerous. Believe it or not, after five years, I still like it.

Carla

Jack says …

My wife's got a good job but she has to travel a lot, both here and abroad. She doesn't have to work long hours. She can only work for twenty minutes at a time and then she has to have a break of at least an hour. She has to prepare a lot before she starts work. She meets a lot of interesting people. She's met a lot of politicians, including Helmut Kohl. She's well-paid, although she doesn't get a regular salary. Some months she earns a lot, and others very little. She says it's stressful but satisfying and also, she doesn't have to work full-time so she can spend more time with me and our three children.

Danielle and Jack

2

B

1 **a** Name these jobs.

b List five more jobs with a partner. Which jobs would you like / hate?

I'd hate to be a dentist.

2 **a** Read the article. Complete the sentences with 'Carla' or 'Danielle'.

1 _____ often travels abroad.

2 _____ works outside.

3 _____ gets a good salary when she works.

4 _____ works in a different part of the city each week.

5 _____ sometimes meets famous people.

6 _____ wears a uniform.

b ○ **3** ○ Guess the two jobs. Listen and check.

3 **a** Find ten adjectives in the article that describe their jobs. Positive or negative? Underline the stress.

+	**—**
good	*boring*

b Look at your list from ex.1. Use one adjective to describe each job.

GRAMMAR FOCUS

have to / don't have to

a (Circle) five examples of *have to* in the article. How do you say *I have to* and *I don't have to* in your language?

b Complete the chart.

+ and −		
I You We They	have to don't _____ to	
		wear a uniform.
He She It	_____ to doesn't have to	

?		
Do	you	have to work tomorrow?
Does	he	

✓✗
Yes, I _____ . / No, I don't.
Yes, he does. / No, he _____ .

c Use *have to / don't have to* + infinitive to talk about obligation / no obligation.
I **have to** wear a uniform. It's part of my job.
I **don't have to** work tomorrow. It's Sunday.

Remember, don't contract *have to* and *has to*.
I **have to** travel a lot. NOT ~~I've to travel a lot.~~

PRACTICE

a Which of these do / don't you have to do? Make six sentences.
During the week, I have to get up early.

During the week	At the weekend
get up early	cook
use public transport	do housework
wear a uniform	study / work
look after children	go shopping

b Ask what a partner has to do. Ask follow-up questions.
Do you have to get up early?

PRONUNCIATION

a ∘ 4 ∘

 full photo enough fantastic after uniform

 teacher doctor regular concentrate enjoyable tomorrow

b ∘ 5 ∘ Listen and write the sentences.

c Listen again. Do you pronounce *have to*:
1 /ˈhæf tuː/ OR 2 /ˈhæftə/?

4 a ∘ 6 ∘ Listen to the introduction to *Guess my job*.
1 How many questions can they ask?
2 What can the mystery guest answer?

b ∘ 7 ∘ Listen and ✓ or ✗ Martin's answers on the **Job analysis** form.

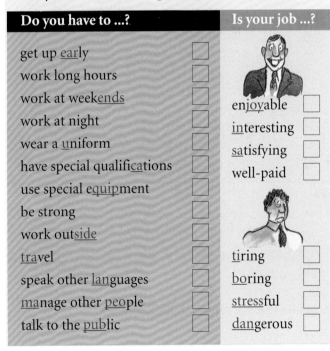

JOB ANALYSIS

**What's your job really like? Is it always the same?
Do you have a lot of responsibilities? ✓ or ✗ the list.**

Do you have to ...?	Is your job ...?
get up early	
work long hours	
work at weekends	enjoyable
work at night	interesting
wear a uniform	satisfying
have special qualifications	well-paid
use special equipment	
be strong	
work outside	
travel	tiring
speak other languages	boring
manage other people	stressful
talk to the public	dangerous

c ∘ 8 ∘ What does he do? Listen and check.

5 Play *Guess my job*. **A** Write a job on a piece of paper. **B** and **C** You have ten questions. Guess the job.
Do you have to …? Is your job …? Are you a …?

6 Write a paragraph about your job / a friend's job.

Going back to the past

> They can eat hot dogs
> but they can't have TVs.

An unusual community

❶ The Amish live in Pennsylvania, USA. They came from Switzerland and Germany in the eighteenth century and live together on farms. Although they live just 240 kilometres from New York City, their lifestyle hasn't really changed in the last 250 years. They've turned their backs on modern materialism: cars, high technology, videos, fax machines, etc. and they have very strict rules which they all have to follow.

❷ They can't use electricity, so they have to use oil lamps to light their houses. They're allowed to use banks and go to the doctor's but they can't have phones in their houses. They use horses for transport because they aren't allowed to fly or drive cars or tractors. They can play baseball and eat hot dogs but they can't have TVs, radios, carpets, flowers, or photos in their houses. Although the Amish don't have churches they're very religious.

1 **a** Look at the photo of an Amish family. Where are they? Do you know anything about the Amish?

b Read paragraph 1. Find out three things about the Amish.

2 **a** Read paragraph 2 in one minute.

b Cover the text. Put the words in the right column with a verb.

~~cars~~	electricity	hot dogs	a phone
a TV	the do<u>c</u>tor's	<u>base</u>ball	banks

They can …	They can't …
_____	*drive cars*
_____	_____
_____	_____
_____	_____

PRONUNCIATION

a ∘**9**∘ Listen and repeat. How do you pronounce *can* and *can't*?

They <u>can't</u> <u>drive</u>.

They can <u>use</u> <u>horses</u>.
Can they <u>play</u> <u>baseball</u>?

<u>Yes</u>, they <u>can</u>.

b ∘**10**∘ Listen. Write positive ☐+☐ or negative ☐−☐.

1 ☐+☐   2 ☐   3 ☐   4 ☐   5 ☐   6 ☐

2

C

GRAMMAR FOCUS

can / can't (permission)

> The Amish can use banks. (It's allowed.)
> They can't have TVs. (It's not allowed.)

a Use *can / can't* to say what is or isn't allowed.

b Remember, *can* has different meanings:
Can I have a coke, please? = request
I **can** swim but I **can't** ski. = ability

PRACTICE

Complete with *can / can't*.

1 Her parents aren't very strict. She ____ do what she wants.
2 You ____ park here. It's only for taxis.
3 ____ I smoke here? No, you ____.
4 They ____ eat pork because they're Muslims.
5 ____ we pay by credit card? Yes, you ____.
6 In England, you ____ vote when you're 18.

3 **a** ✎ **The body A** *p.136*

b Look at the photo again. Describe the Amish.
They've got … / They're wearing …

4 **a** Do you think the sentences are true (T) or false (F)?
1 Amish women can't have short hair.
2 They can wear watches, but not other jewellery.
3 They can't wear glasses.
4 Amish men can't have zips.
5 Amish men can't have beards until they're married.
6 Their children can't go to university.
7 The Amish can't marry people from outside their community.
8 The community is getting smaller each year.

b Read paragraphs 3 and 4. Check your answers. What do / don't you like about their way of life?

---

❸ Amish women have to cover their heads all day. They can't curl or cut their hair. They can't wear buttons or jewellery, wedding rings or watches, but they can wear glasses. The men can't have pockets on their shirts, or belts or zips on their trousers. Single men can't have beards. If an Amish marries somebody from outside the community, he or she has to leave. Children leave school at thirteen or fourteen because the Amish don't believe in higher education.

❹ For the Amish the family is very important, and everybody helps their neighbour. They live in an old-fashioned way because they think that modern technology and habits have destroyed community life. There are now more than 100,000 Amish, and the number is growing every year.

5 ◦**11**◦ Read the rules. Which country do you think each one is from? Listen and check.

Different countries, different rules

1 You have to be over 21 to vote in *Switzerland*.
2 You can't have a dog if you live in the town in _____.
3 Women can't wear trousers at work in _____.
4 You can drive as fast as you like on some motorways in _____.
5 All cyclists have to wear a helmet in _____.
6 If you drink and drive you have to go to prison for six months in _____.
7 You don't have to have an identity card in _____.
8 Women have to do military service for three years in _____.
9 You can't buy or eat chewing-gum in _____.

Australia

Britain

Germany

Iceland

Israel

Japan

Singapore

Sweden

~~Swit~~zerland

> **Impersonal *you***
> • We often use *you* (*can / can't / have to* …) to talk about rules. Here, *you* = people in general.
>   You have to be over 18 to vote.

6 *Talk about … rules*
1 Are these rules the same or different in your country?
2 Do you think they're good or bad?

What's the word?

A civil servant is a person
who works for the government.

What shape is it?	What's it made of?
round rectangular	metal plastic
square	wood glass

1 Look at the **V** box. Answer the questions about pictures 1 to 5.

2 **a** `°12°` Listen. How do you play the game?

b `°13°` Listen. Write the answers, 1 to 6.

1 *a civil servant*

GRAMMAR FOCUS

Relative pronouns

a Complete the chart with *who* / *which* / *where*.

It's a person _____ works for the government.	
It's a thing _____ tells you the time.	
It's a place _____ you can buy aspirins.	

b Use *who*, *which*, and *where* to connect sentences.
A zebra is an animal. It lives in Africa.
A zebra is an animal **which** lives in Africa.

PRACTICE

Complete with *who*, *which*, or *where*, and a word.

a cook   trainers   a thief
a cooker   an estate agent's

1 _____ is a machine _____ cooks food.

2 _____ is a person _____ cooks food.

3 _____ are things _____ you wear for sport.

4 _____ is a person _____ steals things.

5 _____ is a place _____ you can rent a flat.

3 Do the puzzle. What's the mystery word?

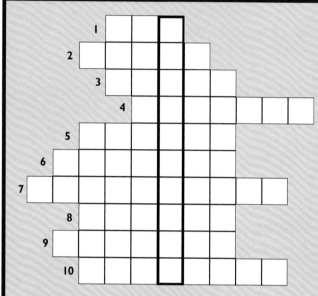

I It's a verb which means *finish*.
2 It's a place where people stay on holiday.
3 They're machines which take you up and down.
4 It's a thing which you put on your wall. It's often square or rectangular.
5 It's a kind of fruit. It's like a grapefruit, but smaller and sweeter.
6 It's a person who looks after your teeth.
7 It's a small, rectangular thing which is made of plastic. You can buy things with it.
8 It's an adjective which means the opposite of *interesting*.
9 They're small, round things which are usually made of plastic. You have them on shirts, coats, etc.
10 It's an expression which you use when a person gives you something.

Definitions	
It's a verb / adjective.	It's a word / expression …
It's the opposite of …	It's a kind of …
It's made of …	It's like a …

4 In pairs, write definitions of these words.

1 sleep   4 a knife
2 a bus stop   5 Excuse me.
3 a banana   6 nurses

5 ►◄ Crossword A *p.120* B *p.123*

2
D

From the airport to the hotel

Changing money

1 **a** ∘**14**∘ Listen and (circle) the number you hear.

1 15 / 50   3 17G / 70G   5 £2.19 / £2.90
2 $16 / $60   4 14 / 40

b ✦ **High numbers** *p.135*

Today's exchange rate £1.00 = US $1.50

Bureau de Change

P Hello. *Can* I _____ 300 US dollars, _____?

A Certainly, sir. Could I have your passport, please?

P _____ you are. _____ the _____ rate?

A A pound is one dollar fifty. _____ £200.

P Thanks … _____ do I _____ to the station?

2 **a** ∘**15**∘ Pieter Okker's at Gatwick airport. Guess the missing words in the dialogue. Listen and check.

b Roleplay the conversation. Use:
$150 $60 $1,200 $1,500

Getting a train

GATWICK EXPRESS services leave the airport for London Victoria every 15 minutes during the day and every 30 minutes early in the morning and late at night. The journey takes just 30 minutes and 35 minutes on Sundays and in the evening. With this high frequency service from early morning until late at night, seat reservations are not required.

3 Quickly read about the Gatwick Express.

1 How often are the trains?
2 How long does the journey take on Sundays?
3 Do you have to reserve a seat?

4 **a** ∘**16**∘ Listen and complete the information.

1 Destination   _____
2 Single / return _____
3 Price   _____
4 Next train   at _____ in _____
5 Platform   _____
6 Journey time   _____

b Practise the dialogue.

Getting a taxi

5 **a** ∘**17**∘ Cover the text. Listen. What's the problem?

Hilton	P	Taxi. Can you take me to the Hilton Hotel, please?
✓	T	Sure.
back?	P	Can you put *these* in the back?
Here	T	OK. Here we are.
much?	P	Thanks. How much is *that*?
£5.50	T	£5.50.
15?	P	£5.15?
50	T	No, fifty. £5.50.
change?	P	Can you change *this*?
smaller?	T	No, I can't. Have you got anything smaller?

b Read the dialogue. What do the words in *italics* mean?

c Look only at the words on the left. Practise in pairs.

6 ▭ **Travel phrasebook 2** *p.132*

The verb have

'I never think I'm going to die'

Cristina has a very unusual but exciting job. ¹*Although* it's hard and very ²_____, she loves it. She's travelled a lot in her job and has been to ³_____ every city in her country. 'I've tried other jobs – I've worked as a hairdresser and as a secretary, but I hated it. When I was eighteen, my parents ⁴_____ me do what I always wanted.' In the winter she has to ⁵_____ and do exercises ⁶_____ morning, and in the afternoon she practises, reads books, and studies videos. She usually works in the summer months. She ⁷_____ works one day a week, but she ⁸_____ over £30,000 each time. She pays half the money to her team, and she also has to ⁹_____ special clothes which are very expensive. She still lives with her parents, and she's got two sisters, ¹⁰_____ also live at home. 'On a working day I have lunch, usually a steak and some salad, and then I get ¹¹_____. I do my hair – I don't wear any make-up – and then I put on my suit. My job's very dangerous but I never feel ¹²_____, and I never think I'm going to die.'

1 a Read and guess Cristina's job.

b Complete the text with the words.

earns	wear	~~although~~	let	nearly	every
only	who	stressful	afraid	train (*v.*)	ready

c °**18**° Listen to Cristina working. Were you right? Would you do this for £30,000?

2 a Look at *have* in the text. Find examples to complete the chart.

The verb *have*	
1 _____	present perfect
2 _____	obligation
3 _____	*have = eat / take*, etc.
4 *She has an unusual job.*	possession

b Are these sentences 1, 2, 3, or 4?

I always have coffee for breakfast. ☐

I've done all the exercises. ☐

He's got / He has a new car. ☐

She has to work on Saturdays. ☐

3 Complete with a form of *have*.

1 Joe's lucky – he *doesn't have to* work.

2 I _____ a cat, a dog, and a canary.

3 What _____ you usually _____ for breakfast?

4 They _____ been to India twice.

5 What time _____ she _____ to get up?

6 _____ Jane _____ any brothers or sisters?

**Have you got ...? /
Do you have ...?**
a big family?
a car?
any pets?

Do you have ...?
a bath or a shower every day?
lunch at home during the week?
a holiday every summer?

Do you have to ...?
wear a uniform at work / school?
use public transport a lot?
work / study at the weekend?

Have you (ever) ...?
seen a bullfight?
been to an opera?
eaten Indian food?

4 Ask a partner the *have* questions above. Ask a follow-up question if you can.
A *Have you got a big family?*
B *Yes, I have.*
A *How many brothers and sisters have you got?*

5 a °**19**° Listen to three dialogues. Where are they? Who are the people?

b Listen again. What are they talking about?

°**20**° ♫ *You don't have to say you love me*, Dusty Springfield

34

Focus on listening

Students often find listening to English stressful, especially listening to cassettes. Why?

1 Understanding spoken language is more difficult than reading because you don't have time to translate every word.
2 In conversation, people use a lot of contractions and weak forms (words which aren't stressed) so it's impossible to hear every word clearly.
3 When you listen to a cassette you can't see the speaker's face. This makes it more difficult.

Can you think of any other reasons?

Listening to cassettes or watching videos is a very good way to practise understanding different voices, accents, and situations. Here are some tips to help you understand better.

Listening for the general idea

Tip 1 Relax. Don't stop listening when you don't understand words or phrases. It's normal not to understand everything. The first time you listen, just try to get an idea of what you're listening to.

1 ∘21∘ Listen to a radio programme. Don't write anything. Close your books, relax, and listen. What kind of programme is it?

Tip 2 You don't need to hear or remember every word. Try to listen for the key words – the words which carry the important information. These are usually stressed. Focus on understanding the general idea.

2 **a** Listen again. Number the topics in order, 1 to 4. Compare with a partner.

The weather ☐ Sport ☐
International news ☐ Business news ☐

b Listen again. Write down all the key words you hear for each topic. Compare with a partner.

Tip 3 If you're listening to a cassette and have the script, use it to check what you have and haven't understood.

3 **a** Look at the listening script on *p.127*. Compare the highlighted key words with your list from ex.2b.

b ∘22∘ Practise again. This time, listen to someone telling a story they read in the newspaper. Listen three times. Follow Tips 1 to 3.

Listening for specific information

Tip 4 When you listen for specific information (e.g. a train time, a price in a shop) you usually know more or less what you're going to hear. Concentrate on listening for what you need to know. Don't worry about understanding the rest.

4 **a** ∘23∘ Read and check what you need to know. Then listen and complete.

1 The British Airways office opens at _____.
2 The next train to Brighton leaves from platform _____.
3 You're going to meet outside _____.
4 A double room during the week costs £ _____.

b Listen again. Read the listening script on *p.127*. Which words didn't you understand? Why?

Tip 5 It isn't enough to listen only in class. You need to practise outside class too. You can:

- record and listen to satellite TV news in English.
- practise with the 'Listen and speak' cassette.
- listen to songs (and read the words if you can).
- read *Easy Readers* with a cassette.
- watch English films with subtitles.
- talk to English-speakers as much as possible.

5 Choose one thing from Tip 5 to do this week.

2

Vocabulary file 2

How can a good dictionary help me?

A good bi-lingual dictionary is very important for efficient language learning. A dictionary doesn't only tell you the meaning of a word. It also tells you the grammar, pronunciation, and stress. It sometimes gives you an example sentence too.

stress   pronunciation   meaning

listen /'lɪsn/ *v.* (to sth / sb) écouter   He often listens to the radio.

grammar   example sentence

1 Dictionary abbreviations What do they mean?

1 sth   *something*
2 sb   _____
3 n.   _____ (e.g. house)
4 adj.   _____ (e.g. fat)
5 v.   _____ (e.g. go)
6 prep.   _____ (e.g. in)
7 adv.   _____ (e.g. slowly)
8 pron.   _____ (e.g. we / us)

■ **Learn verbs with their prepositions if they have one.**

2 Prepositions Complete with the prepositions.

at   to (x 2)   with   after   for   as

1 I want to go too. Wait _____ me.
2 Please write _____ me when you're away!
3 He has to look _____ the children because his wife's at work.
4 I'm sorry, I don't agree _____ you.
5 Have you ever worked _____ a waiter?
6 Excuse me. Can I speak _____ the manager, please?
7 Look _____ those clouds! I'm sure it's going to rain.

3 Word-building Job words often end in -or, -er, and -ist. How do these jobs end? Check in your dictionary. Underline the stress.

1 conduct*or*   6 lawy____
2 psycholog____   7 bus driv____
3 chem____   8 sail____
4 interpret____   9 journal____
5 hairdress____   10 scient____

4 Key words Complete.

also   al<u>though</u>   ever   <u>only</u>   still

1 Have you _____ been to Brazil?
2 _____ it was very windy, they went to the beach.
3 She can't come tomorrow. She can _____ come on Tuesday.
4 I speak Italian, and I _____ speak a little Spanish.
5 I wrote to him a month ago, but I'm _____ waiting for an answer.

5 Pronunciation Cross out the word with a different vowel sound.

  1 bone   coat   ~~wood~~   although   only

  2 ticket   surprised   tiring   file

  3 ring   zip   strict   equipment   climb

  4 gone   want   motorway   offer   opposite

  5 square   wear   prepare   earn   hair

6 ✎ The body B *p.136* Close your book. How many words can you remember?

Organize your vocabulary learning!

■ **Use your dictionary.**

a Find the meaning of new words.

b Check grammar, spelling, and pronunciation.

c Extend your vocabulary.

Try it!

■ Each of these words has a spelling mistake. Correct it. Underline the stress. Check the spelling, stress, and meaning in a dictionary.

1 jewelery   4 salery
2 helmit   5 consentrate
3 qualificacions 6 motor-way

2

v

Grammar file 2

1 Present perfect or past simple?

'**Have** you **ever been** to Paris?'   Yes, I **went** there **in** 1994.'

Present perfect

Have you ever **been** to South America?	**Have** you ever **broken** your leg?
Yes, I **have**.	Yes, I **have**.

☐ Use the present perfect to talk generally about past experiences when you don't say / ask 'when'.

☐ Use *ever* in ? for experiences at any time in your life until now.

☐ Use *never* in −.
I've **never** broken my leg. NOT ~~I haven't never …~~

Past simple

When **did** you **go** to South America?	When **did** you **break** your leg?
I **went** to Venezuela in 1995.	I **broke** it last July.

☐ Use the past simple to say / ask exactly when an action happened.
When **did** you **arrive**? I **arrived** ten minutes ago.

A **Have** you **been** to …?
B Yes, I **have**.
A When **did** you **go** there?

☐ Conversations often begin with the present perfect, then change to the past simple.

2 *have to / don't have to* (obligation)

+ and −

I You We They	**have to** **don't have to**	travel a lot. get up early every day.
He She It	**has to** **doesn't have to**	

?	✓✗

Do	you	**have to** work at weekends?	Yes, I **do**. / No, I **don't**.
Does	he		Yes, he **does**. / No, he **doesn't**.

☐ Use *have to / don't have to* + infinitive to talk about obligation.
I **have to** work tomorrow. It's Monday.
I **don't have to** work tomorrow. It's Sunday.

☐ Don't contract *have / has to*.
NOT ~~She's to wear a uniform.~~

3 *can / can't*

+	He **can** wear jeans at work.
−	Amish women **can't** have short hair.
?	**Can** we smoke here?
✓✗	Yes, you **can**. / No, you **can't**.

☐ Use *can / can't* + infinitive to say what is or isn't allowed.

☐ Remember three meanings of *can / can't*. Ⓖ◀◀9 *p.4*

4 Impersonal *you*

You have to be over eighteen to vote.
How do **you** spell it?
You can't smoke in hospital.

☐ *you* = people in general (not you personally).

5 Relative pronouns (*who / which / where*)

A nurse is a person **who** works in a hospital.
A fridge is a thing **which** keeps food cold.
A post office is a place **where** you can buy stamps.

☐ Use *who / which / where* to connect sentences.

☐ You can also use *that* for people and things.
She's the person **that** won the lottery.
A microwave is a machine **that** cooks food quickly.

▶ Progress chart File 2 *p.8*   ▶ Workbook *p.21* Do **Grammar check 2**.

2
Ⓖ

Love me tender

> *Whose are these keys?*
> *They're mine.*

1 Read about Christie's. What is an auction? Have you ever been to one?

Inside **CHRISTIE'S**

Christie's is one of the most famous auction houses in the world. It was opened in London by James Christie in 1766 to auction books, antiques, and paintings. In 1801 they sold a painting by Velázquez for only £41. Nearly 200 years later, in 1987, they sold Van Gogh's *Sunflowers* for £22,500,000. This was more than three times the world record price for a picture! Today, Christie's auction all kinds of objects which belonged to famous people. Recently they sold the following things:

JOHN LENNON

DAVID BOWIE

KEITH RICHARD

ELTON JOHN

PRINCE

ELVIS PRESLEY

MICHAEL JACKSON

2 **a** In pairs, try to match the objects and people.
  A *Whose is the guitar?*
  B *I think it's Keith Richard's. Whose are the boots?*

  b ◦ **1** ◦ Listen to the beginning of the auction. Were you right?

3 ⎸2⎸ 🎵 Listen and complete the song with the words. Use some of them more than once.

I   me   my   mine   you   your   yours

Song

ELVIS PRESLEY

Love Me Tender

and Any Way You Want Me

1 Love _____ tender
   Love _____ sweet
   Never let _____ go
   _____ have made _____ life complete
   And _____ love _____ so

   Chorus
   Love _____ tender
   Love _____ true
   All _____ dreams fulfil
   For _____ darling _____ love _____
   And _____ always will

2 Love _____ tender
   Love _____ long
   Take _____ to _____ heart
   For it's there that _____ belong
   And we'll never part
   Chorus

3 Love _____ tender
   Love _____ dear
   Tell _____ _____ are _____
   _____ 'll be _____ through all the years
   Till the end of time
   Chorus

Glossary
tender = tenderly, lovingly
sweet = sweetly, lovingly
so = a lot
true = truly
fulfil (*v.*) = make real
for = because
It's there that I belong. = It's my home.
part (*v.*) = separate

Who's or Whose?	🅥

Who's that man? It's my father. = *Who is* (verb *be*)
Whose is that car? It's my father's. = possession

GRAMMAR FOCUS
Possessive pronouns

Whose	is this hat?
	are these ear-rings?

Possessive adjectives			Possessive pronouns	
It's	my	hat.	It's, etc.	_____.
That's	_____			yours.
This is	_____			his.
	_____			hers.
They're	our	ear-rings.	They're, etc.	_____.
These are	_____			theirs.
Those are	John's			John's.

a Complete the chart.
1 Which pronoun doesn't end in *s*?
2 Which form do you use without a noun?

b Use *Whose …?* to ask about possession.

PRACTICE
Complete with possessive adjectives or pronouns.
1 **A** Is this bag Jane's?
   B No, it isn't h_____. H_____ bag's brown.
2 Are these o_____ coats? Yes, they're o_____.
3 Those aren't y_____ keys, they're m_____.
   Y_____ are on the table.
4 I don't know h_____ wife. Have you met h_____?
5 I invited them to m_____ party, but they didn't invite me to th_____.
6 O_____ flat's bigger than th_____, but th_____ flat is more modern.

PRONUNCIATION
a ⎸3⎸ Listen and write the sentences.

b ⎸4⎸ Listen and repeat. 🐍 or 🦓 ?

/z/	whose	☐	this	☐	these	☐	those
☐	miss	☐	books	☐	sing	☐	chairs

4 📖 **Classroom language B** *p.143*

5 🎲 **TB** *p.43* Play *Guess whose.*

Old friends

> *What are you doing on Sunday?*
> *I'm going to Vienna.*

1 **a** How do you say these dates?

3rd May	**21/9/96**	**August 12th 1999**
5.2.84	**30th July**	

b Match the verbs and phrases.

arrive at   arrive in   have
leave   meet   ~~see~~   stay

1 *see* a film, a friend
2 _____ at the hotel, a friend
3 _____ home, a message
4 _____ London, Italy
5 _____ Heathrow, the station
6 _____ dinner, a meal
7 _____ in a hotel, for a week

3
B

at, in		**V**
arrive	**at** a building	
	in a town or country	

2 **a** ○ 5 ○ Debbie calls and leaves a message on Tim's answerphone. Listen and answer.

1 When's Debbie going to Budapest?
2 Why?
3 How long's she staying?

b ○ 6 ○ Listen to Debbie's second message. Complete her travel details.

Name	*Ms Debbie Morgan*
Date of journey	_____
Dep.	London (Heathrow) 7.45 a.m.
Arr.	Budapest _____ a.m. (local time)
Flight number	_____ (Malev Airlines)
Hotel	_____
Phone number	_____

c Then Tim got a postcard from Debbie. Use the travel details to complete her card.

Dear Tim

How are you? I hope you're well. Your mother gave me your address. She said you were fine, but busy. I've got a surprise for you. I'm ¹going to Budapest soon, on March 14th. Here are my travel arrangements. I'm ² _____ London at ³ _____ a.m. and I'm ⁴ _____ in Budapest at ⁵ _____ a.m. I'm ⁶ _____ at the ⁷ _____ hotel. I'm ⁸ _____ for a week. I'm ⁹ _____ with ¹⁰ _____ Airlines (flight number ¹¹ _____).

I'm really looking forward to seeing you again.

Love

Debbie xx

PS I hope you get this card before I arrive!

Debbie's an interpreter.
She's going to Budapest.
Her friend Tim works at
Budapest University and
she really wants to see
him when she's there.

GRAMMAR FOCUS

Present continuous (future)

> I'm flying to Tunisia on Saturday. (I've got a ticket.)
> He's meeting his manager tomorrow. (He's got an appointment.)

a Look at Debbie's postcard.

1 What tense does she use for travel arrangements?
2 Is she talking about now or the future?

b Use the present continuous (*be* + verb + *-ing*) + a future time expression to talk about future arrangements (e.g. things you write in a diary).

c Translate the examples. What tense do you use in your language?

PRACTICE

Look at Tim's diary. Make sentences with the verbs.
On Sunday he's flying to Vienna.

have ~~fly~~ go (× 2) meet play see

Sunday 14th	Vienna (flight YL71G)
Monday 15th	the dentist's
Tuesday 16th	squash
Wednesday 17th	Viktor (University)
Thursday 18th	Terminator III
Friday 19th	dinner (Erika)
Saturday 20th	the ballet

3 a ∘ 7 ∘ Tim calls Debbie in England. Listen and answer.

1 What days can't they meet? Why?
2 What day can they meet?

Listen again. Complete the invitations. Tick the answers you hear.

Invite / suggest	Accept / refuse
1 What _____ _____ _____ on Sunday night?	Well actually, I'm … ✓
	Nothing special.
2 Are you _____ Tuesday evening?	No, I'm …
	Yes, I am.
3 _____ _____ Wednesday?	Sorry. I'm busy.
	Yes, that's fine.
4 _____ you _____ _____ have dinner?	Sorry, I can't. I'm …
	I'd love to.
5 Where can we _____? At the hotel?	Fine.
	No, let's meet at the station.

PRONUNCIATION

Intonation

a ∘ 8 ∘ Listen to phrases from the dialogue. Repeat. Copy the intonation.

b ∘ 9 ∘ Listen to six invitations. Accept or refuse.

4 Complete your diary for three evenings. Ask another student.

Are you free on … evening? / What are you doing on … evening?

If they're free, invite them to do something, and write down your arrangement. Swap partners. Try to fill your diary.

Mon.	_____
Tues.	_____
Wed.	_____
Thur.	_____
Fri.	_____
Sat.	_____
Sun.	_____

5 ∘ 10 ∘ Tim meets Debbie. Listen. What happens?

6 *Talk about …* ***arrangements***

Today
Where / go after class?
How / get there?
What / do this evening?

Tomorrow
What / do tomorrow?
/ go out / evening?

Next weekend
/ do anything special / Friday night?
Where / go / Saturday?
What / do / Sunday?

Ask and answer in pairs. Remember the answers.

A *Where are you going after class?*
B *I'm going home.*

3

B

The slowest journey in history?

> *Finally he sailed across the sea to Ithaca.*

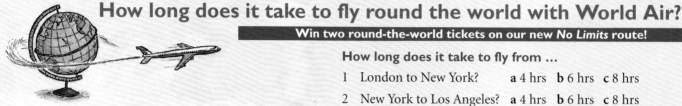

How long does it take to fly round the world with World Air?

Win two round-the-world tickets on our new *No Limits* route!

1 Do the competition in pairs. Make sentences.

1 *We think it takes six hours to fly from London to New York.*

How long does it take to fly from …

1	London to New York?	**a** 4 hrs	**b** 6 hrs	**c** 8 hrs
2	New York to Los Angeles?	**a** 4 hrs	**b** 6 hrs	**c** 8 hrs
3	Los Angeles to Sydney?	**a** 12.5 hrs	**b** 14.5 hrs	**c** 16.5 hrs
4	Sydney to Singapore?	**a** 8 hrs	**b** 10 hrs	**c** 12 hrs
5	Singapore to London?	**a** 10.5 hrs	**b** 14.5 hrs	**c** 18.5 hrs

Time		**V**
about	ten minutes /ˈmɪnɪts/	
	a quarter /ˈkwɔːtə/ of an hour	
	half /hɑːf/ an hour	
	three quarters of an hour	

2 a ・11・ Read and answer.

1 Where was Odysseus from?
2 How far was his home from Troy?
3 How long did it take him to get home?

b Draw Odysseus's route from Troy to Ithaca on the map.

GRAMMAR FOCUS 1

How long does it take? It takes …

How long does it take to	fly get	from London to New York?
(It takes) about eight hours		(to get there) by plane. to fly there.

How long does it take you **to get**	to work? home?
(It takes me) about twenty minutes (by bus / car).	

Use *It takes…* to talk about the duration of a journey.

PRACTICE 1

a Write three true sentences about places in your country.

It takes about seven hours to | *drive to Milan.*
| *get to Milan by car.*

b Ask a partner.

How long does it take you to …

1 wake up in the morning?
2 have a shower?
3 get dressed?
4 have breakfast / lunch / dinner?
5 get to work / class?
6 go to sleep at night?

In Homer's story, Odysseus was a Greek leader who fought a terrible war against the Trojans in Troy. The Greeks finally won, and after the last battle Odysseus wanted to return home to the island of Ithaca. Although
5 it was only about 500 km, the journey took him a very long time.

First a strong north wind blew him round Crete to a big island where the one-eyed giants called Cyclops lived. They kept him prisoner, but after many adventures he
10 escaped. Because of terrible storms, he sailed north again, away from Ithaca, up to the island of the goddess Circe. Circe was kind, and sent him down to Hades, the land of the Dead, to get help for his journey home. From there he went back to Circe's island. When he left the island he
15 went along the coast past the beautiful but deadly Sirens and through the dangerous waters between Cyclops island and the mainland, where two terrible monsters lived. With great difficulty, he sailed past them, and finally he sailed across the sea to Ithaca. His journey took
20 him ten years – an average of 50 km a year. But after all that time, his wife Penelope was still waiting for him!

3

C

GRAMMAR FOCUS 2

Prepositions of movement

> He sailed across the sea.
> He went past the Sirens.

Use a verb (e.g. *sail*) + a preposition (e.g. *across*) to describe movement.

PRACTICE 2

a 🖊 Prepositions B *p.135* Test a partner.

b Cover the text and use the map. In pairs, describe Odysseus's journey.

First he went from Troy to …

3 a Quickly read the newspaper article. Where exactly is Pascale?

French tourist missing in Snowdonia

A young French woman, Pascale Hartman, aged 24, is missing in north-west Wales after two days of strong winds and heavy snow. She was last seen at 11.45 on Friday morning when she left the Youth Hostel to go climbing. A mountain rescue team is looking for her.

---

b Match pictures 1 to 10 to the words in the **V** box.

The country   **V**

a field	☐	a <u>v</u>alley	☐
a <u>mou</u>ntain	☐	a bridge	*1*
a <u>fo</u>rest	☐	a hill	☐
a path	☐	a lake	☐
a <u>ri</u>ver	☐	a <u>ca</u>stle	☐

c ◦12◦ Listen to a man from the rescue team. He's found Pascale. Tick the pictures you hear.

d Listen again. Complete the instructions.

Go _____ the _____, _____ the _____.

Go _____ the _____ for about 300 metres.

Go _____ the _____ on your left.

Go _____ the _____ and then _____ _____ the _____.

Go _____ the _____ and _____ the _____.

4 ►◄ Emergency A *p.120* B *p.123*

It was a cold, dark night …

> *She was driving along the road when she hit a cat.*

1 Match the words and definitions.

2 Read paragraph 1 of the story.

1 What was the weather like?
2 Why was there a lot of traffic?
3 Where was Diana going?

1	**murderer** /ˈmɜːdərə/	☐ a	(*adj.*) very afraid
2	**be in a hurry** /ˈhʌrɪ/	☐ b	(*n.*) a large gun
3	**a shotgun** /ˈʃɒtgʌn/	☐ c	(*n.*) a person who has killed somebody
4	**van** /væn/	☐ d	(*v.*) want to do something quickly
5	**continue** /kənˈtɪnjuː/	☐ e	(*n.*) a kind of vehicle to carry things
6	**terrified** /ˈterɪfaɪd/	☐ f	(*v.*) not stop

(box c contains the number 1)

3

D

1 It was a cold, dark night in November, and it was raining. It was six o'clock and people were going home from work. There was a lot of traffic. Diana was in a hurry, but she wasn't going home. She was driving to her friend Daniel's house to have dinner.

☐ **Suddenly** she hit something in the road. She stopped, and got out of the car. It was a cat, but it was dead. So she got back in the car.

☐ Diana continued her journey. She looked in the mirror and saw a black van behind her. It was very near. She began to feel a bit afraid. It was following her! **Then** the seven o'clock news started on the radio.
  "The police are looking for a murderer who escaped from a north-London prison last night. He is very dangerous …" Now Diana was really afraid.

☐ **At** ten to seven, Diana was driving along the A1. Her friend Daniel was a farmer and he lived 30 km north of London. She was listening to the radio, and beginning to relax after a hard day at the office.

☐ **When** the doorbell rang, Daniel was making dinner. He heard Diana shouting, quickly took his shotgun, and ran to the door. At that moment, the black van stopped next to Diana's car. A tall man got out …

☐ She began to drive faster, but the van drove faster too. It was right behind her. She left the A1 but the black van followed her. Now Diana was terrified. **At last** she arrived at Daniel's farm. She ran up to the house, and rang the doorbell. 'Help, help, Daniel,' she shouted.

AND THE HEADLINES TONIGHT…

GRAMMAR FOCUS 1

The past continuous

a Look at the highlighted verbs in paragraph 1. Complete the rule.

To form the past continuous use:
_____ / *were* + verb + -_____.

b Complete the chart.

Present continuous	Past continuous
I'm working.	I was working.
They're going home.	They _____
Where are you going?	Where _____
It isn't raining.	It _____
Is it snowing?	_____
Yes, it is.	_____
Are you studying?	_____
No, we aren't.	_____

c Use the past continuous to describe actions in progress at a specific time in the past.

It was six o'clock and people **were going** home.

PRACTICE 1

What else was happening at six o'clock? In pairs, make seven more sentences about picture 1.

1 *Two people were going into a pub.*

PRONUNCIATION

was / were

·13· Listen and repeat. Underline the stressed words. When are *was/were* stressed?

1 He was <u>going</u> <u>home</u>.
What <u>were</u> they doing?

2 It <u>wasn't</u> raining.
Yes, it <u>was</u>.

3 They <u>weren't</u> sleeping.
Yes, they <u>were</u>.

3 a Look at pictures 2 to 6. Read and number the paragraphs in the right order.

b **·14·** Listen. What happened?

GRAMMAR FOCUS 2

Past simple or past continuous?

a Look at paragraphs 2 to 6 again. Highlight the past continuous verbs. What tense are the other verbs?

she hit a cat
⬇
she was driving along the road

b Look at the time line. Which action was in progress when the other action happened?

c Complete the rule with 'simple' or 'continuous'.

Use the past _____ for an action in progress and the past _____ for a shorter, completed action.

PRACTICE 2

a Write sentences with past simple / past continuous.

1 When Diana (leave) work it (rain).
When Diana left work it was raining.
2 She (kill) a cat when she (drive) to her friend's house.
3 Suddenly she (see) a black van. It (follow) her.
4 When Diana (arrive) she (get) out of the car and (ring) the doorbell.
5 Daniel (cook) when he (hear) the doorbell.

b In pairs, cover the text and remember the story. **A** tell pictures 1 to 3. **B** tell pictures 4 to 6.

4 Ask what your partner was doing yesterday at these times. Ask follow-up questions.
 A *What were you doing at (8.05) yesterday?*
 B *I was working.*
 A *Do you usually start work at 8.00?*, etc.

5 *Talk about ... what was happening*

Ask and answer in pairs.
 A *What was happening when you got home last night?*
 B *My father was sleeping in front of the TV ...*

What was happening		you got home last night?
What were you wearing		you came to class on the first day?
What were you thinking about	when	you woke up this morning?
How were you feeling		you got to class today?

3

D

At the hotel

Checking into a hotel

1 Pieter's in Stockholm. Read about his hotel. Would you like to stay there?

FOGG'S
HOTEL

Located in a residential area of Stockholm, just 5 km drive from the city centre, with good connections by bus. All 146 rooms have shower and WC, telephone, radio and colour satellite TV.

• **A la carte restaurant (waiter service)** • **Breakfast room (buffet service)** • **Bar lounge** • **Sauna** • **Jacuzzi** • **Roman bath and fitness area** • **Sun terrace** • **Solarium** •

P Hello. *I've got _____ _____*. My name's Okker. Pieter Okker.

R Just a moment. _____ _____ _____ _____, please?

P O-double K-E-R.

R Right, Mr Okker. A _____ room with a _____ for two nights, is that right?

P No, it's _____ nights. From the _____ to the _____ of November.

R No problem, I'll _____ it. May I see your passport, please? Thank you. _____ you _____ in this form, please?

P Sure. _____ _____ _____ _____ _____? Thanks.

R OK. Here's your key, sir, room _____, on the _____ _____. The lift's over there.

P Thanks. _____ _____ _____?

R From 7.00 to _____. The dining-room's on the _____ floor.

2 **a** ° 15 ° Listen and answer.

1 What kind of room did Pieter reserve?
2 How long's he staying?
3 What's his room number?

b Listen again and complete the dialogue.

c Write two words next to each line to help you remember the dialogue. Cover and roleplay.

Calling Reception

3 **a** ° 16 ° Listen and write the room number under each picture. Why are they phoning Reception?

b Listen again. What are the guests' requests?

1 Could I _____ ?
2 Could you _____ ?
3 Could you _____ ?
4 Could you _____ ?

4 **a** Look at the listening script on *p.128*. Underline key words for each dialogue.

b Roleplay the four situations. **A** You're the hotel guest. Change the information. **B** You're the receptionist. Swap roles.

A is the guest	**B is the guest**
– a white <u>coffee</u>	– a beer and a <u>sand</u>wich
– the <u>air</u>-con<u>di</u>tioning	– the <u>heat</u>ing
– <u>blan</u>kets	– <u>toi</u>let <u>pa</u>per
– 7.30	– 7.45

5 🕮 **Travel phrasebook 3** *p.132*

There's always a first time

1 **a** ◦17◦ Listen to five dialogues. What are they doing tonight?

1 *They're going to the theatre.*

b Talk to a partner about your plans for tonight, tomorrow, and next weekend.

2 **a** Complete the text with the verbs in the past simple or past continuous. What do you think the scientists saw?

Lost in the Loch!

In the summer of 1980 a Spanish tourist, Gaspar Carner, ¹*went* to Great Britain on holiday. When he ²_____ in Scotland, he ³_____ to visit Loch Ness, the famous lake where people say there is a monster. But while he ⁴_____ across the lake in a boat, his bag ⁵_____ into the water. In the bag were his passport, car keys, pen, and all his money. Loch Ness is 150 metres deep, so he ⁶_____ to see his possessions again!
Fourteen years later, in 1994, some scientists in a mini-submarine ⁷_____ the bottom of the lake. They ⁸_____ the Loch Ness monster. Suddenly one of them ⁹_____ something black in the water. They went nearer …

go

travel
decide

go
fall

not expect

explore
look for

see

b ◦18◦ Listen to Mr Carner. What happened?

3 ◦19◦ Listen to the sounds and make sentences.

1 *They were having a party when the police arrived.*

4 Read and match the titles to paragraphs 1 to 4.

My first best friend	**My first record**
My first memory of a news event	**My first home**

There's always a first time

Jack Charlton is one of Britain's best-known footballers and managers. He and his brother Bobby were in the English team which won the World Cup in 1966. In 1994 he took Ireland into the World Cup. Here he talks about some of his first experiences.

❶ _____
A flat in Ashington, near Newcastle. My brother and I were born there. The toilet was on the other side of the road. There were no bathrooms in Ashington.

❷ _____
A boy called Jimmy Goldsworthy. We met at school. Later, when I was playing football away from home a lot, we lost touch. He died a few years ago.

❸ _____
I remember the day when World War II finished. I was eight or nine at the time, and we heard it on the radio when we were having lunch. We all stopped eating and got up and cheered.

❹ _____
Frank Sinatra's *Nancy with the laughing face*, which I bought when Sinatra was touring round England in the early fifties.

5 *Talk about … your first …*

Talk to a partner about the topics in ex.4.

◦20◦ 🎵 *Don't you want me?*, The Human League

47

Focus on Easy Readers

1 **a** What kind of books do you enjoy reading in your language? Tick and compare with a partner.

biographies ☐   science fiction ☐

thrillers ☐   romantic books ☐

detective stories ☐   short stories ☐

historical books ☐   autobiographies ☐

non-fiction (e.g. science) ☐

b What do you read in English? Have you ever read an *Easy Reader*?

Q1 **What are *Easy Readers*?**
Easy Readers are books with simple grammar and vocabulary to help students practise reading in English. There are different levels of difficulty, e.g. beginner, elementary, etc.

Q2 **What kind of books are there?**
There are all kinds of books, both fiction and non-fiction. Choose the kind of book you enjoy reading in your own language. Look at the front cover and read the back cover. Then read the first page. Does it interest you?

2 Quickly look at the three extracts and match them to the covers. What kind of books are they? Which one would you like to read?

Extract 1

A woman, Helen Stoner, dressed in black, comes to see Sherlock Holmes at his house in Baker Street in London. She's very unhappy and asks for his help. In this extract she's telling Holmes about the mysterious death of her sister.

5   'Please go on', said Holmes.
   'I couldn't sleep that night. It was a very stormy night, with a lot of wind and rain. Suddenly I heard a woman scream. It was my sister's voice. I ran into the corridor, and just then I heard a whistle, and a minute later the sound of falling metal. I didn't
10 know what it was. I ran to my sister's door. She opened it and fell to the ground. Her face was white and afraid, and she was crying, 'Help me, help me, Helen, I'm ill, I'm dying!' I put my arms around her, and she shouted in a terrible voice, 'Helen! Oh my God, Helen! It was the band! The speckled band!' She wanted to
15 say more but she couldn't. I called my stepfather, who tried to help her, but we could do nothing. And so my dear, dear sister died.'

Extract 2

My name is Catherine Parr. A month ago I was the Queen of England, the wife of King Henry the Eighth. Henry died and we buried *him* last week in St George's Church, Windsor. Two days ago, on 16th February 1547, I went back to the palace of
5 Whitehall, *which* was once my home. I wanted to take my letters and books and bring *them* back to my house. … When we arrived at the palace *it* was cold and dark. I walked into Henry's room. I sat down in one of Henry's large chairs in front of *his* wooden writing desk and looked at the pictures around the
10 room. Next to me there was a big picture of Henry when he was young. *He* was very handsome then, not like the fat old man *he* was later. …
   On the desk in front of me there was a wooden box with a large gold H on the top. I opened *it* slowly and took out some
15 old letters. Each letter was in different writing and some of *them* were old and yellow. One letter had a picture of a large bird on *it*. It was from Anne Boleyn, *who* was Henry's second wife. …

Extract 3

Why are we destroying the rainforests? There is a short answer to that question: money! Countries with rainforests cut down about 50,000 square kilometres of trees every year, and sell the wood to the rich countries of the North. Most rainforest wood
5 from Latin America goes to North America; wood from Africa goes to Europe; and wood from the forests of Asia goes to Japan.
   Switzerland stopped buying rainforest wood in 1982. Has your country stopped buying rainforest wood?
   International businesses buy rainforests in Latin America
10 where land is very cheap. They cut down the trees and sell the wood, and then they use the land for cows. Thousands of trees and animals have died, and forest people have lost their homes, so that today North Americans can eat cheap meat.

Q 3 How do I choose a book which is the right level for me?

Generally, it's best to choose one which you can read quickly and enjoy. If you aren't sure of the level, read the first page. If there are more than eight words that you don't know the book is probably too difficult for you to enjoy reading.

3 Quickly read **Extract 1**. How many words don't you know?

a 0 to 5 **b** 6 to 10 **c** more than 10

Q 4 What do I do when there are words in the story that I don't know?

First decide if the word is a noun, verb, adjective, etc. Then try to guess the meaning from the other words around it (= the 'context').

If you can't guess the meaning, you can either:

continue reading if you can still follow the story.	check if the word is in the Glossary at the back of the book.

use your dictionary.

4 **a** Find these words in **Extract 1**. In pairs, try to guess their meaning from the context.

stormy *l.6*	scream *l.7*	corridor *l.8*
whistle *l.9*	ground *l.11*	dying *l.12*
speckled band *l.14*	stepfather *l.15*	

b Check if any of the words are in the **Glossary**.

c Finally, use your dictionary to check their meaning.

Glossary for Extract 1

band *n.* = a thin piece of metal or material

corridor *n.* = the passage between rooms in a house

speckled *adj.* = with small marks of one colour on top of another colour

stepfather *n.* = your mother's second husband (not your real father)

whistle *v.* = a high sound made by blowing through the lips

Q 5 Sometimes I don't understand exactly who is who. Why?

It helps if you look carefully at the pronouns in the story.

5 Read **Extract 2** and write what each pronoun means.

l.3 him = Henry VIII

Q 6 I can often understand most of the words but I can't follow the story.

When people read in a foreign language they often translate every word and forget to concentrate on the story. Stop regularly and ask yourself questions about the story: Who's speaking? What are they doing? What's happened? What's going to happen next? Many *Easy Readers* include questions to answer after every chapter, to help you check your understanding of the story.

6 Read **Extract 3** and answer the questions.

1 Do these places buy or sell rainforest wood?

Africa	Europe	Japan
North America	Latin America	

2 Why do you think Switzerland doesn't buy wood from the rainforests?
3 What's the connection between cheap meat and rainforest wood?

Q 7 If I read *Easy Readers*, how will it help my English?

Easy Readers are a great way to revise grammar and learn new words. If you want to remember new words you need to write them down. Choose the important words in the story. For example, in *Henry VIII and his Six Wives*, the important words include: *King, Queen, palace*, etc.

7 Read **Extract 3** carefully. Write down four words that you think will be important in this book. Compare with a partner. Do you agree?

Q 8 I'd like to read more, but books are expensive.

Look for *Easy Readers* in your library. Or, if you haven't got a library, students in your class can buy just one book each, then swap them. Try to build a class library. Start reading!

3

Vocabulary file 3

☐ How can I remember new words?

The way you record and learn a word helps you remember it. For example, you can:
- imagine the word.
- write a personal example.
- make a word map.
- associate the word with a similar word in your language.

But you can't learn new words just by writing them down once. You have to revise them and try to remember them regularly. If you test yourself often on new vocabulary you can remember up to 80% of the words.

1 Word groups

a Imagine the words. Order them from large (1) to small (3).

1	elephant	[1]	dog	[3]	horse	[2]
2	van	[ ]	car	[ ]	lorry	[ ]
3	motorway	[ ]	path	[ ]	road	[ ]
4	village	[ ]	town	[ ]	city	[ ]
5	tree	[ ]	forest	[ ]	flower	[ ]

b Think of a real example you know to help you remember these words.

a bridge   a castle   a forest   an island   a lake
a mountain   a palace   a river   a square   a valley

2 Pronunciation Cross out the consonant (b, c, d, etc.) which isn't pronounced. Use a dictionary to check.

1	Wednesday	5	foreign
2	island	6	answer
3	castle	7	climb
4	half	8	listen

3 Key words Complete. Use a dictionary to check.

actually	even	now	suddenly	while

1 _____ the door opened and a man came out.
2 He's been to lots of countries. He's _____ been to Fiji!
3 We met _____ we were on holiday in Egypt.
4 **A** Would you like to come to a party tomorrow?
   B Well, _____ I can't. I'm working.
5 **A** What's your brother doing _____?
   B He's working in France.

■ Remember words with their opposites.

4 Verbs + prepositions Write the opposites of these verbs.

1	climb up *climb down*	a mountain
2	get in _____	the car
3	get on _____	a bus
4	go downstairs _____	
5	go under _____	a bridge

5 Extend your vocabulary

a Add words to the word map. Underline the stress.

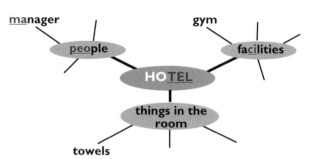

b Which of the words are like a word in your language (with the same or a different meaning)?

Organize your vocabulary learning!

■ **To remember words or phrases, follow this routine:**

a Record the new word with the correct stress.

b Try to remember it after a minute.

c Test your memory again after an hour.

d Remember it again the next day.

e Test yourself after a week, then after a month.

Try it!

■ Do 🗒 **Food A** *p.137* Then look at the pictures and test yourself on the words. After the lesson, look at the words again to see how many you can remember. Test yourself again the next day / week, etc. Can you remember 80%?

Grammar file 3

1 Possessive pronouns

It's my dog.
No, it's **mine**.

Subject pronoun	Object pronoun	Possessive adjective	**Possessive pronoun**
I	me	my	**mine**
you	you	your	**yours**
he	him	his	**his**
she	her	her	**hers**
it	it	its	
we	us	our	**ours**
they	them	their	**theirs**

Whose are these keys?   They're her keys.   They're **hers**.

☐ Use possessive pronouns to talk about people's possessions.

☐ You can use a name + *'s* with or without the noun. It's **Peter's** car. OR It's **Peter's**.

☐ Remember, don't use *the*. This is **mine**. NOT ~~This is the mine~~.

2 Present continuous (future)

> **+** I'**m meeting** some friends tomorrow evening.
>
> **−** They **aren't coming** to the party on Saturday.
>
> **?** What **are** you **doing** tonight?

☐ Use the present continuous (+ a future time expression) to talk about future arrangements. I'**m going** to the theatre on Friday.

> **Friday**
>
> *7.30 theatre*

☐ (*be*) + *going to* is also possible for future plans. I'**m going to** meet some friends tonight.

☐ Remember, we also use the present continuous to talk about things happening now / at the moment.
Ⓖ◀◀ 3 *p.2*

3 *How long does it take? It takes …*

How long does it take to fly from Paris to Lisbon?
(**It takes**) about three hours (by plane).
How long does it take (you) to get home?
(**It takes** me) about half an hour (by bus / car).

☐ Use *It takes …* (+ time) to talk about the duration of a journey.

☐ Remember: It takes … = general time
              It takes me … = a specific journey

4 Prepositions of movement

We walked **along** the street past the cinema.
Go **up** to the seventh floor.

☐ Use a verb of movement + preposition to describe movement. 📖 **Prepositions B** *p.135*

☐ *into* and *out of* are always followed by a noun. Come **in**. Come **into** the living-room. He went **out** last night. He went **out of** the house.

5 Past continuous

+			**−**		
I He She It	**was**	work**ing**.	I He She It	**wasn't**	work**ing**.
You We They	**were**		You We They	**weren't**	

?			**✓✗**
Was **Were**	he they	work**ing**?	Yes, he **was**. / No, he **wasn't**. Yes, they **were**. / No, they **weren't**.

What **were** you **doing** at six o'clock? I **was watching** TV.
It **was raining**, and we **were driving** home.

☐ Form the past continuous with *was* / *were* + verb + *-ing*.

☐ Use the past continuous:
1 to describe an action in progress at a specific time in the past.
2 to describe the scene at the beginning of a story.

I was working as a waitress when **I met** my boyfriend.

☐ Use the past continuous for an action in progress. Use the past simple for a short completed action.

▶ **Progress chart** File 3 *p.8*   ▶ Workbook *p.27*   Do **Grammar check 3**.

51

Same language, different people

> London isn't as dangerous as San Francisco.

1 **a** ✎ **Adjectives A** *p.138*

b Describe the photos. Use the **V** box to help you.

Towns / cities	**V**
a bay	buildings
a <u>c</u>able-car	a <u>mon</u>ument
a <u>sta</u>tue	a square (*n.*)
a <u>fou</u>ntain	

c Which photos are London and which are San Francisco?

2 Read the introduction to **Changing places**. Do you think these sentences are true (T) or false (F)?

1 San Francisco is more violent than London.
2 People have a higher standard of living in San Francisco.
3 Public transport is better in London.
4 Food in the United States is better than in England.

3 **a** In pairs, **A** read paragraphs 1 and 2, **B** read paragraphs 3 and 4. Tell your partner about the differences.

b Read your partner's texts. Decide together which place Julie prefers.

Changing places

Julie Willis is an artist from San Francisco who moved to London in 1988. We asked her to compare life in San Francisco and London. Here's what she told us.

❶ The cities
San Francisco is a lovely city in a beautiful bay. It's got lots of great buildings and places. It's smaller and much more modern than London, but it's less interesting. London has a lot more theatres and museums. The Americans are usually more interested in money than culture! The architecture in London is incredible and very stimulating, and the parks and markets are wonderful. London isn't as dangerous as San Francisco, and it's less violent. I feel much safer living here – nobody carries a gun, not even the police!

❷ The cost of living
People have a higher standard of living in the States because generally, it's much less expensive than England. For example, petrol is less than half the price and things like food, clothes, and cameras are much cheaper. It's a shopper's paradise and I always spend a fortune when I go back! It's a bit more expensive to rent a flat in London and my bills are much bigger than they were in San Francisco. So, although my salary in London is about the same as it was in the States, I have to work harder to get the same quality of life as I had before.

❸ Public transport
In San Francisco you can walk everywhere because it's a small city. There's less traffic than in London, and public transport is great. There are cable-cars to go up all the hills and electric buses which make the city much cleaner. Public transport in London is terrible and really expensive. It takes me an hour to get to work and the journey is usually stressful. London's dirtier too and much more polluted. The traffic is awful, because there are too many cars and the streets are narrow. But English drivers aren't as aggressive as American drivers!

❹ The food
Food in the States is generally much better. It's fresher, cheaper, and there's much more choice. Restaurants aren't as expensive as in London and the service is much better. In some restaurants they put a clock on the table when you arrive, and if they haven't served your meal in five minutes, they'll give you the food free! I'm usually disappointed when I eat out in London, although the Indian restaurants are excellent.

4

A

GRAMMAR FOCUS 1

Comparatives

> San Francisco is smaller than London.
> London is more / less interesting than San Francisco.
> London is / isn't as dangerous as San Francisco.

> San Francisco is much cleaner than London.
> It's a bit more expensive to rent a flat in London.

a To compare people, places, and things, use:
1 a comparative adjective + *than* ⓖ◄◄13 *p.5*
2 (*not*) *as* + adjective + *as*

b Use *much* for a big difference, *a bit* for a small difference.

PRACTICE 1

Make two sentences for each pair.

1 Moscow / Paris (big)
   Moscow is bigger than Paris.
   Paris isn't as big as Moscow.
2 Casablanca / Warsaw (hot)
3 Tokyo / Helsinki (noisy)
4 Chicago / San Francisco (violent)
5 the traffic in Bangkok / in Venice (bad)

PRONUNCIATION

○ 1 ○ Listen and repeat six sentences about cities.

 Remember, *-er*, *-as*, and *than* = /ə/.

4 ○ 2 ○ Listen to Julie. Tick the right box.

	🇺🇸	🇬🇧
• watch more TV	☐	☐
• worry more about their health	☐	☐
• do less sport	☐	☐
• can't drink in bars until they're 21	☐	☐
• dress more stylishly	☐	☐
• have less freedom	☐	☐
• leave home when they finish school	☐	☐

GRAMMAR FOCUS 2

Comparative adverbs

Adverbs	Comparative adverbs	
Regular		
slowly	more	slowly
healthily	less	healthily
Irregular		
hard	harder	
fast	faster	
well	better	
badly	worse	
a lot	more	
a little	less	

The Americans	live more healthily	than the English.
	dress less stylishly	

a Make regular comparative adverbs with *more / less* + adverb. Learn irregular adverbs.

b Use a comparative adverb + *than* to compare two actions.

PRACTICE 2

Make six sentences comparing men and women.

Women drive more slowly than men.

Men?   drive slowly   Women?
       dress badly
       listen well
       work hard
       talk a lot
       think logically

5 *Talk about ... your town*

In pairs, compare your town / city to another one.

the cities	the cost of living
the weather	the lifestyle
the food	public transport

If ...

> *If I lend you my newspaper, we'll start talking.*

1 Match the adverts and places.

- [ ] a department store
- [ ] a travel agency
- [ ] an insurance company
- [1] a car phone company
- [ ] a language school

2 IF YOU WANT TO LEARN ENGLISH QUICKLY, YOU WON'T FIND A BETTER PLACE.

3 If you find it cheaper anywhere else, we'll refund the difference.

1 What will you do if you break down on the motorway at night?

4 Will you have enough money when you're 65?

5 If you enjoy good food, great weather and beaches, and friendly people, you'll love Ghana.

GRAMMAR FOCUS

First conditional

If it rains	we'll stay in.
	we won't go out.

a Highlight the verbs in the adverts. Complete the rule.

Form the first conditional with:

if + _____ simple

AND

_____ / _____ + infinitive

b Use the first conditional to talk about a possible future situation (*if* = 'possible', *will / won't* = 'future').

will / won't

c Complete the chart with *will / won't*.

+		−	
I'll		I	
You'll		You	_____ find a better place.
He'll	love Ghana.	etc.	
She'll			
It'll			
We'll			
They'll			

?		✓✗	
_____ you have enough money?		Yes, I _____.	
		No, we _____.	

Contractions 'll = _____   _____ = will not

PRACTICE

a Match the two parts of the sentences.

1 You won't need cash
2 If you buy a new car today
3 You'll get 10% discount on your holiday
4 We'll deliver your shopping
5 If you buy two bottles

a if you spend more than £50. [ ]
b we'll give you another one free. [ ]
c you won't pay until next year! [ ]
d if you use our credit card. [1]
e if you book before April. [ ]

b Complete the sentences with the verbs.

1 Hurry up! We*'ll miss* the train if we *don't run*. (miss, not run)
2 I know it's a secret, but if you _____ me, I _____ anybody. (tell, not tell)
3 It's expensive to fly. If we _____, it _____ cheaper. (drive, be)
4 Their house is difficult to find. You _____ lost if you _____ a map. (get, not take)
5 She's very lazy. If she _____ harder, she _____ the exam. (not work, not pass)
6 It's midnight. If you _____ to bed now, you _____ tired in the morning. (not go, be)

54

AN AMERICAN IN PARIS

A young American was travelling by train across Europe to Paris. It was a long journey and he was bored. Sitting opposite him was a Frenchman of about fifty. There was a newspaper on the seat next to him.

'Excuse me', the American said. 'Can I borrow your newspaper, please?'

'No,' the man answered. 'I'm sorry. You can't.'

'Why not?' the American asked.

'Well,' the man said, 'it's quite simple. If I *lend* you my paper …'

PRONUNCIATION

a ○ 3 ○

he'll   she'll   they'll
bottle   simple   possible

b ○ 4 ○ Listen and write six phrases.

1 *I'll be there.*

2 ✎ **Verbs A** *p.139*

3 **a** Read the beginning of the story. Guess why the Frenchman doesn't want the American to read his paper.

b Look at pictures A to H. Imagine the story.

4 **a** Read and complete the story with the verbs in the right form.

| become | fall in love | invite | ~~lend~~ |
| find | run away | meet | kill | start |

b ○ 5 ○ Listen and check. Answer the questions.

1 Who's Yvette? Where does she live?
2 Why doesn't the Frenchman want the American to meet her?
3 Does the Frenchman lend the American his paper?

5 Roleplay the story. **A** You're the Frenchman. Look at the pictures. **B** You're the American. Help and correct **A**'s pronunciation. Swap roles.

B *Excuse me. Can I borrow …?*

6 🎲 **TB** *p.59* Play *If …*

1 If I *lend* you my newspaper, we _____ talking.
2 If we _____ talking, we _____ friends.
3 If we _____ friends, I'll _____ you to my house.
4 If I _____ you to my house, you _____ my beautiful daughter, Yvette.
5 If you _____ Yvette, you _____ with her.
6 If you _____ with her, you _____ together.
7 If you _____ together, I _____ you.
8 If I _____ you, I _____ you.
9 So, that's why I don't want to _____ you my paper.

4

B

55 is page number

Somebody told me

> I don't want to do anything tonight.

1 **a** ° 6 ° Julie is Zandra's secretary. Cover the dialogue and listen. Why does Julie call Zandra? What's Julie going to do?

Z Hello? Nova Fashions.
J Is that Zandra? It's me.
Z Who? Oh, Julie! What's the matter with you? You sound terrible!
J I know. I feel awful. ¹_____ _____ A really bad cold, or flu.
Z Oh dear. ²_____
J ³_____ But I'm going to take something now. I'm sorry but I really can't come to work today. I'm going to stay in bed.
Z Of course. I understand. You can't go anywhere with a cold like that. ⁴_____ _____
J Yes, my mother's coming this afternoon. I'll come to work tomorrow if I feel better.
Z Of course, Julie. Well, stay at home today, and get better soon.
J Thanks very much, Zandra. Bye.

b Complete the dialogue with these phrases. Listen again to check.

No, nothing.
Is there anybody to look after you?
Have you taken anything?
I think I've caught something.

GRAMMAR FOCUS

some / any / no + body / thing / where

a Highlight the *some / any / no …* words in the dialogue. Complete the chart.

	+	− and ?	− and as subject
People	somebody	anybody	_____
Things	*something*	_____	_____
Places	somewhere	_____	nowhere

b Look at rules 1 to 4. Find an example from the dialogue for each rule.

1 In + use *some…*
   I'd like to go **somewhere** this evening.

2 In ? use *any…*
   Did you see **anybody**?

3 In − use *any…*
   I didn't buy **anything**.

4 In − short answers, and as the subject, use *no…*
   Did you see **anybody**?
   No, **nobody**. / **Nobody** was there.

PRACTICE

a Complete with *somebody / anybody,* etc.
1 Eric lives *somewhere* in Argentina.
2 Are you doing _____ tonight?
3 Do you know _____ who speaks Hungarian?
4 I met _____ interesting last night.
5 Look! There's _____ strange in your soup.

b Answer with *Nobody., Nowhere.,* or *Nothing.*
1 What did you do last night?   _____
2 Where did you go yesterday?   _____
3 Who did you see?   _____

c Answer the questions in **b** with a full sentence.
1 *I didn't do anything.*

---

else Ⓥ
else = another thing / person / place
Would you like anything **else**?
I don't like this place. Let's go somewhere **else**.

2 ◦ 7 ◦ Julie went back to work the next day. Listen and write true (T) or false (F).

1 Julie saw the doctor.
2 Julie says she didn't go anywhere yesterday.
3 Zandra spoke to Julie on the phone.
4 Zandra went to see Julie yesterday afternoon.
5 Zandra's husband was at home yesterday.
6 Zandra is angry with Julie.

3 **a** Ask the teacher questions 1 to 8 below. Ask follow-up questions too.

1 *Have you been anywhere interesting recently?*

How interesting is your life?

Find somebody who ...	Name
1 has been somewhere interesting recently.	
2 has seen something funny recently.	
3 has bought something expensive recently.	
4 watched something awful on TV last night.	
5 is going somewhere special tonight.	
6 is meeting somebody after the class.	
7 is going to do something exciting this weekend.	
8 is going to go away somewhere soon.	

b Ask other students. Find positive answers to all the questions.

PRONUNCIATION

Cross out the word with a different vowel sound.

1 some   one   done
  once   ~~home~~   nothing

2 nobody   told   wrote
  spoken   woke   not

3 on   door   borrow
  along   cost

4 before   born   work
  boring   important

4 **a** Have you ever been trapped in a lift? Do you know anybody who has?

b Read about Mrs Poor. Use the pictures. Number the paragraphs 1 to 7.

Poor Mrs Poor!

a ☐ On Monday morning, somebody phoned to say the lift didn't work. Workers immediately came and repaired it.

b ☐ When the doors opened, Mrs Poor came out, after 67 hours in the lift. But when she left the car park, the attendant didn't believe her story, and made her pay extra.

c [1] Mrs Moira Poor, aged 69, got into the lift at the Auckland City car park in New Zealand last Friday afternoon. She didn't get out again until Monday morning.

d ☐ She slept on the floor, and continued shouting all day Saturday and Sunday, but nobody came.

e [6] 'I was very worried when she didn't come home on Friday,' said Mrs Poor's husband. 'I phoned the police, but we couldn't find her anywhere.'

f ☐ A few days later the city council gave her $2,100 and free parking in Auckland for life.

g ☐ When she got into the lift, Mrs Poor was carrying only a handbag. After a few seconds, the lift stopped between floors. She shouted and shouted, and rang the alarm, but nobody heard her.

The best and the worst

> *The most cosmopolitan city in Europe.*

1 **a** Read the slogans. What do you think they are advertising?

① THE WORLD'S MOST POPULAR KING-SIZE FILTER CIGARETTE.

② *The most beautiful drink in the world.*

③ Probably the best lager in the world.

④ *The greatest film ever made.*

⑤ **The world's friendliest airline.**

⑥ The oldest university in Europe.

⑦ *The most famous building in the world.*

⑧ **The happiest place on earth.**

b ◦ **8** ◦ Listen and write the names of the products / places. Do you agree with the slogans?

PRONUNCIATION

a ◦ **9** ◦ Listen and repeat the superlatives. Is -*est* pronounced /est/ or /ɪst/?

b ◦ **10** ◦

 the   their   them   than   another

drink   old   made   advert   world

c ◦ **11** ◦ When do you say /ðə/? When do you say /ðiː/?

the oldest   the world   The End
the Italians   the sun   the city centre

GRAMMAR FOCUS

Superlative adjectives

a Complete the chart.

He's the **tallest**.

Adjective	Comparative	Superlative
old	_____	the oldest
big	bigger	_____
friendly	friendlier	_____
famous	more famous	_____
popular	_____	_____
Irregular		
_____	_____	the worst
good	_____	_____

Comparatives: spelling rules ⑬ ◄◄13 *p.5*

b Complete the rules.

To make superlative adjectives:

1-syllable adjectives	+ _____
1 vowel + 1 consonant	double consonant
1 or 2-syllable adjectives ending in *y*	_____
other 2-syllable adjectives and 3-syllable adjectives	_____ + adjective

c Use *the* or a possessive adjective before a superlative.
the oldest university, **my** best friend

PRACTICE

a Complete with a superlative adjective.

Did you know that ...?

1 The _____ hotel in the world is in Kiruna in Sweden. (cold)

2 Astronomers have recently discovered the _____ star in our galaxy. (young)

3 The _____ man in the world is the Sultan of Brunei. (rich)

4 The _____ animal in the world is the koala bear. (lazy)

5 The _____ team sport is rugby. (dangerous)

6 The _____ hotel room in the world is the Galactic Fantasy suite at the Crystal Palace in Nassau. (expensive)

b Match sentences 1 to 6 with a to f.

a More players get injured than in any other sport. ☐

b It sleeps for about 22 hours a day. ☐

c It's made only of ice. [1]

d He once left a tip in a hotel in Cyprus of £115,000. ☐

e It costs $25,000 a night to stay there, and includes a personal robot-servant called Ursula. ☐

f It's only 10,000 years old. ☐

2 a ∘12∘ Listen to six quiz questions. Circle the answers.

1 India China Berlin
2 Canada Brazil Russia
3 San Marino Vatican City Andorra
4 Tokyo New York London
5 Mars Jupiter the Earth
6 chimpanzees dogs dolphins

b Listen again. Write sentences.

1 *The longest wall in the world is in China.*

3 Talk about ... the best in town

Talk about the town where you're studying.
A and **B** You know the town. **C** You're a tourist. Ask questions about the town. Swap roles.

- What are (interesting) monuments in this town?
- Where's (good) shopping area?
- What's (easy) way to get around the city?

- What's (dangerous) area to walk?
- What's (old) building?
- What's (beautiful) park?

- What's the (nice) place to eat typical food?
- Where's the (exciting) nightlife?
- Where's the (good) place to buy souvenirs?

4 a Read the advert for Edinburgh. Have you ever been there? Do you agree?

Come to *Edinburgh*, the most beautiful city in Britain!

It's got the most impressive castle, the friendliest and most generous people, the greatest dancers, the best whisky and the biggest and most important arts festival in the world.

b What pictures would you use to advertise your town?

c Write an advert for your town or country. Invent some good slogans.

At the restaurant

~MENU~

Starters
Smoked salmon with mustard sauce
Tomato and orange soup
Chef's green salad

Main courses
Pepper steak
Roast chicken with lemon
Smörgåsbord (a Swedish cold buffet with seafood, fish, and cold meat)
Mushroom and spinach lasagne

Desserts
Lemon cheesecake
Fresh fruit salad and cream
Chocolate gateau

3 courses 140 krona

4

Ordering a meal

1 📖 **Food B** *p.137*

2 Pieter's meeting two old friends, Benni and Hana, for dinner in a restaurant in Stockholm. Read the menu.

1 How many meat dishes are there?
2 Is there anything for vegetarians?

3 **a** ◦**13**◦ Listen. On the menu, tick the food you hear.

b Listen again. Which word is missing in each phrase?

for A table⁄three, please.	C
Are you ready order?	☐
What you recommend?	☐
I have the pepper steak.	☐
Rare, medium, well-done?	☐
The roast chicken me, please.	☐
What you like to drink?	☐
I like some mineral water too, please.	☐

c Who says what? Write C (customer) or W (waiter). Find three ways to order food.

4 Roleplay. **A** is the waiter. **B** and **C** are customers.

Complaining

5 **a** ◦**14**◦ Listen to five dialogues. What do Benni and Hana say? Listen again. What does the waiter say?

b Use the pictures. Practise the dialogues.

6 **a** ◦**15**◦ Listen. True (T) or false (F)?

1 Nobody has a dessert.
2 They all have coffee.
3 Pieter pays for the meal.
4 There's a mistake in the bill.

b Listen again and complete the phrases.

1 Would you *like any dessert*?
2 Just a black _____ _____ _____.
3 What about _____ _____?
4 I'll have _____ _____ _____.
5 Nothing for _____, _____.
6 Could I _____ _____ _____?
7 We're in _____ _____.
8 I'll _____ _____.
9 There's a _____ here.
10 The bill's _____.

7 📖 **Travel phrasebook 4** *p.132*

Focus on speaking

Learning to speak a language is like learning to drive. You have to practise a lot to get better.

Read what these students say about speaking English. Which is your biggest problem?

> I haven't got enough vocabulary to say what I want to.

> I always worry that I make too many mistakes.

> I speak too slowly because I have to translate everything I want to say before I can say it.

> I feel embarrassed when I speak English and I can't express my personality.

> I feel strange speaking English in class to people who speak my language.

Tip 1 If you don't know a word or phrase, don't just stop. Try to find another way to express it with words you know.

1 **a** Which words is this student trying to say?
I don't know the word in English but …

1 it's like a cat but bigger. It's yellow and black.
2 you use it to wash your hands. It smells nice.
3 it's something you do on holiday when you want to get brown.
4 you win them at the Olympic games. They're made of gold or silver.
5 it's how you feel before an interview or an exam.

b Describe a picture to a partner who points to the right one. Swap.

Tip 2 You can always say more than you think. Don't worry about making mistakes. The important thing is to communicate what you want to say.

2 ►◄ **Find the differences** A *p.121* B *p.124*

Tip 3 Think what you want to say before you speak. It gives you confidence.

3 *Talk about … your living-room*

a You're going to describe your living-room. Think for one minute about what you can say.

b Describe your room to a partner.

Tip 4 Practise speaking English as much as you can. The more you practise, the more confident you'll feel.

In class you can:
a take every opportunity to speak English. Never use your language if you can say it in English. Use
📖 **Classroom language** *p.143*.
b talk as much as you can when you work in pairs / groups.
Outside class you can:
c learn and practise the words you need to talk about your job, family, etc.
d use the 'Listen and speak' cassette.
e practise before and after class with another student.

4 **a** Read ideas **a** to **e**. Which of them have you tried?

b Choose an 'outside class' activity. Try it this week.

Another day in Paradise

1 **a** Look at the photos. What can you see?

A world of difference

1 Which is the richest country in the world?
   a Saudi Arabia **b** Switzerland **c** the USA
2 Which is the largest continent?
   a Africa **b** Asia **c** America
3 Which is the world's busiest international airport?
   a Frankfurt **b** Chicago **c** London Heathrow
4 Which nationality drinks the most coffee?
   a the Brazilians **b** the Finns **c** the British
5 Which is the most addictive?
   a coffee **b** alcohol **c** tobacco
6 Which nationality eats the most chocolate?
   a the Swiss **b** the Belgians **c** the Germans
7 Which nationality lives the longest?
   a the Americans **b** the Japanese **c** the Spanish
8 Which is the most popular spectator-sport in the world?
   a golf **b** football **c** basketball

b **○16○** Listen to the politician. Write her promises.

1	jobs	create 800,000 new jobs
2	houses	
3	taxes	
4	education	
5	pensions	

c Listen again. Say what her party will do if they win the elections.
1 *If they win … they'll create 800,000 new jobs.*

2 **a** In groups, imagine you are politicians. Write three promises for the next election.
If you vote for us, we'll build more houses.

b Tell the class your promises. Whose are the best?

3 **a** Do the quiz in pairs. Decide on the order for **b** and **c**.
1 *We think (that) Saudi Arabia is the richest. We think Switzerland is richer than the USA.*

b Compare with another pair. Check with the teacher.

4 **Talk about … the best and the worst**

Make superlative sentences. Tell a partner. Do you both agree?
A *I think the most beautiful city in this country is Avignon.*
B *I agree. / I don't agree. I think Montpellier is more beautiful.*

I think …
(beautiful) city in this country is …
(attractive) actor / actress in the world is …
(good) place for a holiday is …
(exciting) sport to watch is …
(good) film I've seen recently is …
(bad) programme on TV is …

4

Song

5 ｜ 17 ｜ ♫ *Another day in Paradise*, Phil Collins

a This is a song about a homeless woman in a big city. Listen and ⟨circle⟩ the right word.

b Complete the song and read it with the **Glossary**. Why does the singer think 'it's another day for you and me in Paradise'?

c Complete the sentences with the words.

anything   anywhere   nobody
something   somewhere

1   She hasn't got _____ to live.
2   She needs _____ to sleep.
3   The man doesn't do _____ to help her.
4   _____ wants to know her.
5   The singer asks somebody to do
    _____.

d What do you think of the song? There are over 350,000 homeless people in England. What about in your town?

She calls out to the man on the _____	(seat / ⟨street⟩)
'Sir, _____ you help me?	(can / could)
It's cold and I've nowhere to _____	(sleep / stay)
Is there somewhere you can _____ me?'	(tell / show)
5 He walks on, doesn't _____ back	(look / go)
He pretends he can't _____ her	(see / hear)
Starts to whistle as he crosses the _____	(road / street)
_____ embarrassed to be there	(Seems / Feels)

Chorus
Oh, think twice
10   'Cause it's another day for you and me in Paradise
Just think about it

She calls out to the man on the _____	(street / seat)
He can see she's been _____	(crying / flying)
She's got blisters on the soles of her _____	(foot / feet)
15 She can't _____ but she's trying	(talk / walk)

Chorus

Oh Lord, is there nothing more _____ can do?	(anybody / anyone)
Oh Lord, there must be something you can _____	(say / do)
You can tell from the lines on her _____	(face / hands)
You can see that she's been _____	(here / there)
20 Probably been moved on from every _____	(town / place)
'Cause she didn't fit in _____	(here / there)

Chorus

Glossary
l.5   **walks on** = continues walking
l.6   **pretends** = wants her to think
l.8   **embarrassed** = uncomfortable
l.14 **blisters** = if you walk a lot you get blisters on your feet
l.14 **sole** = the bottom of your foot
l.16 **Lord** = God
l.20 (**she's**) **been moved on** = people have told her to leave
l.21 **she didn't fit in** = people didn't accept her

4

◁▷

63

Vocabulary file 4

Are British and American English the same?

The British and the Americans speak the same language, although they have a different accent. But sometimes they use a different word, e.g. *autumn* (*n.* Br.) = *fall* (*n.* US). There are also some differences in spelling, e.g. *centre* = *center* (US), *colour* = *color* (US). You will find examples of these differences in songs and films, and when you travel.

1 British and American English Complete the chart.

highway ~~candy~~ pharmacy cookies
gasoline a check subway

	British	American
1	sweets	*candy*
2	biscuits	_____
3	underground	_____
4	petrol	_____
5	chemist's	_____
6	road	_____
7	a bill	_____

2 Word groups Put the food in the right group. Add one more to each.

lamb peach ~~spinach~~ ice-cream
salmon chicken strawberry beans
apple pie peas pineapple cheesecake

Vegetables	Fruit	Meat and fish	Desserts
spinach	_____	_____	_____
_____	_____	_____	_____
_____	_____	_____	_____
_____	_____	_____	_____

3 Restaurant Number the words in the order you ask for them in a restaurant (1 to 6).

bill ☐	coffee ☐	main course ☐
starter ☐	menu ☐	dessert ☐

■ **Synonyms are words with the same meaning. Try to record and learn them together.**

4 Synonyms Complete the words.

1	small = *little*	6	just = o _ _ y
2	hard = d _ _ _ _ _ _ t	7	polluted = d _ _ _ y
3	normally = u _ _ _ _ _ y	8	fast = q _ _ _ _ _ y
4	maybe = p _ _ _ _ _ s	9	kind (*n.*) = t _ _ e
5	big = l _ _ _ e		

5 Key words Complete.

else probably recently as than

1 I don't like this sweater. Have you got anything _____?
2 This car isn't as fast _____ mine.
3 If you go by train it'll _____ be cheaper.
4 How's Maria? I don't know. I haven't seen her _____.
5 She works much harder _____ me.

6 Verbs Complete with the right verb. Use 📖 **Verbs A** *p.139* to check.

1 Excuse me. Can you _____ me the time? (say / tell)
2 Tonight I'm going to _____ a football match on TV. (watch / look at)
3 Hurry up. If we don't leave now, we'll _____ the bus. (lose / miss)
4 Can you _____ me a pen? I can't find mine. (lend / borrow)
5 Where did you _____ your husband? (know / meet)
6 Lawyers _____ a lot of money. (win / earn)
7 When I go out I always _____ a handbag. (carry / wear)

7 Adjectives Test yourself on 📖 **Adjectives A** *p.138.* Think of a place you know for each adjective. *exciting – New York*

Organize your vocabulary learning!

■ **Use your dictionary to check if words are British or American English.**
Record both words.
film = movie (US)

Try it!

■ **Are these words British or American? Use your dictionary. What's their equivalent?**

1 sidewalk *(US)* pavement *(Br.)*	4 apartment
2 truck	5 vacation
3 elevator	6 chips

Grammar file 4

1 Comparative adjectives, *as ... as*

San Francisco is **cheaper than** London.
New York is **more / less dangerous** than LA.
Restaurants are(n't) **as** expensive **as** in London.
The service is **much / a bit** better.

☐ To compare people, places, and things, use:
  1 a comparative adjective + *than* Ⓖ◄◄13 *p.5*
  2 (*not*) *as* + adjective + *as*

☐ Use *much* (+ comparative) for a big difference, *a bit*
  (+ comparative) for a small difference.

2 Comparative adverbs

	Adverb	Comparative adverb
Regular	quickly	**more / less quickly**
Irregular	fast	**faster**
	hard	**harder**
	well	**better**
	badly	**worse**
	a lot	**more**
	a little	**less**

Women drive **more slowly than** men.
Men drive **faster than** women.

☐ To compare two actions use a comparative
  adverb + *than*.

3 First conditional

will / won't

+		−	
I You etc.	**'ll** miss the train.	I You etc.	**won't** catch it.

?		✓✗	
Will you tell him?		Yes, I **will**. / No, I **won't**.	

Contractions 'll = will   won't = will not

☐ Use *will / won't* + infinitive for all persons.

If ... + will / won't

If you don't work, you **won't** pass the exam.
She**'ll** miss the train **if** she doesn't hurry.

☐ Make the first conditional with *if* + present simple
  and *will / won't* + infinitive. The *if*-phrase can
  come first or second.

☐ Use the first conditional to talk about a possible
  future situation.

4 *some... / any... / nobody*, etc.

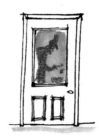

Somebody's in the bathroom.

Is **anybody** in the bathroom?

There isn't **anybody** in the bathroom.

	+	? and −	− and as subject
People	somebody someone	anybody anyone	nobody no one
Things	something	anything	nothing
Places	somewhere	anywhere	nowhere

☐ Use *somebody / anything / nowhere* when you don't
  know exactly who / what / where.

☐ in + use *some...*

☐ in ? and − use *any...*

  BUT in − short answers, and as the subject, use *no...*,
  etc.
  Who's in the bathroom? **Nobody**.
  Nobody's in the bathroom.

☐ Remember, (*some*)*body* and (*some*)*one* mean the same.

5 Superlative adjectives

Adjective	Comparative	Superlative	Spelling
tall happy	taller happier	**the** tall**est** **the** happi**est**	+ est
modern expensive	more modern more expensive	**the most** modern **the most** expensive	+ the most
good bad	better worse	**the best** **the worst**	irregular

Everest is **the highest** mountain in the world.
French champagne is **the most expensive**.

☐ Use superlative adjectives to say that someone or something
  is the biggest / tallest in a group.

☐ Use *the* + *est* or *most* to make superlative adjectives.
  Spelling rules Ⓖ◄◄13 *p.5*

▶ **Progress chart** File 4 *p.8*   ▶ Workbook *p.33* Do **Grammar check 4**.

65

4

Ⓖ

Born in the USSR

> *I've had this T-shirt for 15 years.*

5

A

A Russian star

Natalia Morskova is probably the top player of a very hard sport: women's handball. She was born in Rostov in Russia in the former USSR on 17th January 1966. She first started playing when she was twelve, and she has been a professional player since she was sixteen. She was the star member of the Russian women's team, and in 1988 they won the Olympic bronze medal. Two years later they became world champions, and Natalia was voted the top player in the world. Then she decided to leave Russia and went to Spain to play for the Spanish league champions, Mar Valencia. She has lived in Spain since 1991. She has been married for ten years and has a daughter, Natasha, aged nine.

1 **a** Look at the photo of Natalia. What's she doing? What do you know about her from the photo?

b Read about Natalia. In pairs, find why these numbers are important to her.

17   12   16   1988   1990   1991   10   9

2 **a** Complete the answers from the text.

1 How long has she lived in Spain?

She _____ _____ in Spain _____ 1991.

2 How long has she been married?

She _____ _____ married _____ ten years.

b Answer 'yes' or 'no'.

1 Does she live in Spain now?
2 Is she married now?

GRAMMAR FOCUS

Present perfect + *for* / *since*

1991 ················· for … years ············ now

She went to Spain in 1991.   She lives in Spain now.
How long has she lived in Spain?
She's lived in Spain since 1991.
She's lived in Spain for … years.

a Complete the rules with *since* or *for*.

To answer the question *How long …?* use:

1 _____ + a period of time:
(10) minutes, (2) hours, (4) days, (3) years

2 _____ + a fixed point in time:
a date (6th June), a month (July), a year (1996)

b Use the present perfect to talk about actions which started in the past and are still true now.

PRACTICE

a Put the expressions in the right group.

three months   my last birthday   I was a child
May   1960   ten days   a few weeks ago   ages
I was eighteen   a long time

for	since
	I was a child

b Complete with the present perfect + *since* or *for*.

1 Natalia started playing handball when she was twelve. She plays handball now.
She's played handball since she was twelve.

2 We bought our car two years ago. We have it now.
We _____

3 Lee moved to Leeds in April. He lives there.
He _____

4 I got married six months ago. I'm still married.
They _____

5 Italy became a republic in 1946. It's a republic now.
Italy _____

c Write the five questions.

1 *How long has she played handball?*

PRONUNCIATION

a ⚬ 1 ⚬ Listen and repeat.

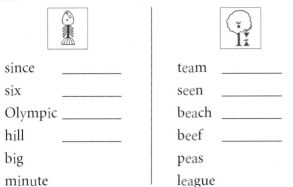

since	_____	team	_____
six	_____	seen	_____
Olympic	_____	beach	_____
hill	_____	beef	_____
big		peas	
minute		league	

b Put these words in the right column.

leave   live   chip   cheap   sit   seat   eat   it

c ⚬ 2 ⚬ Listen and write the four questions. Underline the stressed words.

1 _How long_ have they been _married_?

3 Ask a partner _How long …?_ questions from the chart below. Tell the class any interesting answers.

A _How long have you been in this school?_
B _Since October. How about you?_

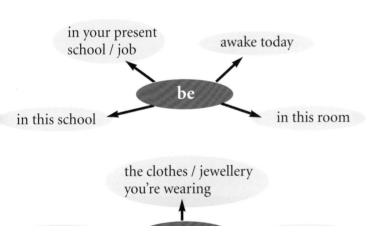

in your present school / job

awake today

be

in this school

in this room

the clothes / jewellery you're wearing

your car / bike   **have**   that hairstyle

the other students in this class

your teacher   **know**   your best friend

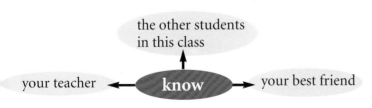

here   **live**   in your present house / flat

4 **a** ⚬ 3 ⚬ Listen to the interview. Number the photos in the order Natalia talks about them (1 to 6).

My favourite things

A ☐
B ☐
C ☐
D ☐
E ☐
F ☐

b Listen again. How long has she had each thing? Where did she get them?

5 _Talk about …_ **your favourite things**

List five possessions that are important to you. Swap lists with a partner. Ask:

How long have you had …?
Where did you get it / them?
Why is it / are they important to you?

> **buy (for) / give (to)**   🅥
> It was / They were a (birthday) present.
> (My boyfriend) bought it / them **for** me.
> (My mother) gave it / them **to** me.
> I got it / them from (a shop in Milan).

As old as you feel?

I want to be free.

You're only as old as you feel ... but how old do you feel?

1 Would you like to …?
go and work in a foreign country? ☐
travel round Europe by bus? ☐

2 Are you planning to …?
go dancing this weekend? ☐
think about a pension soon? ☐

3 Are you hoping to …?
stay in your present job / school? ☐
live somewhere else within five years? ☐

4 Do you want to …?
look younger than you are? ☐
stay at home most evenings? ☐

5 Do you need to …?
worry about cholesterol? ☐
wear glasses for reading? ☐

6 Do you like …?
meeting new people? ☐
wearing the latest fashions? ☐

SCORE

Look at your ✓ answers.
Score 3 points for ✓ to orange questions
Score 1 point for ✓ to green questions

12 to 18	You're young and you have no worries. Enjoy life while you can.
8 to 11	You're young at heart. You have a responsible attitude to life, but you enjoy having fun, too.
0 to 7	Welcome to middle-age. But remember, it's never too late to do something new.

Age-groups Ⓥ

a baby	☐	an adult	☐
a child	☐	middle-aged	☐
a teenager	☐	old	☐

1 a Match the pictures with words from the Ⓥ box.

b How old is 'old'?

2 a Interview a partner with the questionnaire. Ask *Why?*.

b Work out your partner's score.

GRAMMAR FOCUS

Verb + *to* + infinitive

a Look at the questionnaire.

1 Which verbs are followed by *to* + infinitive?
2 Which verb is different?

would like to or *like* + *-ing*?

b Compare:

1 I like learning new things.
2 I'd like to learn Italian this year.

Which one is general? ☐
When does *like* = *want to*? ☐

PRACTICE

a Complete with *to* + a verb.

---

be   bring   do   go   go cycling
~~learn~~   rest   stay   study

---

1 Sue loves languages. At the moment she's trying *to learn* Japanese.

2 Last year we decided _____ to the Bahamas for a relaxing holiday. We really needed _____ .

3 **A** What job would you like _____ after you leave school?

   B Well, I'm planning _____ maths at university because I want _____ an accountant.

4 You don't need _____ your book to class tomorrow.

5 We were hoping _____ but it was raining so we decided _____ at home.

b Complete with *to* + a verb or verb + *-ing*.

1 Would you like _____ tonight? (go out)
2 Do you like _____? (cook)
3 He'd like _____ a new flat. (buy)
4 They don't like _____. (fly)
5 What would you like _____ next? (do)

PRONUNCIATION

a ◦ **4** ◦ Listen and write five sentences.

1 *I'd <u>like</u> to be <u>rich</u>.*

b Underline the stressed words. Is *to* pronounced /tuː/ or /tə/?

3 Finish the sentences. Compare with a partner. Are any of your answers the same?

1 When I was young, I wanted to …
2 This summer I'm hoping …
3 When I retire, I'd like …
4 This weekend I need …
5 At the moment I'm trying …
6 In my free time I like …
7 Next year I'm planning …

4 ►◄ **Would you like to …?** A *p.121* B *p.124*

5 **a** Look at the photo of Charles Bornat. How old do you think he is?

Charles Bornat

b ◦ **5** ◦ Listen to an interview with Charles. How old is he? What are his hobbies?

c Listen again. Complete the sentences.

Past

He was born in …
When he was young, he wanted to be a …
Before he retired he was an …

Present

He's been retired since he was …
He's lived in Coventry since …
He likes …
He's trying to …
He likes listening to …
He's a big fan of …

Future

He wants to …
He'd like to …
He's hoping to …

◦ **6** ◦ 🎵 *I want to break free*, Queen

Love stories

> *He thought she was dead so he killed himself.*

1 Match the words and definitions. Pronounce the words.

1	**des**perate /ˈdesprət/ (*adj.*)	a a person who carries a message
2	**e**nemy /ˈenəmɪ/ (*n.*)	b something you don't want other people to know
3	**me**ssenger /ˈmesɪndʒə/ (*n.*)	c an underground room for dead people
4	**peace** /piːs/ (*n.*)	d make someone think something is true when it isn't
5	**pre**tend /prɪˈtend/ (*v.*)	e the opposite of *friend*
6	**se**cret /ˈsiːkrɪt/ (*n.*)	f ready to do anything to change a situation *1*
7	**tomb** /tuːm/ (*n.*)	g your uncle's or aunt's child
8	**cou**sin /ˈkʌzn/ (*n.*)	h the opposite of *war*

2 **a**   7   Cover the story. While you listen, follow the pictures. Which picture is <u>not</u> in the story?

b   Read and check.

One night

1 **One night** a young man met a girl at a party, and they fell in love at first sight.

2 **That night** he went to her house, ¹*because* he wanted to see her again. He was afraid to go in ²*so* he waited under the balcony until she appeared.

3 They spent the night together, and **the next day** they got married. Their marriage had to be a secret ³_____ their families were enemies.

4 **The following day**, the man had a fight with his wife's cousin and killed him ⁴_____ he had to leave the city.

5 The girl was desperate ⁵_____ she wanted to be with her husband. ⁶_____ she made a plan.

She decided to take a drug and pretend to be dead, and **later**, when she woke up, she planned to escape from the family tomb and run away with her husband.

6 **Then** she sent a message to her husband, and took the drug. But her husband didn't get the message ⁷_____ the messenger couldn't find him.

7 **When** the man heard that his wife was 'dead' he hurried to her tomb. He thought she really was dead ⁸_____ he killed himself.

8 **When** the girl woke up, she saw her husband was dead ⁹_____ she killed herself, too.

9 **Finally**, ¹⁰_____ both their children were dead, the two families made peace.

5

C

GRAMMAR FOCUS 1

so / because

> He went to her house because he wanted to see her.
> He was afraid to go in so he waited under the balcony.

Complete the rules with *so* or *because*.

1 _____ answers the question *Why?* and tells you the reason for something.
2 _____ tells you what happened as a result of something.

PRACTICE 1

a Complete the story with *so* or *because*.

b Finish the sentences.

1 He wanted to see her again so …
2 He had to leave the city because …
3 The messenger couldn't find her husband so …
4 She killed herself because …

PRONUNCIATION

a ∘ 8 ∘ Listen and repeat. Is the /ə/ sound stressed?

desperate enemy messenger
balcony appear family

b ∘ 9 ∘ Underline the stressed syllable. Circle the /ə/ sound. Listen and check.

husb(a)nd afraid immediately
finally together again

3 **a** Look at the story again. Write the connectors (*One night*, etc.) from each paragraph under the right picture.

b In pairs, use the pictures and connectors to tell the story. **A** Do pictures A to E. **B** Do pictures F to J.

GRAMMAR FOCUS 2

had to / didn't have to

> He killed a man so he had to leave the city.

a Complete the chart.

Present	Past
I have to go.	_____
You don't have to go.	*You didn't have to go.*
Does he have to go?	_____

b Use *had to / didn't have to* + infinitive for past obligations.

PRACTICE 2

a Match the sentences.

1 My friend gave me a ticket.
2 I had to borrow an umbrella.
3 I didn't go away in August.
4 I didn't have to work yesterday.
5 I missed the last bus.
6 I had to go to the post office.
7 The hotels were full.

a It was a public holiday. ☐
b I had to get a taxi. ☐
c I didn't have to pay. ☐ *1*
d I needed some stamps. ☐
e I had to stay at a Youth Hostel. ☐
f I had to work. ☐
g I couldn't find mine. ☐

b Say them as one sentence, using *so* or *because*.

1 *My friend gave me a ticket* **so** *I didn't have to pay.*

4 In groups, write your own love story. Imagine as many details as you can.

A man …   (nationality / name)
met a woman …   (nationality / name)
in …   (where / when?)
and they …
The man was …   (age / adjectives / job)
and the woman was …   (age / adjectives / job)
They had to …
because …
One day …
so they had to …
Finally …

5

C

71

Famous in the 20th century

> Who said, 'I'm the greatest.'?

5

D

★ CINEMA ★

1 What did Humphrey Bogart say in *Casablanca* in 1942?
   a Play with me, Sam.
   b Play it, Sam.
   c Play it again, Sam.

2 Who said 'Hasta la vista, baby' in a film in 1992?
   a Arnold Schwarzenegger
   b Mel Gibson
   c Kevin Costner

★ SPORT ★

3 How many times did Ayrton Senna win the Formula 1 championship?
   a three
   b four
   c five

4 Which athlete won the 1988 Olympic men's 100 metres but didn't get a medal?
   a Carl Lewis
   b Michael Johnson
   c Ben Johnson

★ MUSIC ★

5 What song did Gene Kelly sing in a film in 1952?
   a *White Christmas*
   b *Singing in the rain*
   c *My way*

6 Which singer sang with Domingo and Pavarotti before two World Cup finals?
   a Caruso
   b Callas
   c Carreras

★ HISTORY ★

7 When did Germany become one country?
   a 10/11/87
   b 10/11/88
   c 10/11/89

8 Who became President of the USA in 1968 but had to resign in 1974?
   a Richard Nixon
   b Jimmy Carter
   c Lyndon Johnson

★ LITERATURE ★

9 What novel did Boris Pasternak write in 1957?
   a *The Idiot*
   b *Dr Zhivago*
   c *Anna Karenina*

10 Who wrote *A hundred years of solitude*?
   a Gabriel García Márquez
   b George Orwell
   c Alexander Solzhenitsyn

Score ____
10

1 Do the quiz in small groups. Check your answers with the teacher. What was your group's score?

GRAMMAR FOCUS

Questions with / without auxiliaries

> 1 What did Humphrey Bogart say in *Casablanca*?
> 2 Who said 'Hasta la vista, baby'?

a Look at quiz questions 1 and 2. When do we use *did*?

b Complete the rules with 'use' / 'don't use'.

1 When the question word is not the subject _____ *do / does / did*.

2 When a question word is the subject _____ *do / does / did*.

PRACTICE

Write the questions for these answers.

1 Fellini directed *La Dolce Vita* in 1960. (Who?)
   Who directed La Dolce Vita in 1960?
2 Michael Jordan played for the Chicago Bulls. (What team?)
   What team did Michael Jordan play for?
3 Bob Dylan sang *Blowing in the wind* in 1965. (Who?)
4 Albert Einstein won the Nobel prize for physics in 1921. (When?)
5 Anwar Sadat died in Cairo in October 1981. (Where?)
6 Dr J. L. Baird invented the TV in 1926. (Which scientist?)
7 The *Titanic* hit an iceberg in 1912. (Which ship?)

2 In pairs, write a quiz question for the class.

3 ►◄ 20th century quiz **GROUP A** *p.121*
GROUP B *p.124* **GROUP C** *p.125*

Asking the way

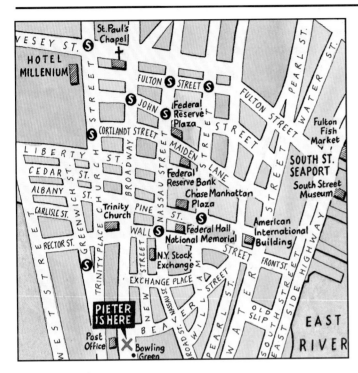

Giving directions

1 **a** Match the phrases and pictures.

1	Go along / up / down this street for about (400 metres).	*E*
2	Take the first turning on the right.	
3	Go past (the Stock Exchange).	
4	Go straight on until you get to (Exchange Place).	
5	It's on the corner, opposite (the church).	
6	Turn left into (Nassau Street).	
7	It's on the / your left.	
8	Go over the traffic lights.	

b Look only at the pictures. Practise the phrases.

Asking the way

2 **a** ·10· Pieter's in New York. Listen and tick the expressions from ex.1a that you hear.

b Listen again. Draw the route on the map. Where does Pieter want to go? What three questions did he ask?

3 ·11· Another tourist is asking for directions. Guess the missing words. Listen and check.

A Excuse *me*, please. Is _____ a post office _____ here?

B Yes, the nearest _____'s at the _____ of Fulton Street. Go _____ this street and _____ left. Go _____ the traffic _____, and take the _____ turning on the _____. It's _____ the corner _____ the left, _____ to the market. You can't _____ it.

---

4 **a** In pairs, choose a place on the map and write directions to get there from the Post Office.

b Swap partners. Read your directions to your new partner who follows them and says where you get to.

5 **a** ·12· Listen. Where does Pieter want to go? How many people does he speak to?

b Listen again. True (T) or false (F)?
1 He's quite near the museum. ☐
2 He has to get a number 7 bus. ☐
3 He needs to get off at 86th Street. ☐
4 It's about ten stops. ☐
5 He gets the wrong bus. ☐
6 A tourist tells him the way. ☐
7 The museum is in Central Park. ☐

6 📖 **Travel phrasebook 5** *p.133*

5

Double lives

1 Number the expressions in a usual order, 1 to 13. Compare with a partner. Do you agree?

Events in your life	Ⓥ
go to university ☐	fall in love ☐
be born [1]	get divorced ☐
go to school ☐	have children ☐
start work ☐	get married ☐
leave school ☐	leave university ☐
die ☐	get engaged ☐
retire ☐	

2 **a** Match the detectives to their pictures.

1 Hercules Poirot ☐
2 Inspector Clouseau ☐
3 Miss Marple ☐
4 Sherlock Holmes ☐
5 Philip Marlow ☐

b Do you like detective stories / films? Tell a partner the name of one you've read / seen.

3 **a** Work in pairs. **A** read **Part 1** of Agatha Christie's biography. **B** read **Part 2**. Remember the important information.

b Tell each other what you remember using the lifelines.

Agatha Christie

Part 1

Agatha Christie was born on 15th September 1890. She didn't go to school because her mother wanted to teach her at home. She studied the piano and singing in Paris.

She got married in 1914 to a pilot and they had one daughter. During the first World War, when she was working as a nurse, she began to write detective stories. In the hospital, she learnt a lot about drugs and poisons, and she used this information in her novels.

She published her first novel in 1920. The main character was a Belgian detective, Hercules Poirot. The book soon became a best-seller and made her famous.

In 1928, Agatha Christie mysteriously disappeared. The police found her two weeks later suffering from amnesia. She couldn't remember anything. This was front-page news in all the newspapers in Britain, and even today nobody knows exactly what happened to her during those two weeks. Soon after that, she got divorced.

Part 2

In 1929, Agatha Christie went on holiday to Baghdad in Iraq. There she met and fell in love with her second husband, who was a famous archaeologist. They went home to England on the Orient Express and got married in 1930.

She travelled with her husband to the Middle East many times, and a lot of her later stories take place there, for example, *Murder on the Nile*. She also created the detective Miss Marple, and began to write plays. One of them, *The Mousetrap*, opened at a theatre in the West End of London in 1952, and is still on today – a world record.

During her life she wrote nearly eighty detective stories, and she also wrote some romantic novels under the pen name of Mary Westmacott. She died in January 1976, when she was eighty-six years old.

Agatha Christie's thrillers are famous for their surprise endings. You sometimes don't know who the murderer is until the last page.

Part 1 ▪15.9.1890 ▪ ▪ ▪ 1920 Poirot▪1928 disappeared ▪divorced

Part 2 ▪1929 Baghdad▪ ▪1930 ▪*The Mousetrap* 1952▪80 books▪ + Mary Westmacott ▪1976

4 **a** Write the questions for these answers.

1 *When was she* born?
   In 1890.

2 *What happened to her* in 1914?
   She got married.

3 _____ to write?
   When she was working as a nurse.

4 _____ in 1928?
   She disappeared.

5 _____ disappear?
   Nobody knows.

6 _____ do?
   He was an archaeologist.

7 _____ write?
   Nearly eighty.

8 _____ died?
   She was eighty-six.

b Find six more words for kinds of books from the text. Complete the **V** box below.

```
Kinds of books                    V

short stories

r_____ _____

d_____ _____

th_____

n_____

p_____
```

5 **a** Read Ruth Rendell's biography. Put the verbs in the past simple or present perfect.

b How is Ruth Rendell's life similar to Agatha Christie's? Find five similarities.

1 *She is also a detective-story writer.*

c Why is Agatha Christie's biography all in the past simple but Ruth Rendell's in the past simple and present perfect?

Ruth Rendell

Many people call Ruth Rendell 'the new Agatha Christie'. She ¹_____(be born) in London in 1930. When she ²_____(leave) school, she ³_____(work) as a journalist. In 1950 she ⁴_____(get) married to another journalist and they had a son. In 1973, after twenty-three years together, they got divorced, but four years later they re-married. Ruth Rendell ⁵_____(publish) her first novel in 1964. It ⁶_____(be) an immediate success.

Since 1964 she ⁷_____(write) many more novels, and is still writing today. Her famous detective is a middle-aged policeman, Inspector Wexford. She ⁸_____(publish) other books under the pen name of Barbara Vine, and she ⁹_____(win) many prizes for her novels. Since 1986 she ¹⁰_____(live) in a sixteenth-century farmhouse.

In her novels, Ruth Rendell is more interested in the characters than the crimes. Her detective novels, short stories, and psychological thrillers are international best-sellers. She's now the sixth highest-earning woman in England.

6 **a** Write questions about Ruth Rendell.

1 How long _____ a writer?
   Since 1964.

2 _____ married?
   Since 1977.

3 _____ farmhouse?
   Since 1986.

b Look at Ruth's lifeline. Why were these dates important in her life?

1930 — 1950 — 1964 — 1973 — 1977 — 1986 ► now

7 *Talk about ... your lifeline*

Draw your lifeline with five important dates. Swap with a partner. Ask about the dates. Ask follow-up questions.

A *What happened to you in 1979?*
B *I was born in 1979, on October 4th.*
A *Where were you born?*

Vocabulary file 5

How many words do I need to know?
Although Shakespeare used 33,000 words, English speakers today use only about 5,000 words in conversation. By the end of this course you will know at least 2,000 English words.

1 Word groups Add two words to each. Underline the stress.
Jewellery: <u>bra</u>celet _____ _____
Age-groups: <u>ba</u>by _____ _____
Family: <u>daugh</u>ter _____ _____
Connectors: <u>Af</u>ter that _____ _____
Kinds of books: bi<u>o</u>graphy _____ _____
Verbs + *to* + infinitive: want _____ _____

2 Prepositions Complete with at on to .
1 Could you tell me the way _____ the station?
2 Take the first turning _____ the right.
3 It's _____ the end of the road, next _____ the post office.
4 Go straight _____, past the church.
5 The bank is _____ the corner.

3 Key words Complete.

as well ex<u>ac</u>tly i<u>mm</u>ediately
<u>nea</u>rly soon to<u>ge</u>ther

1 I've _____ finished. Just give me another minute.
2 When he arrived at the hotel he _____ went to bed.
3 After the party they walked home _____.
4 The meal was delicious and very cheap _____.
5 It's time to go. It's going to get dark _____.
6 You've arrived at _____ the right moment.

4 Verbs

a What are the opposites of these verbs?
1 be awake   *be asleep*
2 win   _____
3 appear   _____
4 arrive   _____
5 be single _____
6 be born   _____
7 buy   _____
8 begin   _____

b Complete with the verb.

become	direct	~~write~~	invent	paint	win

1 *write* a novel   4 _____ a product
2 _____ a picture   5 _____ a medal
3 _____ a film   6 _____ president

5 Word-building Match two words to make a new word / phrase.
1 track   story   [ ]   6 traffic   table   [ ]
2 military call   [ ]   7 table   opener   [ ]
3 detective juice   [ ]   8 car   tennis   [ ]
4 fruit   suit   [1]   9 tin   lights   [ ]
5 phone   service   [ ]   10 coffee   park   [ ]

6 Pronunciation

a Cross out the word with a different pronunciation of 'ea'.

1 break steak ~~meal~~ great

2 near hear heart appear

3 peace east reason wear

4 meat head bread dead

5 heard earn team learnt

b Look at ♪ **English sounds: Vowels** *p.142*. Remember the twenty words and sounds. Test a partner.

Organize your vocabulary learning!

■ **Learn words that are important for you.**
It's impossible to remember every new word you see. Choose words that you think are useful and important. Write them down and revise them regularly.

Try it!

■ Look back at **5** ◁▷ *p.74*. Choose five new words. Record them in a sentence in your vocabulary file.

Grammar file 5

I've **been** up here **for** 431 days …

1 Present perfect + *for* / *since*

How long **have** you **lived** in this flat?
I**'ve lived** here **for** fifteen years.
I**'ve lived** here **since** I was eighteen.

☐ Use the present perfect to talk about actions which started in the past and are still true now.
I've known him for ten years.
NOT ~~I know him for ten years.~~

☐ To answer the question *How long* …? use:
for + a period of time: **for** three years
since + a fixed point of time: **since** 1992 / April

☐ Remember the difference between the present perfect and the past simple.
I**'ve been** a teacher for three years. = I'm a teacher now.
I **was** a teacher for three years. = I'm not a teacher now.

2 Verb + *to* + infinitive

I **want to** go to bed early.
Would you **like to** go out tonight?
He's **hoping to** buy a new car.
They **decided to** go to France.

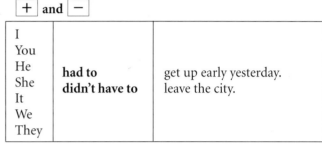

… but I'd really **like to** get down.

☐ Use *to* + infinitive after these verbs:
want need would like hope
try decide plan

I**'d like to** be a doctor.
I **like go**ing to the cinema.

☐ Remember the difference:
Use *would like* + *to* + infinitive to talk about what you want to do now or in the future.
Use *like* + verb + *-ing* to talk generally about what you like / don't like.

3 *so* / *because*

Reason	Result
It was raining.	I took my umbrella.

It was raining **so** I took my umbrella.
I took my umbrella **because** it was raining.
I was tired. **So** I went to bed.

☐ Use *so* and *because* to connect reason with result.

☐ *because* answers the question *Why* …?

4 *had to* / *didn't have to*

☐ + and ☐ −

I You He She It We They	**had to** **didn't have to**	get up early yesterday. leave the city.

?

Did you	**have to**	get up early?

✓ ✗

Yes, I **did**. / No, I **didn't**.

☐ Use *had to* + infinitive to talk about past obligations.

5 Questions with / without auxiliaries

What novel did **Boris Pasternak** write in 1957?
   Pasternak = **subject**

Who wrote Dr Zhivago?
   Who (question word) = **subject**

☐ Remember the normal order for questions (QASI). In these questions, the question word is not the subject.

Question	**A**uxiliary	**S**ubject	**I**nfinitive
What novel	did	Pasternak	write?

☐ If a question word (*Who*, etc.) is the subject of the verb, don't use *do* / *does* / *did*.
Who painted *Guernica*?
NOT ~~Who did paint *Guernica*?~~

5
G

A pain or a pleasure?

> *Trying to shop with young children is a nightmare!*

1 a ✎ Activities C *p.134*

b ∘ **1** ∘ Listen to five people talking about housework. Complete the chart.

	love	like / enjoy	don't mind	don't like	hate
1 *shopping*					
2					
3					
4					
5					

c Talk about housework in pairs.
A *I really hate washing-up. It's boring.*
B *Me too. And I don't like ironing.*

2 a Read the magazine article quickly. Name the people in the pictures.

b Read again and write the names.
1 Who doesn't like shopping?
   Simon and _____
2 Who likes shopping slowly and carefully?
   _____
3 Who likes shopping with certain people?
   _____ and _____
4 Who enjoys shopping alone?
   _____ and _____

c Find words / phrases in the article which mean:
1 a bad dream or experience
2 enjoyable
3 alone
4 a cupboard where you keep clothes
5 a book with pictures of products for sale
6 too many people (*adj.*)
7 a period when prices in shops are cheaper
8 something at a very good price

6

A

Shopping: a pain or a pleasure?

A _____   **B** _____

Some women include shopping in their list of favourite activities. Men traditionally hate it. Here's what some of our readers think.

❶ Aisha, 32
I like shopping , but it depends who I go with. Trying to shop with young children is a nightmare! I don't like shopping with my husband either because he's always in a hurry, and worries about spending money. But shopping with friends is fun, and I like going on my own too.

❷ Simon, 28
I don't really enjoy shopping. In fact it's a pain! I find it stressful because I'm always afraid of making mistakes. I've got a collection of awful 'mistakes' at the back of my wardrobe, which I never wear! But I don't mind going with my girlfriend, because she helps me choose. I think women are better at buying clothes than men. They've got better taste and they always know what's in fashion.

❸ Ivan, 30
I'm not interested in shopping at all – in fact I hate it. My wife buys all my clothes and brings them home. I try them on and if I like them, I keep them. If not she takes them back. Choosing things from catalogues and the TV shopping channels is the only kind of shopping I enjoy.

❹ Rosa, 24
I love shopping, but not on a Saturday or during the sales, when the shops are really crowded. I prefer shopping alone. Buying things often takes me a long time because I never buy the first thing I see. I always look around other shops to see if I can find the same thing cheaper. I'm quite good at finding a bargain. I hate shopping in large supermarkets, and prefer buying food in small shops or street markets.

GRAMMAR FOCUS

Verb + -ing (= gerund)

Highlight six different gerunds in paragraphs 1 and 2. Match them to the rules.

Use the gerund:
1 after verbs of feeling:
   like / love / hate / enjoy / mind / prefer
   I **don't mind cooking** but I **hate washing-up**.
2 after prepositions
   I'm good **at finding** bargains.
3 when we use a verb as the subject of a sentence
   Buying things often takes me a long time.

PRACTICE

a Complete with a gerund.
1 I'm quite good at _____.
2 I'm not very good at _____.
3 When I'm on my own, I really enjoy
  _____.
4 I think that _____ is very relaxing.
5 _____ is my favourite holiday activity.
6 The job I hate most in the house is
  _____.

b Guess what a partner has written.

3 Talk about ... shopping

Ask a partner.

❶ **Do you enjoy shopping? Why (not)?**

❷ **Do you like shopping ...?**
   ☐ **at the sales**
   ☐ **by post from catalogues**
   ☐ **in large supermarkets**
   ☐ **from TV shopping channels**
   ☐ **in street markets**

❸ **Do you prefer shopping alone or with somebody? Who?**

❹ **Are you good at finding bargains?**

❺ **Have you ever bought anything that you've hardly ever worn?**

❻ **Which of the four people in the magazine article are you most like?**

PRONUNCIATION

a ○ 2

 ŋ — shopping   young   thing   belong   ironing

 g — bargain   good   magazine   catalogue   flag

 dʒ — gerund   enjoy   bridge   large   gym

b ○ 3 ○ Listen. Are the words /ŋ/, /g/, or /dʒ/?

Gerund or infinitive?		
● When two verbs are together, the first verb changes the form of the second verb. Remember two groups:		
1 *would like*, want, etc.	*to* + infinitive	I'd like to go to Bali.
2 *like, enjoy, hate*, etc.	verb + *-ing*	I enjoy doing exercise.

4 Put the verbs in the right form.
1 **A** Would you like _____ to a party with me tonight? (come)
   B Oh yes, I love _____ to parties. (go)
2 I don't want _____ in an office because I hate _____ early. (work, get up)
3 _____ the night before an exam makes me nervous. (study)
4 Joe'd like _____ a flat because he doesn't like _____ with his parents. (buy, live)
5 I love _____ but I'm afraid of _____ so I always go by train or bus. (travel, fly)
6 **A** I think _____ is the best exercise. (run)
   B Do you? I think _____ is better. (swim)

5 **a** Complete the sentences.

Happiness is not having to get up in the morning.

This summer I'd like to ...
In my free time, what I most like doing is ...
My idea of happiness is ...

b Class survey. What are the most common endings?

First impressions

> *He looks friendly. He looks like an actor.*

1 Describe these people.
Ⓐ *She's got dark curly hair. She's quite pretty.*

2 **a** How old do you think they are?
Ⓐ *She looks about 35.*

b Guess their jobs.

politician	actor / actress	police officer
tennis player	university teacher	violinist

Ⓐ *She looks like a politician.*

3 **a** ✎ **Adjectives B** *p.138* Think of a person you know for each adjective.

b Guess their personalities.
Ⓐ *She looks friendly and quite intelligent.*

GRAMMAR FOCUS

look or *look like*?

> He looks French.
> She looks like an actress.

a Complete with 'adjective' or 'noun'.

To describe a person use:

look + _____

look like + _____

b Compare.
looks / looks like = my impression / what I think
He**'s** French. / She**'s** an actress. = fact / what I know

PRACTICE

Complete with the right form of *look / look like*.

1 You _____ tired today.

2 I think my son _____ me.

3 I thought Martha _____ really beautiful yesterday.

4 He _____ shy, but in fact he's quite talkative.

5 Do you really think I _____ a model?

6 People say that my brother _____ Tom Cruise.

6
B

PRONUNCIATION

a ° **4** °

 wear pair where they're square

 hear dear we're beer year idea

b ° **5** ° Listen and write /eə/ or /ɪə/.

1 Clare's got fair hair. /___/

2 We're really serious. /___/

3 The theatre's near here. /___/

4 Are you Aries, Aquarius, or Sagittarius? /___/

4 **a** Every month people send their photos and personal information to *Marie Claire* magazine to meet new people. Jerry and Anna wrote to them. Look at their photos. Describe them.

He's got … / He looks … / He looks like …

Would you like to meet these people?

Name	**Jerry Dowles**	**Anna Malik**
● Age		
● Height	*1m 85*	*1m 71*
● Job		
● Home		
● Vehicle		
● Smoker		
● Favourite actress		
● Favourite actor		
● Ideal weekend activities		
● Star sign		
● Personality		

b Look at the chart above. What questions do you have to ask to find out the information?

Age How old is Jerry?

> **(be) like / look like** **ⓥ**
>
> Use *What does he / she look like?*
> to ask about appearance.
> Use *What's he / she like?*
> to ask about personality and appearance.

5 **a** ►◄ Jerry and Anna A *p.121* B *p.124*

b If they meet, do you think they'll get on well? Why (not)?

6 ° **6** ° Anna and Jerry met for an evening. Listen to what they said after the meeting. Write four adjectives for each. Do they want to meet again?

Anna is …	Jerry is …
_____	_____
_____	_____
_____	_____
_____	_____

7 *Talk about … people*

a Look at the chart. Think about a family member / friend.

age ➔ appearance ➔ job ➔ home / car / family ➔ hobbies ➔ star sign ➔ personality

b Ask about a partner's person. Would you like to meet him / her?

A *Who's your person?*

B *My brother.*

A *How old is he? / What does he look like?*, etc.

What's in your rubbish?

> *He doesn't drink much fruit juice.*

One night, when other journalists were trying to photograph famous people in restaurants or nightclubs, Bruno Moran and Pascal Roustain tried something different. They decided to find new information about the stars' private lives by looking in their rubbish bins. This is what they found in Jack Nicholson's bin:

Does Jack Nicholson have the world's healthiest diet? Let's see.

He obviously drinks a lot of alcohol, especially beer, and he likes expensive champagne. He drinks a little mineral water and occasionally a Seven Up, but surprisingly for an American, he doesn't drink any coke. Instead of coke, he drinks lots of Schweppes ginger beer. He doesn't drink much fruit juice. As for food, he doesn't have many meals at home, except for breakfast. He usually has some bacon and perhaps a few frozen peas. When he's hungry between meals he has some corn chips or a few sweets. And as we can see, he smokes a lot of cigarettes, usually Camel.

6

C

1 Look at 📖 **Food B** *p.137*. In pairs, label the words countable (C) or uncountable (U).

2 📖 **Food C** *p.137*. Test a partner.

PRONUNCIATION

Linking

◦ **7** ◦ Listen and repeat. Try to link the words.

1 I eat a lot of oranges.
2 Would you like a bag of crisps?
3 Can I have a jar of coffee, please?
4 I'd like a box of chocolates.
5 How much is a packet of biscuits?

3 **a** Read the introduction to the article. Who are Bruno and Pascal? Where did they look for information about famous people?

b Look at the photo. What can you see?
Four bottles of champagne.

c Read the article.

1 How much alcohol does Jack Nicholson drink?
2 Does he drink much mineral water?
3 How many sweets does he eat?
4 Does he smoke many cigarettes?
5 Do you think he's healthy? Why (not)?

GRAMMAR FOCUS

Quantifiers (*a lot of / much*, etc.)

a Highlight *a lot of / much / many / a little / a few / very few* in the text and in ex.3c.

b Complete the chart.

		Countable	Uncountable
For large quantities	+	a lot of / lots of	_____
	− ?	(not) _____	(not) much
For small quantities		a few	a _____ /
		very few	very _____
		How _____?	How _____?

Remember:
I smoke **a lot of** / **lots of** cigarettes.
BUT I smoke **a lot**. NOT ~~I smoke a lot of.~~

PRACTICE

a Cross out the wrong words.

1 I eat ~~much~~ / a lot of fruit.
2 How much / many tea do you drink?
3 I only eat a few / a little meat.
4 Do you drink much / many coffee?
5 Yes, I drink a lot / a lot of.
6 I don't eat much / many vegetables.
7 I only eat a little / a few sweets at weekends.

b Interview a partner with *How much …? / How many …?* and the food in the picture below. Use short answers.

Short answers	
U	**C**
A lot.	A lot.
Not much.	Not many.
A little.	A few.
Very little.	Very few.
None. (= 0)	None.

c Write six sentences about your partner's diet. Whose diet is healthier?

He doesn't eat much meat but he eats a lot of vegetables.

---

4 ° **8** ° Listen to a radio programme about ru[b...] Complete the text.

The throw-away society

● In Western Europe we throw away millions of tonnes of rubbish every year. [1] 28% of this rubbish is packaging.

● The average person in Los Angeles throws away [2]_____ kilos of rubbish every day, but the average person in the Third World throws away only [3]_____ kilo.

● In Britain we throw away [4]_____ tonnes of paper every year. (That's the same as [5]_____ trees.)

● In one year, a European family with two children throws away:
   [6]_____ kilos of paper
   [7]_____ kilos of metal
   [8]_____ kilos of plastic (the same as [9]_____ supermarket bags)

● In one year, the average person throws away [10]_____ cans.

5 *Talk about … the environment*

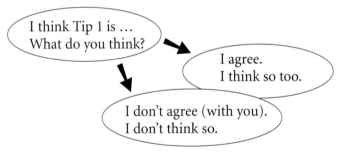

I think Tip 1 is …
What do you think?

I agree.
I think so too.

I don't agree (with you).
I don't think so.

a Read five tips to help the environment. Which do you think are the most and least important?

1 Separate your rubbish into different containers (bottle banks, paper banks, etc.).
2 Re-use plastic bags, e.g. from supermarkets.
3 Use recycled paper and environmentally-friendly products.
4 Buy food that doesn't have a lot of packaging.
5 Don't drive in the city. Use public transport.

b Which ones do you do? How often?

The day the birds died

> There are too many people and there isn't enough fresh air.

The day the birds died

Mexico City is the oldest and most historical capital city in North America. It's an exciting, beautiful, and magical city, which for the past few years has been fighting against serious environmental problems. It has a population of over 22 million people and it's
5 getting bigger all the time. It's more than three times bigger than New York City and it's the largest city in the world. Every day, thousands of people move in from the country to look for work, but there aren't enough jobs for all of them, and the result is extremely high unemployment and over-population.

10 The city is situated at a height of 2,255 metres above sea level and is surrounded by snow-capped volcanoes. For the Aztecs, who first built the city, it was a beautiful, sunny capital, but today Mexico City is almost always covered by an enormous brown cloud of smog which is caused by the pollution coming from hundreds of factories around the city and from over three million cars waiting in endless traffic jams. Just breathing the air is the same as smoking 40 cigarettes a day! One day in the 1980s, the level
15 of pollution in the air in one part of the city was so high that thousands of birds fell from the sky and died.

Since then, the Mexican government and private organizations have worked very hard to clean the air and control the levels of pollution, and the situation is improving. But the problem of over-population is more difficult to solve – by the year 2010, over 30 million people will live in Mexico City.

1 Complete the **V** box with *'s* or *are*. What's the difference between the two columns?

Cities	**V**
There _____ a lot of	There _____ a lot of
jobs	work (*n.*)
people	unemployment
cars	traffic
cigarettes	smoke (*n.*)
clouds	pollution
factories	

2 **a** Look at the photos of Mexico City. What can you see? Have you been there? / Would you like to go?

b You're going to read about Mexico City. Why do you think these phrases are in the text?

22 million   New York City   2,255 metres
the Aztecs   40 cigarettes a day
thousands of birds   30 million

c Read the text and see if you were right.

3 **a** Find words in the text which mean:

1 (*prep.*) more than
2 the noun from *unemployed*
3 (*n.*) too full of people
4 (*adj.*) covered with snow
5 (*n.*) smoke and fog together
6 (*n.*) a line of cars which have stopped
7 (*gerund*) taking in air
8 (*v.*) getting better

Complete the sentences with one word.

1 The world is over-populated. There are too many _____.
2 There are thousands of cars. There's too much _____.
3 There's a lot of unemployment. There aren't enough _____.
4 The town is too small for its population. It isn't _____ enough.
5 It's difficult to breathe. The air's too _____.

c What major problems does your capital city have?

GRAMMAR FOCUS

(*not*) *enough, too, too much / many*

a Look at the sentences in ex.3b. Complete the rules with 'C noun', 'U noun', or 'adjective'.

too + _____
too much + _____
too many + _____
(not) enough + *C / U nouns*
(not) _____ + *enough*

b Circle the more negative sentence.

1 The film was very long.
   The film was too long.
2 She eats a lot.
   She eats too much.
3 We haven't got any money.
   We haven't got enough money.

a Complete with *too, too much / many*, or *enough*.

1 I can't go out. I've got _____ work.
2 Paul can't buy a car. He hasn't got _____ money.
3 We aren't going by plane because it's _____ expensive.
4 There's _____ food! We'll never eat it all.
5 The party was terrible. There were _____ people.
6 Kay can't vote. She isn't old _____.
7 I'm _____ hot. I'm wearing _____ clothes.

b Look at pictures 1 to 4. Write two sentences for each with *too, too much / many*, or *enough*.

4 ⟨9⟩ Jean François lives in Fanlac, a tiny village near Périgueux in south-west France. Listen to him describe it. Note down two positive points and two negative points.

5 *Talk about … your town / city*

In groups, talk about where you live. What's it like? What are the good / bad points? Do you think there is / are enough / too many / not enough …?

public transport	libraries
parks	museums / art galleries
car parks	nightlife (bars, clubs, etc.)
shopping centres	cinemas / theatres
sports facilities	schools

6

D

Shopping

Buying food

> **Zabar's**
> Probably the best delicatessen in the city. The variety and quality of the coffee and cookies, cheese, and croissants is breathtaking. 2245 Broadway, at 80th Street (787 2000).
>
> **The Original Levi's Store**
> This enormous store sells everything Levi's have ever designed. Customers are limited to buying six pairs of jeans at one time.

1 Read about the shops in Pieter's guidebook. Which would you prefer to go to?

2 **a** °10° Listen. What does he buy? How much is it?

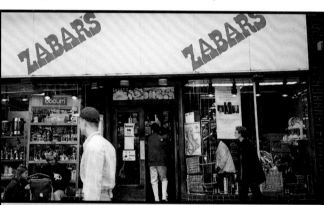

> **P** Can I _____ some of that _____, please?
> **A** Which one? This _____?
> **P** No, _____ one.
> **A** Ah, this _____. How much _____ _____ _____?
> **P** _____ a _____.
> **A** Anything _____?
> **P** No, thanks. How _____ is _____?
> **A** _____.
> **P** _____ you are. _____.

b Listen again. Complete the dialogue.

3 **a** Imagine Pieter wants to buy some apples. Change the dialogue as necessary.

b Roleplay the dialogue with different food.

> tomatoes – 90c a kilo Edam cheese – $9.50 a kilo
> cookies – $16.75 a kilo roast beef – $21.99 a kilo

> **one / ones**
> ● If you don't want to repeat a noun, use *one(s)*.
> Which one(s) do you want?
> The big one(s) or the small one(s)?

Buying clothes

4 **a** °11° Pieter's at the Levi Store. Listen. What does he buy?

Clothes _____ Colour _____

Size _____ Price _____

b In pairs, write the dialogue. Use these words.
Have you got those jeans in my size?

> **P** those / size?
> **B** Which?
> **P** black
> **B** size?
> **P** 32
> **B** Let's / Here
> **P** try / on?
> **B** changing room
> **P** bit / small / bigger?
> **B** ones / 34
> **P** fine / take
> **B** else?
> **P** No / much?
> **B** $49.95

c Practise the dialogue with the words above.

Taking things back

5 **a** °12° Listen. What did they buy?

b Listen again and complete.

1 The *zip's* _____ on _____ _____. Can I _____ them?

2 _____ volume control doesn't _____. I'd _____ my _____ _____.

3 _____ a button _____ on this shirt. Have _____ got _____ one?

6 📖 **Travel phrasebook 6** *p.133*

Going, doing, playing, watching

1 **a** Put two sports in each column. Then add one more to each.

~~football~~   <u>ta</u>ble-<u>te</u>nnis   <u>scu</u>ba-<u>di</u>ving
gym<u>na</u>stics   <u>jo</u>gging   <u>ru</u>gby   <u>sai</u>ling   squash

Ball sports	Racket / bat sports	Water sports	Other
football	_____	_____	_____
_____	_____	_____	_____
_____	_____	_____	_____

> **go / play / do** **V**
> go + verb + *-ing* (e.g. go swimming)
> *play* + sports with a ball / racket (e.g. volleyball)
> *do* + exercise / martial arts (e.g. yoga / karate)

b Which verb goes with each of the sports in ex.1a?

2 *Talk about ... sports*

Interview a partner. Ask follow-up questions.
Who watches the most sport? Who does the most?

> Which sports do / did you like playing? When?
> Where? Who with? How often? Why (not)?

> Which do you like / not mind / hate
> watching live / on TV?
>
> Which do you think is the most exciting /
> boring to watch?
>
> Do you think there's too much sport on
> TV in your country?

> Which sport do you think is the best exercise /
> most dangerous?

3 **a** Look at the statistics. Do any of them surprise you?

Most popular sports done in Britain				
Men	**%**		**Women**	**%**
Walking	44		Walking	38
Snooker	24		Aerobics, etc.	16
Swimming	14		Swimming	15
Cycling	12		Cycling	7
Darts	11		Snooker	5
Football	10		Darts	4

b What are the three most popular sports in your country: a) on TV   b) that people do?

c Write five sentences about your country using the sports.
In Italy not many men play darts and very few people play snooker. A lot of women do aerobics.

4 **a** Look at photos A to D. Describe the people.

b Guess their nationalities and sports.
He looks American.
He looks like a basketball player.

5 **a** ∘**13**∘ Listen to a radio programme about Arantxa Sanchez-Vicario. Make notes about:
1   her training routine.
2   her diet.

b Would you like to be a professional sportsperson? Why (not)?

6

◁▷

Vocabulary file 6

Why do I remember some words and forget others?

Some words are easy to remember, because, for example, the word is similar to a word in your language, or it's a word that you often use. Other words are more difficult to remember, because the spelling or pronunciation is unusual, or because you don't often see or hear the word.

When you revise a group of words, focus especially on the ones that you find difficult to remember. Try to think why.

1 Remembering verbs

a Try to remember six housework verbs from ✎ **Activities C** *p.134*. Which one(s) couldn't you remember?

b ✎ **Do, Make, Get A** *p.140* Focus on the expressions which are difficult for you.

2 Word groups Add three more words to each group.

CITY PROBLEMS	SHOPPING
pollution	*fashion*
smog	*take back*

3 *go, play,* or *do*? Complete the chart. Add one more in each column.

~~jogging~~ foot̲ball t̲ennis y̲oga aer̲obics
sw̲imming ba̲sketball cy̲cling kar̲ate

go	play	do
jogging	_____	_____
_____	_____	_____
_____	_____	_____
_____	_____	_____

4 Word-building Write the opposites. How many begin with *un-*?

big	*small*	hard-w̲orking	_____
emp̲loyed	_____	ta̲lkative	_____
full	_____	co̲mfortable	_____
se̲lfish	_____	fri̲endly	_____
u̲sual	*unusual*	mo̲dern	_____
ex̲trovert	_____	ti̲dy	_____

5 Key words Complete.

a̲gain   a̲nother   o̲ther   rea̲lly

1 We're _____ hungry. Have you got anything to eat?
2 Could you say that _____, please?
3 Would you like _____ drink?
4 All the _____ students in my class were ill yesterday.

■ **Learn adjectives with their prepositions.**

6 Prepositions Complete with about at in of.
1 Her mother's very good _____ languages.
2 I'm not interested _____ politics.
3 Are you worried _____ your exams?
4 My father's afraid _____ flying.
5 I'm very bad _____ remembering names.

7 Odd one out ⟨Circle⟩ the different word. Why is it different?
1 potatoes spinach rice meat
2 karate exercise cycling gymnastics
3 love hate mind want
4 dark slim good-looking quiet
5 box kilo can packet
6 generous selfish friendly extrovert

Organize your vocabulary learning!

■ **If you forget the same word again and again, try to think of a special way to remember it.**

a Think of an image in your mind.

b Try to associate it with another word in English or your language.

c Write down the word and say it a few times.

d Write it on a card and keep it in your pocket to test yourself from time to time.

Try it!

■ Look at ✎ **Food** *p.137*. Which words do you find difficult to remember? Choose a way to remember them. Test yourself after a day, a week, etc.

Grammar file 6

1 The gerund (verb + -ing)

I don't mind **washing-up** but I hate **ironing**.
I'm afraid of **flying**.
Smoking is bad for your health.

☐ Use the gerund:
   1 after verbs of feeling:
     like, love, hate, enjoy, mind, prefer
     I **love shopping**.
   2 after prepositions
     I'm good **at cooking**.
   3 as the subject of a sentence
     Swimming is the best form of exercise.

☐ Remember the spelling changes for -*ing*. *p.2*

☐ Remember:
   I **like** travel**ling**.   BUT   **I'd like to go** to Australia.

2 Describing people (*look* / *look like*)

Ah, he **looks like** his father.

He l**ooks** friendly.
She **looks like** her sister.

☐ Use *look* + adjective. Use *look like* + noun.

☐ Use *look* / *look like* to describe the impression a person gives you.

☐ Remember the difference.
   What does he **look like**? He's tall, with blue eyes.
      = appearance
   What's he **like**? He's quite shy but he's very nice.
      = personality / appearance

3 Quantities

I've got **a lot of** books, but I haven't got **many** CDs, and I've only got **a few** tapes.
They drank **a lot of** wine, **not much** beer, and **very little** lemonade.
How much coke did they drink? **How many** crisps did they eat?
Were there **many** people? Was there **much** noise?
There was **a lot of** noise. There were **lots of** children.

☐ For large quantities

	a lot / lots of	a lot / lots of
+	a lot / lots of	a lot / lots of
−	(not) many	(not) much
?	How many …?	How much …?

| For small quantities | a few / very few | a little / very little |

☐ A lot of food words are **U** but the containers are **C**.
   How much coke did they drink?
   BUT   **How many cans** of coke …?

4 *too, too much* / *many*, (*not*) *enough*

I don't want to go out. I'm **too** tired.
I'm stressed. I've got **too much** work.
There are **too many** chairs in this room.

☐ To say there's more than you need, use:
   too + adjective
   too much + **U** nouns
   too many + **C** nouns

☐ *too*, *too much* / *many* have a negative meaning.
   My house is **very big**. (It's got five bedrooms.)
   My house is **too big**. (I'd like a smaller one.)

Have you got **enough** money?
The table isn't big **enough** for six people.
There isn't **enough** food for everybody.

☐ *enough* = all that you need

☐ Use *enough* after an adjective but before a noun.

5 *one* / *ones*

Which bag do you prefer, the blue **one** or the red **one**?
Which shoes are you going to buy? The cheap **ones**?

☐ Use adjective + *one* / *ones* in place of adjective + noun.
   the blue car = the blue **one**   NOT   ~~The blue.~~

6

Ⓖ

A business trip

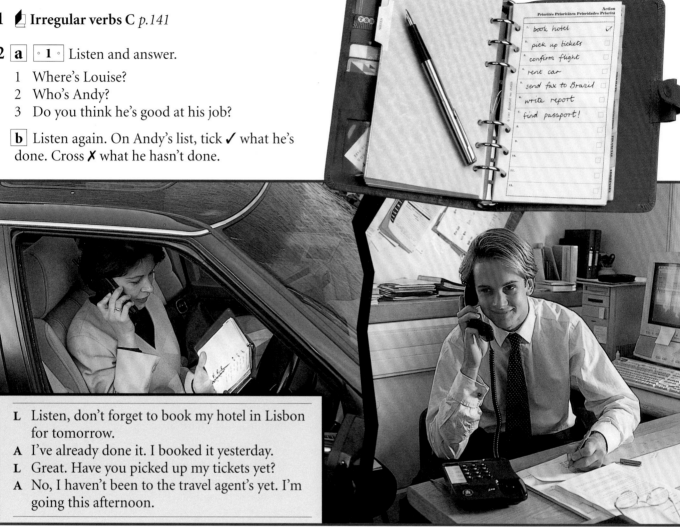

I've already done it.

1 📖 Irregular verbs C *p.141*

2 **a** · 1 · Listen and answer.

1 Where's Louise?
2 Who's Andy?
3 Do you think he's good at his job?

b Listen again. On Andy's list, tick ✓ what he's done. Cross ✗ what he hasn't done.

> **L** Listen, don't forget to book my hotel in Lisbon for tomorrow.
> **A** I've already done it. I booked it yesterday.
> **L** Great. Have you picked up my tickets yet?
> **A** No, I haven't been to the travel agent's yet. I'm going this afternoon.

GRAMMAR FOCUS 1

Present perfect + *already* / *yet*

a Look at the dialogue. Complete the rules with *already* and *yet*.

1 Use _____ in + sentences.
2 Use _____ in − sentences and ? .
3 Put _____ before the main verb.
4 Put _____ at the end of a sentence.

b Use *already* to emphasize that someone has done something.

I've **already** seen that film.

Use *yet* to say / ask if someone has done something.
Have you tidied your room **yet**?
He hasn't finished **yet**.

PRACTICE 1

a Write sentences from Louise's filofax notes with *already* and (*not*) *yet*.

1 *Andy's already booked the hotel.*
2 *He hasn't* _____
3 _____
4 _____
5 _____
6 _____
7 _____

b Practise in pairs with Louise's notes.
A *Have you … yet?*
B *Yes, I've already done it. / No, not yet.*

PRONUNCIATION

a ° 2 °

yet	_____	just	_____
yesterday	_____	juice	_____
few	_____	enjoy	_____
yellow	_____	generous	_____
student		January	
usually		village	

b Put these words in the right column.

young	June	new	job
music	jam	jogging	use

3 ▶◀ **Have they done it yet?** A and B *p.121*

4 **a** ° 3 ° Louise phones Andy from Lisbon. Listen. What's happened? What does she ask Andy to do?

b Complete the dialogue.

> **L** I've *just* arrived in Lisbon. But I've _____ something really stupid.
>
> **A** What?
>
> **L** I've _____ my _____. I _____ it in the _____ when I was _____ to the hotel.
>
> **A** Oh no! What _____ inside it?
>
> **L** Everything. My _____ with my credit cards, my _____, my _____ …
>
> **A** Have you called the police _____?
>
> **L** Yes, I've _____ _____ to them. _____ you phone the bank and cancel my _____ _____?
>
> **A** Don't worry. I'll do it right now.

GRAMMAR FOCUS 2

just

> I've just arrived in Lisbon. (I arrived five minutes ago.)
> She's just started a new job. (She started yesterday.)

a Use *just* + present perfect to say that something happened very recently.

b We don't usually use *just* in ⁻ sentences.

PRACTICE 2

Write sentences.

1 *The plane from Manila has just landed.*

5 ° 4 ° Listen to the sounds. Imagine what's just happened.

> **Verbs**
> Remember to learn verbs in phrases.
> send *a fax / a letter / a postcard*

Heart of gold

> He went to Romania to help in the orphanage.

1 Match the words and definitions. How do you pronounce the words?

1 **aid** /eɪd/ (*n.*)
2 **award** /əˈwɔːd/ (*n.*)
3 **isolated** /ˈaɪsəleɪtɪd/ (*adj.*)
4 **mayor** /meə/ (*n.*)
5 **orphanage** /ˈɔːfənɪdʒ/ (*n.*)

a the top person in local government [ ]
b a home for children with no parents [ ]
c a prize [ ]
d help [*1*]
e very far from other places [ ]

2 **a** Read the story. Where is Negru Voda? Why did the people there need money? Who's John Keeping?

● **Negru Voda is a small town in Romania, on the border with Bulgaria. The town is very isolated – the people there call it 'the town that God has forgotten'. They desperately needed money to look after the hundreds of children in the local orphanage. In 1991 John Keeping, a builder, heard about the problems in Romania and decided to go to Negru Voda with an aid organization to help in the orphanage there. Five years later, the BBC invited him to appear on their TV programme *Hearts of Gold* …**

b ° **5** ° Listen to the interview. Answer the questions.

1 Why did the BBC invite John onto the programme?
   To _____

2 Why did he go straight back to Britain?
   To _____

3 What was the first thing they had to do?
   They had to _____

4 Why did they need more people?
   To _____

5 How long did the work take?
   About _____

6 Who opened the new orphanage?
   _____

GRAMMAR FOCUS 1

Why …? To + infinitive

> *Why* did John go to Romania? *To help* in the orphanage.
> They needed money *to rebuild* the orphanage.

a Use *to* + infinitive to answer the question *Why …?*

b Compare with *Because* + subject + verb.
Why did they need money?
(**Because they wanted**) to rebuild the orphanage.

PRACTICE 1

a Make sentences with *to* + a verb.
1 *He needed a visa to go to China.*

1 He needed a visa	have a rest.
2 He's gone to the bank	~~go to China.~~
3 I'm going back to the hotel	confirm our flight.
4 He drove to the airport	cancel her ticket.
5 We phoned the travel agency	order some dollars.
6 She sent a fax	pick up his friend.

b List three places that you've been to recently and three you're going to soon. Swap lists with a partner. Ask *When?* and *Why?* for each one.
A *When did you go to the theatre?*
B *Last week.*
A *Why did you go there?*
B *To … / Because …*

> Recently
> theatre
> the shopping
>   centre
> my parents' flat
>
> Soon
> the beach
> Munich

PRONUNCIATION

a ° **6** °

organization international dictionary profession station

children church natural beach future picture

b Underline the stress. Where do we stress words ending in *-tion* / *-sion*?

c ° **7** ° Underline the stress. Listen and check.

emergency	animals	elephant
medical	environment	disaster
nuclear	salary	provide

7
B

3 **a** Quickly read paragraphs 1 to 4. Complete with the name of the organization.

1   The United Nations International Children's Emergency Fund started in New York in 1946 to help children after World War II. Today, _____ collects money for children in the world's poorest countries.

2   _____ began in 1971 in British Columbia to stop US nuclear testing at Amchitka Island in Alaska. It tries to protect the environment and animals in danger, for example, whales, tigers, and elephants.

3   Started in Belgium in 1971, _____ is an organization of doctors and other medical professionals to provide help for victims of war and natural disasters. Their doctors and nurses work all over the world for no salary.

4   The _____ started in Switzerland in 1863 to help soldiers who were wounded in war, friend or enemy. Today it provides help for both soldiers and civilians in countries which are at war. In Muslim countries it is called the Red Crescent.

b In pairs, complete the chart below with short notes. Guess the meaning of any words you don't know. Check with a dictionary or ask the teacher.

Organization	Started where?	When?	Why?
UNICEF	_____	_____	*To* _____
Greenpeace	_____	_____	_____
Médecins sans frontières	_____	_____	_____
The Red Cross	_____	_____	_____

GRAMMAR FOCUS 2
to or *for*?

UNICEF started in 1946 to help children.
Today it collects money for children.

Highlight *to* and *for* in paragraphs 2 to 4. Then complete the rules.

1   Use _____ + a verb (infinitive).
2   Use _____ + a noun.

PRACTICE 2

Complete with *for* or *to*.

1   He's got an interview _____ a job next week.
2   We stopped at a café _____ have a drink.
3   They took a taxi _____ get to the station on time.
4   I've bought a book _____ my mother.
5   She got some souvenirs _____ give to her friends.
6   Have you got a stamp _____ a letter to Japan?
7   I just called _____ say I love you.

4 **a** Work in groups. In five minutes finish each sentence with *for* and *to* in as many ways as you can.

I gave him some money | *for something to eat.*
| *to buy some food.*

1   I'm learning English …
2   Please come to my flat next Saturday …
3   She's going to stop at the next petrol station …
4   He's going to Brazil …

b Which group has the most correct sentences?

Problems

What should I do?

Dear Maggie...

Have you got a problem that you can't solve?
Write to Maggie for some good practical advice.

A **Are these feelings normal?**
When I first got married I was really happy. My wife and I were always together. But we've just had our first child and now everything has changed. My wife doesn't have time for me any more. She's only interested in the baby. Is this normal? Should I say something to her?

B **I can't remember!**
I'm worried because I've got a terrible memory. I forget people's names and important appointments. I forget where I put things and I can never remember where I parked my car. I'm always late in the mornings because I forget to set my alarm clock. I've just got a new job in a bank and I'm afraid of losing it. Please help me!

C **Why does she do it?**
I've got a problem with one of my friends. I've known her for four years and I really like her. But she always copies everything I do. If I buy some new clothes, the next day she'll go out and buy exactly the same ones. It's the same with music, films, even my friends! It's really annoying. What should I do?

D **How can I tell her?**
I've fallen madly in love with a wonderful girl who has just started in my English class. The problem is I don't know how to tell her. I thinks she likes me but every time I'm near her I feel too embarrassed to say anything. I've never felt like this before. What should I do?

❶ ☐
Have you ever told her that you don't like it? Perhaps she thinks you're pleased? She's probably very unsure of herself and she wants to be like you. Perhaps that's really why you like her? You should talk to her about it, and explain how you feel.

❷ ☐
You shouldn't be afraid of her. Maybe she's just as shy as you. What about giving her a single red rose and a short note? Say something like this: 'I'd really like to get to know you but I don't know how.' She'll probably be excited to know she's got a fan!

❸ ☐
You shouldn't worry too much, because there's an easy answer. Why don't you write things down? You should keep a list of everything you want to do, every name you want to remember and finally you'll begin to remember things. But don't lose the piece of paper!

❹ ☐
I think that, like most men, you're probably still a child yourself, and you want to be the centre of attention. You haven't found out yet that marriage is for adults. Your wife's probably too tired looking after the baby. You should think of her for once, not of yourself, and you should help her more with the baby. Then she'll have more time for you.

---

1 **a** ✎ **Adjectives C** *p.138*

> *bored* or *boring*?   **V**
>
> My job is bor**ing**. = The job makes me feel bored.
> I'm bor**ed** (with my job). = I feel bored.

b Cross out the wrong word.

1 My job's very ~~tired~~ / tiring. I have to stand up all day.
2 Thrillers are usually quite excited / exciting.
3 She's very interested / interesting in politics.
4 The news on TV was a bit worried / worrying.
5 I was embarrassed / embarrassing because I couldn't remember her name.
6 He was depressed / depressing because he was having problems at work.

7
C

2 **a** Read letters A to D. Which writer is …?

forg<u>e</u>tful? ☐   shy? ☐
<u>se</u>lfish? ☐   a<u>nnoy</u>ed? ☐

b Read Maggie's answers 1 to 4. Match them to problems A to D. Do you agree with her advice?

GRAMMAR FOCUS

should / shouldn't

> What should I do? (= What's your advice / opinion?)
> You should talk to her. (= I think it's a good idea.)
> You shouldn't be afraid of her. (= Don't be afraid of her.)

Highlight examples of *should / shouldn't* in Maggie's answers. Complete the rule.

Use *should / shouldn't* + _____ to give advice / say what you think is right.

Remember, *should / shouldn't* is the same for all persons.

PRACTICE

a Cover Maggie's answers. Can you remember her advice?

Letter A *You should …*

b Look at problems 1 to 5. Write two sentences giving advice for each.

1 I can't sleep at night.

2 I need to learn English as quickly as possible.

3 I feel very stressed.

4 I want to meet new people.

5 I've got an interview for a job tomorrow.

PRONUNCIATION

a ∘ 8 ∘ Listen and write the advice. Match to **Grammar Practice** problems 1 to 5.
You shouldn't work too hard. = 3

b ∘ 9 ∘ Listen and repeat. Write the words.

1 /wʊd/   = *would*
2 /kʊd/   = _____
3 /ʃʊd/   = _____
4 /pʊt/   = _____
5 /ʃʊdnt/ = _____
6 /wʊdnt/ = _____

3 **a** 10 Listen to a radio phone-in programme. What's the listener's problem?

b Look at the phrases in the **V** box below. Listen again and complete Maggie's advice. Can you think of any other advice?

> **Giving advice**   **V**
> Why don't you _____
> What about _____
> I think you should _____

4 ►◄ **What should I do?** A *p.121* B *p.124* C *p.125*

True stories

> *They turned off the gas and picked up the canary.*

1 **a** Look at story **1**. Describe pictures A to D.

b | ° **11** ° | Number the paragraphs 1 to 6. Use the pictures to help you. Listen and check.

c | **12** | Why do you think the old lady screamed? Listen and check.

GRAMMAR FOCUS 1

Phrasal verbs

You have already learned many verbs + prepositions. (See ✎ **Irregular verbs** *p.141* for a list.)

Look at the highlighted verbs in the story.

turn off = stop	a machine	Turn off the TV.
turn on = start		
pick up = lift into the air		

Sometimes a verb + particle (= preposition or adverb) has a new meaning. These are phrasal verbs.

PRACTICE 1

a ✎ **Verbs B** *p. 139* Test a partner.

b Complete with a phrasal verb in the right tense.

1 The music was too loud so she *turned down* the volume.

2 A babysitter is a person who _____ _____ children when their parents go out.

3 I'm _____ _____ my glasses. I can't find them anywhere.

4 Jim got home from work, _____ _____ his suit and _____ _____ a tracksuit.

5 Can you _____ _____ the number of the bus station in the phone book?

6 Could you _____ _____ this form?

2 **a** Cover stories **2** and **3**. In pairs, **A** describe one picture to **B**. Then **B** describe the other picture to **A**.

b **A** read story **2**, **B** read story **3** in two minutes. Then tell your partner the story.

c | ° **13** ° | Answer the questions. Then listen and check. Which of the three stories do you like best?

Story 2 Why were they in Copenhagen?

Story 3 Who was in the woman's bed?

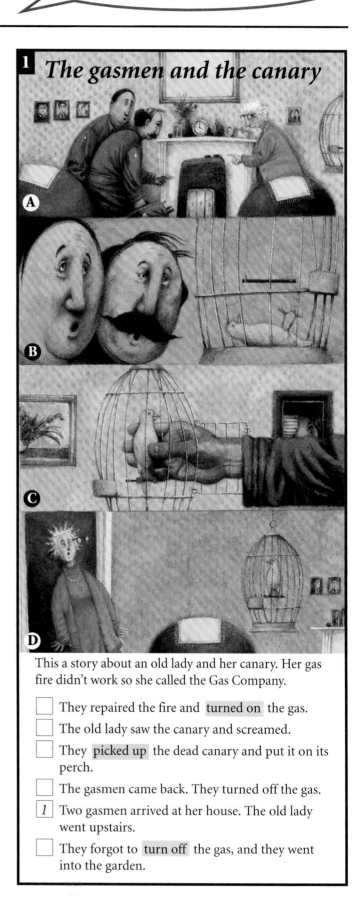

1 *The gasmen and the canary*

This a story about an old lady and her canary. Her gas fire didn't work so she called the Gas Company.

☐ They repaired the fire and turned on the gas.

☐ The old lady saw the canary and screamed.

☐ They picked up the dead canary and put it on its perch.

☐ The gasmen came back. They turned off the gas.

☐ *1* Two gasmen arrived at her house. The old lady went upstairs.

☐ They forgot to turn off the gas, and they went into the garden.

7

D

2

Take me home

A few years ago a Danish businessman from Copenhagen went to a business meeting in Frankfurt. On his last night he went to a party, and drank too much. He called a taxi to take him back to his hotel. He got into the taxi and said to the driver, 'My hotel, please.' 'Where is it?' the taxi-driver asked. The businessman took out his wallet and gave the driver a card. Then he immediately fell asleep. But when he woke up some hours later he was very surprised to see that they were driving past Tivoli Gardens, a famous park in Copenhagen. 'What are we doing here?' he shouted at the taxi-driver. …

3

Bath time

In 1987 in King's College Hospital, London, a new student nurse was looking after a room of elderly patients. It was only her third day at work. She saw a woman sitting on one of the beds. 'It's time for your bath', said the nurse. 'But I've already had one', the old woman replied. She looked a bit confused. 'No, you haven't,' said the nurse. 'Come on, take off your clothes and put on this dressing-gown.' The old woman looked surprised, but she put it on. Then the nurse took her to the bathroom and gave her a bath. When they came back to the room the nurse said, 'That's strange. There's somebody in your bed.' …

GRAMMAR FOCUS 2

Word order of phrasal verbs

verb ⟶ take out ⟵ particle

object   object

He took out his wallet .   He took it out.

a Highlight these verbs in stories **2** and **3**. Then circle their objects.

take back   take out   look after   take off   put on

b Complete the rule with 'noun' or 'pronoun'.

If the object is a _____, put it between the verb and the particle.

c With most phrasal verbs, if the object is a noun you can put it between or after the verb and particle. He **took out** his wallet. OR He **took** his wallet **out**.

- Remember, with some verbs, the object <u>always</u> goes <u>after</u> the particle, e.g. *look after, look for, get on with*. A nurse looks after **people**. / She looks after **them**. NOT ~~A nurse looks people after.~~

PRACTICE 2

a Write a request for each picture.

1 Can I _____ _____ *this dress*, please?

2 Can you _____ _____ _____ _____?

3 Could you _____ _____ _____ _____?

4 Hey! _____ _____ my towel – now!

b Say pictures 1 to 4 with object pronouns.

1 *Can I try it on, please?*

3 Talk about … your habits

Ask a partner. Compare answers.

What are the first two things you turn on in the morning? And the last two things you turn off before you go to sleep?

What clothes do you put on …?
– on a very cold day   – to relax   – to go to a wedding

What do you often have to look for when you get up in the morning (e.g. your glasses)?

Have you ever looked after children or pets? Did you enjoy it?

7

D

Talking on the phone

Using the phone

1 Pieter's now in a hotel in Rio de Janeiro. Read the **Telephone information**. What number should he dial if he wants:

1 a cup of coffee in his room?
2 somebody to wash and iron his shirt?
3 to speak to a friend in room 217?
4 to make an international call?

2 `°14°` Pieter makes three calls. Listen and answer.
Call 1 Why does Pieter phone Varig airlines?
Call 2 Who answers? When will Ronald be back?
Call 3 Who pays for the call? What time is it in Amsterdam?

3 **a** Read the dialogues. Guess the missing words.

b Listen again and complete. Write **P** next to Pieter's lines. Practise the dialogues.

4 ▶◀ **On the phone A** *p.122* **B** *p.124*

Leaving a message on an answerphone

5 `°15°` Pieter left Ronald a message. Listen and complete Ronald's notes.

> **Message from:** Pieter
>
> Here until _____
>
> Staying at _____, room _____,
>
> phone_____
>
> Call him between _____

6 **a** Write a message like Pieter's to leave on a friend's answerphone. Invent your name, city, hotel, and room number.

b In pairs, **A** read **B** your message quite fast. **B** take notes. If you don't understand all the message, 'rewind the answerphone' (ask **A** to say it again).

B *Sorry, I'm not at home at the moment. Please leave a message after the beep.*
A *Hi. This is …*

7 📖 **Travel phrasebook 7** *p.133*

Telephone information

Welcome to the Hotel Copacabana. If you require information or assistance, please dial 0 for the hotel operator, who will be pleased to help you.

Internal dialling

Manager	80
Reception / Messages	81
Room service	82
Laundry	84
Room to room	3 + room no.
Outside line	9

National dialling
Dial 9 + area code + number

International dialling
Dial 9 + 00 + country code + area code + number

1 Phoning a company

P Hello, is _____ Varig Airlines?

_____ _____ _____ Reservations, please?

Just _____ moment, I'll _____ you through.

Sorry, it's _____. Can you _____?

2 Calling a friend

Can I _____ _____ Ronald, please?

_____ calling?

_____ _____ Pieter Okker.

What time _____ he be _____?

Can _____ _____ a message?

Can you _____ him I called?

I'll _____ _____ later.

3 Reversing the charges

I'd _____ to _____ a _____ charge call to Holland.

Hold the _____, please _____.

Go _____, caller. _____ through _____.

Message in a bottle

Karen Jary

1 **a** Read the article. Number the paragraphs 1 to 6.

A ☐

Then, almost 25 years later, Karen got the reply she was waiting for. Her mother phoned to say that there was a letter for her from Holland. The letter, including a copy of her original letter, came from Emilie Bambach in the Dutch city of Harlingen.

B 1

On a quiet afternoon in April 1970, Karen Jary went with her school friends to Great Yarmouth. When they got to the beach they each put a carefully-written letter into a bottle and threw it into the North Sea.

C ☐

In her letter Emilie said that she found the bottle in 1970, when she was walking on the beach in Vlieland, northern Holland, with her husband Frans. They were on their honeymoon.

D ☐

The 'little girl' is now 36 and married with two children. 'I got very excited when Emilie's letter arrived. I'm going to reply to her soon and my daughter says she's going to write to Emilie's youngest son.' Emilie also said, 'I'm hoping to go to England to meet Karen and her family. I'm sure I'll get on with her very well.'

E ☐

'Then the letter got lost in the house. I looked for it everywhere, but I didn't find it until this Christmas, 25 years later, when I was cleaning the attic. I decided to write to Karen because I was curious about the little girl that wrote the letter.'

F ☐

Eleven-year-old Karen was sure that somebody was going to find her message in a bottle. Her letter, addressed to 'Dear Reader', was in a Heinz ketchup bottle. But days passed, then weeks, then months, and Karen didn't get an answer. Finally she forgot about her letter, until last week …

b Write sentences. Are they true (T) or false (F)?

1 already has Karen letter replied the to
2 haven't met the yet two women
3 Emilie got has just married
4 attic bottle Emilie found has in just the the
5 daughter Emilie's hasn't Karen's son to written yet

2 **a** ⟨Circle⟩ five examples of *get* in the article. Find:
1 two examples of *get* = *receive*
2 two examples of *get* = *become*
3 one example of *get* = *arrive*
4 one example of *get* = a phrasal verb

b ✎ *Do, Make, Get* B *p.140*

3 **a** Complete the questions with (a phrase using) *get*.

1 Have you ever sent a message in a bottle? Did you *get a reply*?

2 Do you have a good sense of direction or do you often _____ ?

3 How long does it take you to _____ home?

4 What time do you usually _____ on Sunday mornings?

5 What present(s) did you _____ for your last birthday?

6 How often do you _____ a taxi?

b Interview a partner. Ask follow-up questions.

4 ►◄ **I'm sorry, I don't agree** A *p.122* B *p.125*

5 🎲 **TB** *p.105* Play *Noughts and crosses*.

∘16∘ 🎵 *Message in a bottle*, The Police

Vocabulary file 7

☐ **Words often have more than one meaning. How do I know which one I want?**

Where do you **work**? In a bank.
The lift doesn't **work**. It's broken.

In these sentences, the verb *work* has two different meanings. Many other English words have different meanings, and they can also be grammatically different. For example, the same word can be a verb or a noun, e.g. *book* (read a **book** (n.) / **book** (v.) a ticket*). Look carefully at the context to decide which meaning is correct.

1 Verbs Look at ✎ *Do, Make, Get* B *p.140*. How many different meanings of *get* are there?

2 Key words

just

Does *just* = **a** now / a very short time ago **b** exactly **c** only?

1 I'm not hungry. Just a sandwich for me. `c`
2 We've just finished. ☐
3 I'm ready. I'm just coming. ☐
4 Thank you. That's just what I wanted. ☐
5 Just a moment, please. ☐

3 Word-building Make nouns with *-tion* or *-sion*. Underline the stress.

Verb	Noun
1 re<u>ceive</u>	*re<u>cep</u>tion*
2 de<u>cide</u>	_____
3 pro<u>tect</u>	_____
4 in<u>form</u>	_____
5 re<u>vise</u>	_____
6 re<u>serve</u>	_____
7 po<u>llute</u>	_____

■ **Practise reading phonetics to help you pronounce words correctly.**

4 Pronunciation Look at the phonetics for five words from File 7. Write the words. Check the spelling in a dictionary.
1 /'aksɪdənt/
2 /ə'nɔɪd/
3 /ɪn'vaɪrənmənt/
4 /flaɪt/
5 /'hʌnɪmuːn/

5 Phrasal verbs Complete. Check with ✎ **Verbs B** *p.139*.

after   away   in   off   on (x 2)   out   up (x 2)

1 I can't hear the radio. Can you turn it _____, please?
2 We're looking _____ my neighbour's cat.
3 The room was dark so she turned _____ the lights.
4 They picked _____ all the papers and threw them _____.
5 He took _____ his jacket and tie, and put _____ a sweater.
6 Are you going to take any money _____ of the bank?
7 I filled _____ the insurance forms.

6 Adjectives Answer with an adjective ending in *-ed*. Check your answers with ✎ **Adjectives C** *p.138*. How do you feel if …
1 you haven't slept well? *tired*
2 you've got a lot of work and very little time? _____
3 a film is very boring? _____
4 you fail all your exams? _____
5 you have a problem _____
6 you break a glass at a party _____

Organize your vocabulary learning!

■ **When you look up a word in a dictionary, you sometimes find more than one meaning.**

  a Decide if the word in your sentence is an adjective, noun, verb, etc.

  b If there is still more than one meaning, look at the context again, and choose the best meaning.

Try it!

■ What do the highlighted words mean in these sentences? Look them up in a dictionary. Find another meaning for each word.
1 I'm going abroad for a year, so I'm going to let my flat.
2 He used a saw to cut the wood.
3 She had to pay a £25 fine .
4 Open the safe , and give us all your money!
5 Isn't it great! Geoff and Angela are engaged .

Grammar file 7

1 Present perfect + *yet / already*

Have you had breakfast **yet**?
No, I haven't had it **yet**.
Yes, I've **already** had it.

- ☐ Use *yet* in ⊟ sentences and ❓.
  Use *already* in ⊞ sentences.

- ☐ Put *yet* at the end of the sentence.
  Put *already* before the main verb.

- ☐ Use *yet* to ask if someone has done something or to say that someone hasn't done something.
  Use *already* to emphasize that someone has done something.

2 Present perfect + *just*

I've **just** arrived. Can you pick me up?

- ☐ Use *just* + present perfect in ⊞ sentences to say that something happened very recently.

- ☐ Put *just* before the main verb.

3 *Why …? To* + infinitive / *For* + noun

I went to Ireland.

Why did you go there?

I went there **to see** some friends.
I went there **for a holiday**.

- ☐ Use *to* + verb (infinitive) or *for* + noun to answer the question *Why …?*

- ☐ Compare *Because* + subject + verb.
  Why did he go to the bank?
  (**Because he wanted**) to get some money.

- ☐ Don't use *for* with *to* + infinitive.
  I came here **to learn** English.
  NOT … for to learn …

4 *should / shouldn't* (advice / opinion)

I can't sleep at night. What **should** I do?
You **should** see a doctor.
You **shouldn't** drink coffee.
I don't think people under 18 **should** drive cars.

- ☐ *should / shouldn't* + infinitive is the same for all persons.

- ☐ Use *should / shouldn't* + infinitive to give advice / your opinion.

5 Phrasal verbs

| **Turn on** the light. It's dark in here. | **Turn** it **on**. |
| It's hot. Can I **take off** my jacket? | Can I **take** it **off**? |

- ☐ A phrasal verb = verb + particle (preposition or adverb) with a new meaning.
  Turn up the TV. = make the TV louder

- ☐ With most phrasal verbs, if the object is a noun, you can put the object between the verb and the particle.
  Put on **your coat**.   OR   Put **your coat** on.

- ☐ When the object is a pronoun it always goes between the verb and the particle.
  Put **it** on.   NOT   Put on it.

| She's **looking after** my cat. | She's **looking after** it. |
| I'm **looking for** my keys. | I'm **looking for** them. |

- ☐ Remember, with some phrasal verbs the object always goes after the particle, e.g. *look after, / look for*.

▶ **Progress chart** File 7 *p.9*   ▶ Workbook *p.51* Do **Grammar check 7**.

101

What types of film do you like?

I love westerns.
Do you? So do I.

1 Look at the photos. What types of film are they?

A   B   C   D

Types of film Ⓥ

an ad<u>ven</u>ture film	a car<u>toon</u>	a <u>wes</u>tern
a <u>com</u>edy	a <u>dra</u>ma	a <u>thri</u>ller
a <u>hor</u>ror film	a <u>mus</u>ical	<u>sci</u>ence <u>fic</u>tion
a love story		

2 **a** Look at the poster below. What type of film is it? Have you seen it? What's it like? Who's in it? What's it about?

b Read the film review. Does it make you want to see it?

8

A

CYRANO DE BERGERAC
Jean-Paul Rappeneau   **132 min**

A superb new version of the classic story of the brave 17th-century soldier who is in love with his young cousin but doesn't tell her until it's too late. Depardieu gives a wonderful and often deeply-moving portrayal of the unhappy main character. The photography is spectacular, and even the English subtitles are very well-written.

A   I saw a really good film last night.

B   _____? What film?

A   *Cyrano de Bergerac*, with Gérard Depardieu.

B   Oh yes, I've seen it too. I didn't like it.

A   _____? Why not?

B   I don't like films with subtitles.

A   _____? I do. And I really like love stories.

B   _____? I don't.

3 **a** ° **1** ° Cover the dialogue. Listen to two people talking about the film. Do they agree?

b Listen again and complete.

GRAMMAR FOCUS 1

Echo questions

We saw a good film last night.	Did you?
My sister didn't like it.	Didn't she?
She prefers thrillers.	Does she?

a Make echo questions with the auxiliary verb and the subject pronoun.

b Use echo questions to show interest or surprise.

PRACTICE 1

Write echo questions.

1	I don't like flying.	*Don't you?*
2	She can't swim.	_____
3	They're going to have a baby.	_____
4	He's got a new girlfriend.	_____
5	I was in New York last weekend.	_____
6	He met his wife in Singapore.	_____
7	We've been married for 20 years.	_____
8	Rome's really expensive.	_____

PRONUNCIATION

Intonation

a ◦ 2 ◦ Listen and repeat the echo questions 1 to 8. Copy the intonation.

b ◦ 3 ◦ Listen and reply.

1   I'm tired. _Are you?_

4 a Write true sentences about yourself.

I like …ing.	I was born in … .
I can't … .	Tonight I'm going to … .
I'd love to … .	I hate … .
I haven't … .	Last night I … .

b Read them to a partner to answer with an echo question and a follow-up question.

A _I like travelling?_

B _Do you? Where have you been?_

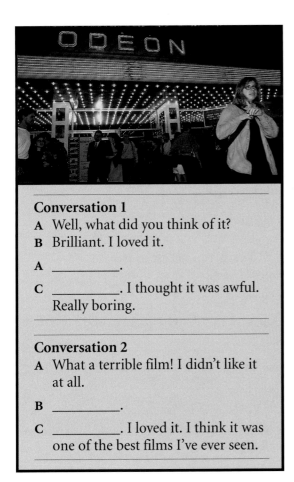

Conversation 1

A Well, what did you think of it?

B Brilliant. I loved it.

A _____ .

C _____ . I thought it was awful. Really boring.

Conversation 2

A What a terrible film! I didn't like it at all.

B _____ .

C _____ . I loved it. I think it was one of the best films I've ever seen.

---

5 a ◦ 4 ◦ Listen. Do they agree about the film?

b Listen again. Complete **Conversations 1** and **2** with the phrases.

I didn't.   I did.
Neither did I.   So did I.

GRAMMAR FOCUS 2

So / Neither do I.

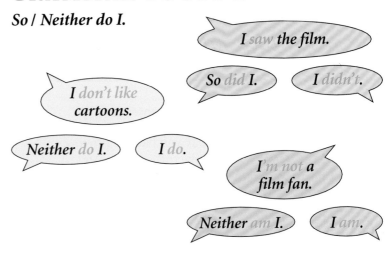

I _saw_ **the film.**

So _did_ **I.**   I _didn't._

I don't like **cartoons.**

Neither _do_ **I.**   I _do._

I'm not a **film fan.**

Neither _am_ **I.**   I _am._

Complete the rules with ⊞ or ⊟ .

1   **To agree**
Use _So_ + auxiliary + subject with a ☐ sentence.

Use _Neither_ + auxiliary + subject with a ☐ sentence.

2   **To disagree**
Use subject + auxiliary.

PRACTICE 2

a Talk about the types of film in the **Ⓥ** box in ex.1.

A _I don't like horror films._

B _Neither do I. / I do. I love comedies too._

b Complete with an auxiliary.

	Agree	Disagree
1 I really like _classical music._	So _____ I.	I _don't._
2 I don't like _mushrooms._	Neither _____ I.	I _____ .
3 I've got a _microwave._	So _____ I.	I _____ .
4 I can't speak _German._	Neither _____ I.	I _____ .
5 I went to _the beach_ today.	_____ I.	I _____ .
6 I didn't _watch TV_ last night.	_____ I.	I _____ .
7 I haven't been to _Venice._	_____ I.	I _____ .
8 I'm going to _stay in_ tonight.	_____ I.	I _____ .

6 Look at **Practice 2** sentences 1 to 8 again. **A** Change the words in _italics_ to make true sentences about yourself. **B** Agree or disagree. Then swap.

A _I really like dancing._

B _I don't. I'm not very good._

We all make mistakes

I'll pay you back tomorrow.

1 Complete cartoons 1 to 6 with the sentences.

I won't do it again.	I'll pay you back tomorrow.
I'll have the steak.	I'll take this one for you.
Shall I take a message?	I'll come back tomorrow.

GRAMMAR FOCUS 1

Uses of *will* / *won't*

a Complete with the sentences from ex.1.

Use *will* / *shall* for:		
1	offers of help	Shall I take a message? _____
2	promises	I'll pay you back tomorrow. _____
3	unplanned decisions	I'll come back tomorrow. _____

Remember, use *Shall I* / *we …?* in offers.
Shall I take you to the station? NOT ~~Will I …~~

b Translate the cartoons. Which verb form do you use in your language?

PRACTICE 1

What do you say? Write a sentence with *will* / *shall* and one of the verbs.

tell	pay	forget	answer	turn on	have

1 You're in a café. You decide to pay for everybody's drinks.

Don't worry. _____ *for these.*

2 You're in a room. It's getting dark. Make an offer.

_____ *the light?*

3 You look at the restaurant menu and decide you want the roast chicken. Tell the waiter.

_____ .

4 You're at a friend's flat. He's cooking. The phone rings. Make an offer.

_____ .

5 A friend tells you a secret. Make a promise.

_____

6 You're going on holiday. Make a promise to a friend.

_____ *to send you a postcard.*

2 **a** Who said what, and when? In pairs, try to match the speakers, dates, and predictions.
We think Margaret Thatcher said … in 19…

> Lord Haldane, politician
> Dick Roe, London record producer
> James Davidson, music critic
> Margaret Thatcher, British Prime Minister 1979–90
> Richard Nixon, President of the USA
> Thomas Watson, chairman of IBM

> 1860   1907   1943   1961   1971   1976

We all make mistakes!

Even experts can be wrong. Here are six of the world's worst predictions:

'I don't think we'll have another war. This one is probably the last.'

'I don't think there'll be a woman Prime Minister in my lifetime.'

3 'Verdi's *Rigoletto* will be famous for a day or two and then will be forgotten.'

4 'There'll only be a world market for about five computers.'

5 'These boys won't be a success.'

'The aeroplane will never be able to fly.'

b ○ 5 ○ Listen and check.

---

will / *won't* (predictions)

> I think pollution will soon be the world's biggest problem.
> There won't be another World War.

a Look at ex. 2a again. Highlight *will* / *won't* + infinitive in predictions 1 to 6.

b Use *will* / *won't* + infinitive to make predictions which are your opinions (what you think / guess will happen in the future).

c We normally use *I don't think* + *will* to make a negative prediction.
I **don't think** I'**ll** get married.
NOT ~~I think I won't get married.~~
Remember: can → **will be able** to NOT ~~will can~~
there is / are → there **will be** (there'**ll be**)

PRACTICE 2

a ○ 6 ○ Listen to five conversations. Number the topics 1 to 5. Do the speakers agree or disagree?

sport ☐	politics ☐	the weather ☐
fashion ☐	films ☐	

b Make predictions about the topics using *will*.
Begin *I think* / *I don't think* …
I think Benfica will win the League.

c Find a student who agrees with each one.

> **Agreeing / disagreeing with opinions** ⓥ
> I think so.   I don't think so.   Definitely (not).
> So do I.   Neither do I.   Probably.
> I hope so.   I hope not.   I'm not sure.
> Possibly. / Maybe. / Perhaps.

3 *Talk about … your future*

Ask a partner.
Do you think you'll ever live in another country?

> **Do you think you'll …**
> **ever**
> live in another country?
> speak English fluently?
> go to Africa or India?
> have your own business?
>
> stay in your present house / flat?
> have more than two children?
> retire before you're 55?
> study English here next year?

8

B

A passion for chocolate!

> *Fifty Kit Kats are eaten every second.*

1 [a] Talk about ... chocolate

Look at all the chocolate products in the photos.

> *Which ones have you tried?*

> *How often do you have chocolate?*

> *Do you think chocolate is addictive?*

> *Are you a chocolate addict?*

[b] Do you know where chocolate comes from? Read the introduction to the article and check.

A PASSION FOR *Chocolate*

Chocolate originally comes from South America. The first European to try chocolate was Hernán Cortés, in Mexico in 1519 at the Aztec court of Montezuma. For a century, it was a secret drink known only in Spain. After that it became expensive, so only rich people could enjoy it. Then in 1847 a British company, Fry & Son, produced the first chocolate bar, and that was the beginning of the 'chocolate revolution'.

Today chocolate is enjoyed all over the world, but most of us don't know very much about it – we just eat it!

Did you know …?

1 Chocolate is *made* from cocoa beans, sugar, and dried milk roasted together.

2 Cocoa trees are _____ mainly in Ghana, Nigeria, and Brazil. They have big leaves, and pink and white flowers.

3 When they grow, the flowers become pods. These are cut off the tree and then _____ in the sun. There are 20 to 50 cocoa beans in each pod.

4 The world's greatest chocolate eaters are the Swiss. More chocolate is _____ per person in Switzerland than in any other country.

5 The best-quality chocolates are made by hand in Belgium and Switzerland.

6 Cocoa powder is _____ to make drinking chocolate, ice-cream, cakes, biscuits, liqueurs, and also some beauty products like face creams.

7 A famous Mexican recipe called Chicken Mole is chicken which is _____ in chocolate sauce with 50 different spices!

8 A bar of chocolate has the same chemical as the one which is _____ in the brain when we are in love.

9 The best-selling sweet in Britain is the Kit Kat. Fifty Kit Kats are eaten every second, and each one has 250 calories.

10 Women buy much more chocolate than men. 42% of all chocolate is _____ by women, 32% by children, and only 26% by men.

2 **a** Read and complete the article with the past participles of these verbs.

buy   cook   dry   eat   grow
~~make~~   produce   use

b Cover the article. In pairs, write true (T) or false (F).

1 Chocolate is used to make face creams.
2 Cocoa trees are grown in Europe.
3 If you eat a lot of chocolate you'll fall in love.
4 Men buy less chocolate than children.
5 Coffee beans are used to make chocolate.
6 The Belgians eat the most chocolate.

c Which fact(s) did you find most surprising?

I didn't know chocolate is made from dried milk.

And sometimes our passion for chocolate can be fatal!

Death by chocolate

A courtier of Louis XIII died after his lover gave him a cup of poisoned chocolate. After drinking it he said to her, 'Don't forget, next time you offer a gentleman chocolate, put in a little more sugar. That will help to hide the taste of the poison.'

GRAMMAR FOCUS

The present passive

+	Chocolate	is	eaten all over the world.
	Cocoa trees	are	grown in Ghana.
−	They	aren't	grown in cold countries.
?	How	is	chocolate made?

a Study the chart above and complete the rule.

To make the passive, use the verb _____ + _____ .

b Do we know who grows the trees? Is it important?

c Underline the right rule.

Use the passive when we **focus / don't focus** on who does the action.
Chocolate **is made** from cocoa beans.
= We're not interested in who makes the chocolate.

PRACTICE

Make passive sentences.
1 *English is spoken by about 1.5 billion people.*

1	English	mine	in the world every second
2	rice	speak	in Japan and Korea
3	gold and diamonds	sell	in fields full of water
4	145 McDonald's hamburgers	grow	by about 1.5 billion people
5	many TVs and videos	make	in South Africa

3 ▶◀ **Where are they made?** A *p.122* B *p.125*

4 Write five sentences about what's grown, produced, or made in your country, and where.
A lot of white wine is produced in the Moselle Valley.
Volvo cars are made in Gothenburg in the south of Sweden.

5 **a** In Britain there's an organization called 'Chocoholics Unanimous'. Guess the answers to these questions.

1 Who do you think the organization is for?
2 Do you think there are more men than women in the club?
3 How often do you think they meet a year?
4 What do you think they do in their meetings?
5 How much chocolate do you think the members eat a day?
6 Do you think members try to stop eating chocolate?

b ° **7** ° Listen to an interview with the president, Caroline Sarll. Were you right? Are you any kind of *-holic*? Do you know anyone who is?

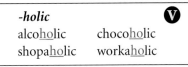

-holic	Ⓥ
alco<u>holic</u>	choco<u>holic</u>
shopa<u>holic</u>	worka<u>holic</u>

8

C

The Tower of London

The White Tower was built by William I.

1 Talk about … London

What are the famous sights of London?
Which places would you most like to visit?

Historically the Tower of London is the oldest and most important castle in England. It is one of London's most famous sights and is ¹*visited* daily by ²_____ of tourists. Last year it was visited by over ³_____ people. The oldest part is the White Tower, which gives the castle its name. It was built by William the Conqueror in about ⁴_____. The rest of the castle was completed by Edward ⁵_____ in ⁶_____. The castle was used as a palace and a prison until the ⁷_____ century. Many famous prisoners were kept there, including Sir Thomas More and Princess Elizabeth, the future Elizabeth ⁸_____. The young princes, Edward II and the Duke of York, were murdered in the Bloody Tower by their uncle, Richard ⁹_____. Anne Boleyn, the ¹⁰_____ wife of Henry VIII, was executed in the Tower. Today it contains the Crown Jewels and several museums, open every day to the public. The ¹¹_____ people who guard the Tower and work as tourist guides are called Beefeaters, the oldest royal bodyguard in the world. They still wear uniforms which were designed in ¹²_____. Large, black ravens have lived in the Tower for ¹³_____ of years. It is said that when they finally leave, the kingdom of England will fall. Today there are only ¹⁴_____ left.

2 **a** Look at photos 1 to 8. Do you know who / what they are?

b ◦ 8 ◦ Listen to the guide. Read and complete the text.

c Find these words in the text. Guess their meaning. Underline the stress. Check with a dictionary.

l.4	<u>daily</u>	*l.23*	several
l.9	Conqueror	*l.25*	guard
l.10	the rest (*n.*)	*l.28*	bodyguard
l.13	prison	*l.30*	designed
l.15	kept	*l.36*	kingdom
l.22	execute		

PRONUNCIATION

a Cross out the word without the sound /ɜː/.

1 murder   hurt   turn   ~~tourist~~
2 third   fire   first   Sir
3 were   verb   person   where
4 bored   work   world   worse

b ◦ 9 ◦ Listen and check. Which spelling patterns are often pronounced /ɜː/?

3 Cover the text. What can you remember about each photo?

GRAMMAR FOCUS

The past passive

> The White Tower was built by William I.
> The Princes were murdered in the Bloody Tower.

a Highlight six more examples of the past passive in the text.

b Complete the rules.

1 To form the past passive use _____ / *were* + _____.

2 To say who did the action, use the preposition _____.

c In which sentence are we more interested in the person / the building?
The White Tower **was built** by William the Conqueror.
William the Conqueror **built** the White Tower.

8

D

PRACTICE

a Make six true sentences with the words below. *Anna Karenina was written by Leo Tolstoy.*

Anna Karenina	build	the Greeks
the 1994 World Cup	invent	Leo Tolstoy
the <u>Py</u>ramids of Giza	paint	the Brazilians
paper	write	Leonardo da Vinci
the *Mona Lisa*	start	the Chi<u>nese</u>
the Olympic Games	win	the E<u>gyp</u>tians

b In pairs, make more sentences about:

1 a sports event   4 a painting
2 a book   5 an invention
3 a building

c Read the first part of your sentences to another pair. Can they complete them?
A *The last Formula 1 championship was won by …?*
B *Michael Schumacher?*

4 **a** Look at the chart below. In pairs, guess what the connection is with Anne Boleyn.
1 *Henry VIII was her husband.*

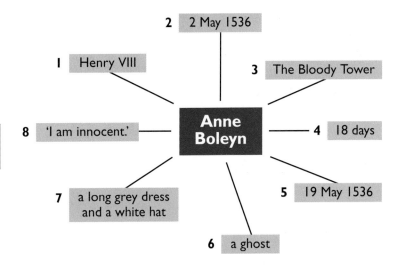

b ◦ 10 ◦ Listen to the guide and check.

5 **a** Think about the most interesting / beautiful building you've visited.

– Where is it?
– When was it built? Who by?
– What can you see there?
– Why is it interesting?

Tell other students.

b Write a paragraph about it for a class guidebook.

Going to the doctor's

Describing illness

1 Test a partner on ⬛ **The body B** *p.136.*

2 **a** Match the pictures and phrases 1 to 8.

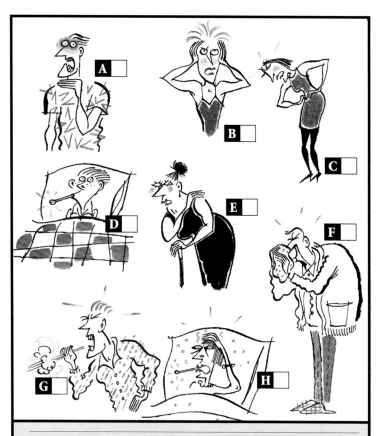

1 She's got a stomachache.
2 She's got a headache.
3 He's got a cold.
4 He's got a sore throat.
5 My shoulder hurts.
6 He's got a temperature.
7 She's got flu.
8 I've got a cough.

b Roleplay. **A** Choose a picture. **B** Ask 'What's the matter?' and give some advice. Swap roles.

B *What's the matter?*
A *I feel … / I've got (a) … / My … hurt(s).*
B *You should … / Why don't you …?*

Advice about illness ⓥ

call a <u>doc</u>tor   go to bed   lie down
go to <u>hos</u>pital   go home and rest
take | an <u>as</u>pirin /'asprɪn/
      | some <u>me</u>dicine /'medsn/

Going to the doctor's

3 **a** ⟨°11°⟩ Pieter's in Bangkok. Listen and answer.

1 What's the time?
2 Where's Pieter?
3 How is he?
4 What should he do?

Dr K _____
Tel _____
Time _____
Take my _____

Address _____

b ⟨°12°⟩ Listen and complete Pieter's notes.

4 **a** ⟨°13°⟩ Listen. What's the matter with Pieter?

b Listen again. Complete the doctor's advice.

You've got a _____ virus.
You must _____
Don't _____
You mustn't _____
Come back _____

---

must / mustn't + infinitive

[+] You must go to bed.
[−] She mustn't go to work.
[?] How many tablets must I take?
● Use *must / mustn't* for strong advice and obligation.

5 Roleplay. **A** You're ill. Describe your illness to the doctor. **B** You're the doctor. Give **A** some advice.

6 📖 **Travel phrasebook 8** *p.133*

8

Coincidences?

1 **a** · 14 · Listen. Match the dialogues and pictures.

A ☐ B ☐ C ☐ D ☐

b Listen again. What are the four coincidences?

2 ▶◀ **What have you got in common?** A *p.122*
B *p.125*

3 **a** What do you know about the two men below?

b Read and cross out the wrong verb.

A coincidence?

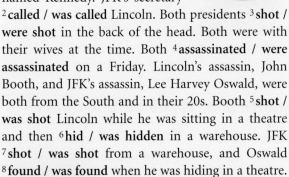

Abraham Lincoln ¹elected / **was elected** President of the USA in 1860, John Fitzgerald Kennedy in 1960. Lincoln had a secretary named Kennedy. JFK's secretary ²**called** / **was called** Lincoln. Both presidents ³**shot** / **were shot** in the back of the head. Both were with their wives at the time. Both ⁴**assassinated** / **were assassinated** on a Friday. Lincoln's assassin, John Booth, and JFK's assassin, Lee Harvey Oswald, were both from the South and in their 20s. Booth ⁵**shot** / **was shot** Lincoln while he was sitting in a theatre and then ⁶**hid** / **was hidden** in a warehouse. JFK ⁷**shot** / **was shot** from a warehouse, and Oswald ⁸**found** / **was found** when he was hiding in a theatre. Lincoln was succeeded by Andrew Johnson who was born in 1808. JFK was succeeded by Lyndon Johnson who was born in 1908. JFK was riding in a Lincoln car when he ⁹**shot** / **was shot**.

c Complete the chart. Which coincidence do you find the strangest? Do you know any other strange coincidences?

	Lincoln	Kennedy
elected in	1860	_____
secretary's name	_____	_____
shot in the back of his	_____	_____
accompanied by	_____	_____
on (day)	_____	_____
assassin was from	_____	_____
succeeded by (who)	_____	_____
who was born in	_____	_____

4 *Talk about … the future*

a In pairs, read the predictions. Choose three that you think will come true in your lifetime.

The USA will have a woman president.

Men will have babies.

It'll be fashionable to be fat.

An African team will win the World Cup.

Everybody will retire at 55.

Smoking will be illegal everywhere in the world.

People won't be able to sunbathe any more.

Cars will stop using petrol.

There won't be any tigers, except in zoos.

b Compare with other pairs. Do you agree or disagree? Why?

· 15 · 🎵 *Imagine*, John Lennon

8

◁▷

111

Vocabulary file 8

How can I continue learning vocabulary after the course?

You can learn more words all the time, from books (e.g. *Easy Readers*), magazines, songs, etc. Remember to check the grammar and pronunciation of new words in your dictionary, as well as the meaning, and to record them in your vocabulary book. And don't forget to revise all the words you've learnt in the course.

1 Word groups Cross out the odd word.
1 platform train ~~flight~~ station
2 western cartoon comedy novel
3 speak jump shout talk
4 bill ticket receipt tip
5 tower palace queen castle
6 temperature teeth headache flu
7 leaf flower plant grow
8 menu starter main course dessert
9 windy hot raining winter

2 Word pairs Write the missing word.
1 cold / freezing   hot / *boiling*
2 boring / exciting   noisy / _____
3 60 seconds / a minute   30 minutes / _____
4 hat / head   trousers / _____
5 go / come   lend / _____
6 biscuits / packet   coke / _____
7 start / finish   turn off / _____
8 pear / fruit   onion / _____
9 stand / up   sit / _____
10 jogging / go   yoga / _____

3 Word-building Complete the chart. Underline the stress. Check in a dictionary.

Verb	Noun
see	*sight*
____	beginning
pro<u>duce</u>	____
____	con<u>tai</u>ner
pre<u>dict</u>	____
in<u>vent</u>	____
____	el<u>ec</u>tion

4 Prepositions

a Complete the sentences.

by (x 2)   for   about (x 2)   without   back

1 *Hamlet* was written _____ Shakespeare.
2 Let me pay _____ the drinks.
3 Are you worried _____ something?
4 She goes to work _____ car.
5 You can't drive _____ a driving-licence.
6 I think she's _____ thirty-five. I'm not sure.
7 I'll pay you _____ tomorrow.

at   for   since   in   on

8 He's worked here _____ 1995.
9 I sometimes have to work _____ the weekend.
10 I was born _____ June 11th.
11 We usually go on holiday _____ August.
12 I've lived in France _____ two years.

b Look at ✎ **Irregular verbs C** *p.141*. Can you remember them all?

5 Pronunciation

a Look at ✎ **English sounds: Consonants** *p.142*. Look at the twenty-four pictures. Remember the words and sounds. Test a partner.

b What's the common sound? Write the sound word (see ✎ **English sounds** *p.142*).

1 English biscuit married mountain *fish*
2 worse third nurse her   _____
3 home coat know go   _____
4 answer father far can't   _____
5 January German bridge job   _____
6 shoe sugar shopping station   _____

Organize your vocabulary learning!

■ Look back at all the study tips (**Vocabulary files 1 to 7**). Which one(s) have you found most useful? Compare with other students.

■ In pairs, test a partner with ✎ **Wordbank 1 to 9**.

Grammar file 8

1 Echo questions

Hana smokes.	**Does she?**
I didn't enjoy it.	**Didn't you?**
I'll help you.	**Will you?**

> I've worked here for twenty-five years and I've never been ill in my life.

> **Haven't you?**

> No, he hasn't. And neither have I.

☐ Make echo questions with the auxiliary verb + the subject pronoun.

☐ Use echo questions to show interest and surprise.

2 *So / Neither do I., I do / don't.*, etc.

	Agree	Disagree
I love football. I played yesterday.	**So do I.** **So did I.**	I don't. I didn't.
I don't like tennis. I'm not a good player.	**Neither do I.** **Neither am I.**	I do. I am.

☐ To agree:
Use *So* + auxiliary + subject pronoun to agree with a
⊞ sentence.
Use *Neither* + auxiliary + subject pronoun to agree
with a ⊟ sentence.

☐ To disagree:
Use subject + ⊟ auxiliary to disagree with a ⊞
sentence.
Use subject + ⊞ auxiliary to disagree with a ⊟
sentence.

3 Uses of *will*

1 **Offers of help**	**Shall** I carry your bags? **I'll** open the door for you.
2 **Promises**	We **won't** be late. **I'll** always love you.
3 **Unplanned decisions**	**I'll** have the steak, please. **I'll** do it now.
4 **Predictions**	I think Liverpool **will** win. I don't think **I'll** enjoy it.

☐ Remember the four uses of *will / won't* + infinitive.

☐ Use *Shall I / we …?* for offers.
Shall I open the window? NOT ~~Will I …~~

☐ Remember:
can → **will / won't be able** NOT ~~I will can~~
there is / are → there **will be** (there**'ll be**)

4 The passive

	⊞	⊟	?
Present	Rice **is grown** in China. Cars **are made** in Brazil.	It **isn't grown** in Germany. They **aren't made** in Monaco.	**Is** it **grown** in France? **Are** they **made** in Korea?
Past	Paper **was invented** by the Chinese. The pyramids **were built** by the Egyptians.	It **wasn't invented** by the Greeks. They **weren't built** by the English.	When **was** it **invented**? **Were** they **built** by the Pharaohs?

☐ Make the present passive with *am / is / are* + past participle.

☐ Make the past passive with *was / were* + past participle.

☐ Use the preposition *by* to say who did the action.

☐ Use the passive when we aren't interested in who does the action.

☐ The passive is quite formal. We use it more in writing than speaking.

5 *must / mustn't* + infinitive

⊞	You must go to bed.
⊟	She mustn't go to work.
?	How many tablets must I take?

☐ *must / mustn't* + infinitive is the same for all persons.

☐ Use *must / mustn't* for strong advice and obligation.

▶ **Progress chart** File 8 *p.9*   ▶ **Workbook** *p.57* Do **Grammar check 8**.

8
Ⓖ

George and Mabel

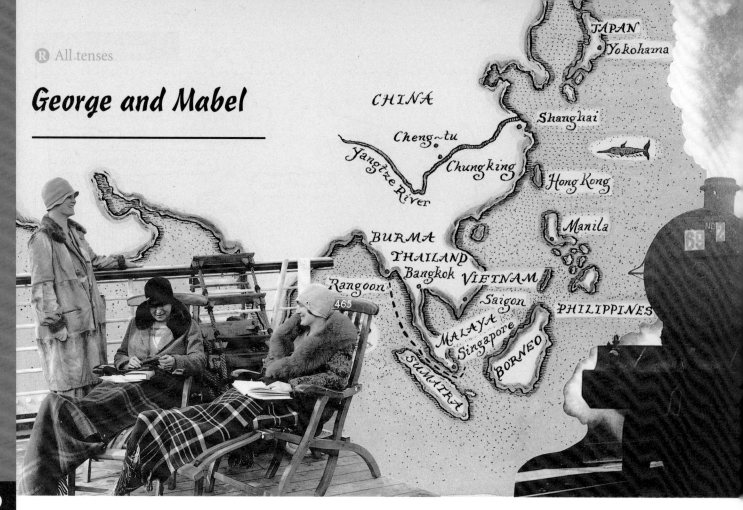

9

A

1 You're going to read a short story by Somerset Maugham. First read about him. Why did some of his friends get angry with him?

Somerset Maugham
Somerset Maugham (1874–1965) was a well-known English novelist and short story writer. Many of his stories take place in the Far East, in countries like China, Singapore, and Malaysia. He was famous for writing stories about real people who he met when he was travelling. Some of these people were very angry when they recognized themselves in his books.

2 What's the difference between …?
  1 get engaged / get married
  2 a stranger / a foreigner
  3 a journey / a trip
  4 a boat / a ship
  5 a servant / a civil servant
  6 terrible / terrified

3 `1–6` Look at *p.115*. Listen and read **Part 1**. Cover the rest of the story.

  1 Who were George and Mabel?
  2 Why couldn't they get married for seven years?
  3 Why do you think George suddenly got nervous?

4 Read **Part 2**. What do you think he decided to do?

5 Read **Part 3**. What do you think Mabel did?

6 Read **Part 4**. Draw George's journey on the map.

7 **a** Read **Part 5**. Use the words to complete the two telegrams.

ARRIVING   AT   DIDN'T   I   MANILA
SEE   SOON   SORRY   YOU

  b Continue George's journey on the map. Where do you think he went next?

8 **a** Read **Part 6**. Guess the missing words.

  b Listen and check. Complete George's journey on the map.

9 `7` Guess how the story ends. Listen and check.

10 *Talk about … the story*

  • Did you enjoy the story?
  • What do you think George and Mabel looked like?
  • Do you think they were real people?
  • Do you think many people get nervous before they get married?

Mabel, by Somerset Maugham

◦ 1 ◦ **Part 1**

George was a civil servant, working in Burma. He met Mabel and they got engaged when George was home on holiday in England. Mabel planned to go to Burma six months later, where they were going to get married. But there was one problem after another: Mabel's father died, the war started, and George had to go to an area which was dangerous for a white woman.

In the end, seven years passed before she could start the journey to Burma. George made all the arrangements for the marriage, which was going to take place on the day of her arrival. He went to the port to meet her ship. Then suddenly, George got really nervous.

◦ 2 ◦ **Part 2**

Seven years was a very long time. He couldn't really remember what Mabel was like. She would be like a complete stranger. He began to feel terrible. He decided he had to tell Mabel that he was sorry, but he couldn't, he really couldn't marry her. But how can a man tell a girl something like that when she has been engaged to him for seven years, and has come six thousand miles to marry him? George didn't know what to do.

◦ 3 ◦ **Part 3**

There was a ship in the port which was going to leave for Singapore the next day. George wrote a letter to Mabel:

> *Dearest Mabel*
> *I have to go away on business. I don't know when I'll be back. I think you should go back to England. My plans are very uncertain.*
> *Your loving George*

He left the letter, and without any luggage, just in the clothes he was wearing, he jumped onto the ship and went to Singapore.

◦ 4 ◦ **Part 4**

When he arrived in Singapore he found a telegram waiting for him:

```
I UNDERSTAND PERFECTLY
DON'T WORRY
LOVE MABEL
```

'My God,' he said. 'I think she's following me!' He checked the passenger list of the next ship arriving in Singapore, and her name was there! He was terrified. There was not a moment to lose. He caught the first train to Bangkok. But he was worried. She could easily follow him there. Fortunately there was a French ship sailing for Saigon. He got on it. In Saigon he would be safe.

The journey took five days and was dirty and uncomfortable. He was happy to arrive, and went straight to the hotel. When he signed his name in the visitor's book, the receptionist gave him a telegram. There were only two words on it:

```
LOVE MABEL
```

◦ 5 ◦ **Part 5**

When he read the telegram he panicked. 'When's the next boat for Hong Kong?' he asked. He sailed to Hong Kong but he didn't stay there. He went on to Manila. But he didn't feel safe in Manila, so he went on to Shanghai. And in Shanghai, every time he went out of the hotel, he imagined he saw Mabel coming towards him. So he decided to go to Yokohama. But at the Grand Hotel in Yokohama a telegram was waiting for him:

```
_____ _____ _____ _____
_____ _____ LOVE MABEL
```

Desperately he looked at the passenger lists of the ships on their way to Yokohama, but he couldn't find her name. Where was she now? He returned to Shanghai and went straight to his club. He immediately asked if there was another telegram for him. There was. They gave it to him:

```
_____ _____ LOVE MABEL
```

◦ 6 ◦ **Part 6**

No, no, she wasn't going to catch him so easily. He made his plans. He could take the last [1]ship along the Yangtze river to Chungking. After that nobody could get there until the following [2]s_____, except in a very small and dangerous [3]b_____. A journey like that was [4]i_____ for a woman alone. When he arrived in Chungking, he still didn't want to take any risks. There was a small place called Cheng-tu and it was 400 miles away. You could only go there by [5]r_____, and the area was full of thieves. He would be [6]s_____ there.

When George arrived in Cheng-tu, he felt that he could [7]r_____ at last. Mabel would never [8]f_____ him there. He stayed with the British consul, who was an old [9]f_____ of his. He enjoyed staying in a comfortable, luxurious house. He enjoyed being [10]l_____ and doing nothing after his exhausting journey across Asia, but above all, he enjoyed feeling safe at last. The [11]w_____ passed happily …

A musician all her life

1 Look at Sinead O'Connor. Describe her. How old do you think she is? What do you think she's like? Then read the **Profile**.

Profile

Sinead Marie Bernarde O'Connor says she has been a musician 'all her life'. She was born in Ireland on 8th December 1966. She went to school in Dublin, and was living there when she made her first record at the age of 14. She moved to London in 1987 which is where she now lives. She's single, and has two children.

2 **a** Cover the questionnaire. Look at her answers. Imagine the questions.

1 Three cats.
2 My bathroom.
3 Ironing.
4 Jamaica.
5 My credit card and my keys.
6 I sing.
7 Only English.
8 My legs.
9 My mother and father.
10 To be a granny.

b Read the questionnaire. Did you guess correctly?

3 Interview a partner with the questionnaire. Try to ask follow-up questions.

A *Have you got any pets?*
B *Yes, a dog.*
A *What's its name? What kind of dog is it?*

🎵 **8** 🎵 *Nothing compares 2U*, Sinead O'Connor

THE ENGLISH FILE QUESTIONNAIRE

Your tastes

Have you got any pets? Yes. Three cats.

What are your favourite possessions? A jewellery box my brother gave me, a small jar which was my granny's, and my piano.

What's your favourite room in the house? My bathroom.

Do you like cooking? Yes.

What housework do you hate doing? Ironing.

Which place in the world would you most like to visit? Jamaica.

What are the main differences between the Irish and the English? Irish people are passionate and English people are not.

What sort of music do you listen to at home? All kinds. I love all music but especially songs.

Your habits

What things do you always carry with you? My credit card and my keys.

How do you relax? I sing.

What languages can you speak? Only English.

Do you watch much TV? Not really.

Do you have a healthy diet? Yes, I'm quite careful about what I eat.

Your personality

What are you afraid of? Being afraid.

Is there anything you don't you like about your appearance? My legs.

Who has been the biggest influence on your life? My mother and father.

What are your best and worst qualities? I am a very loving, mothering type of person. But I am not often a loving mother to myself.

Your future

What are your plans for the next couple of weeks? I live in the present moment.

Where are you going for your next holiday? Ireland.

What would you like to do when you retire? To be a granny.

9
B

Going home

1 **a** Pieter is flying back to Amsterdam this morning. What do you think he has to do before he leaves the hotel?

b ∘ **9** ∘ Listen. True (T) or false (F)?

1 Pieter's bill is wrong.
2 He pays by credit card.
3 He gets a taxi to the airport.
4 He's left his ticket at the hotel.
5 His flight leaves at 8.10.
6 He misses his flight.

2 📖 **Travel phrasebook 9** *p.133*

3 **a** Look at pictures 1 to 12. What was Pieter doing in each place?

b 🎲 **TB** *p.122* Play the *Travel with English* game.

you a good citizen?

What would you do if you saw two people fighting?

Are *you* a good citizen?

1 What would you do …?
… if you were in the street and you saw two people fighting?

a I'd try to stop them.
b I wouldn't do anything. I'd walk past quickly.
c I'd call the police.

2 What would you do …?
… if a shop assistant in a department store gave you too much change?

a I wouldn't say anything but I'd feel bad.
b I'd leave the shop quickly and I'd feel happy.
c I'd say 'Excuse me! I think you've made a mistake.'

3 What would you do …?
… if you were sitting on a crowded bus and an elderly woman got on?

a I'd give her my seat immediately.
b I wouldn't get up if I was tired.
c I'd look out of the window.

4 What would you do …?
… if you wanted to have a noisy party in your flat?

a I'd tell my neighbours the day before.
b I'd invite my neighbours too.
c I wouldn't tell my neighbours.

5 What would you do …?
… if you found a homeless woman sleeping in the entrance to your flat?

a I'd tell the police.
b I'd ask her to go away.
c I'd try to help her.

How to score		
1 a = 3	b = 1	c = 2
2 a = 1	b = 0	c = 3
3 a = 3	b = 1	c = 0
4 a = 2	b = 3	c = 0
5 a = 1	b = 0	c = 3

What your score means	
12–15	You're a model citizen. Are you sure you told the truth?
7–11	You're a typical citizen, like most of us. You're quite civilized but you could do better.
3–6	You are not a very good citizen. Try to think of other people sometimes, not just yourself!
Less than 3	Have you ever heard of the words 'citizen' and 'community'?

9
C

1 Look at the quiz. Read only question 1. (Circle) your answer. Compare with a partner.

GRAMMAR FOCUS

Second conditional

a Highlight the verbs in question 1 of the quiz.

b Look at the chart. Complete the rule.

+ and −					
If	I you he she it we they	saw two people fighting, didn't see anything,	I you he she it we they	would wouldn't	call the police.

?				
If	you	saw two people fighting	would you	try to stop them?

✓✗
Yes, I would. / No, I wouldn't.

Contractions 'd = would   wouldn't = would not

Make the second conditional with:

if + _____ tense AND _____ / _____ + infinitive

c Use the second conditional to talk about an imaginary situation.
If I **were** rich, **I'd travel** a lot. (but I'm not rich so I don't travel)

Remember:
1 Don't use *if* + *would*. NOT ~~If I would saw …~~
2 With the verb *be*, you can say:
If I **was** rich, I'd … OR If I **were** rich, I'd …

PRACTICE

a Do the rest of the quiz. Check your score.

b Put the verbs in the right tense. Use contractions.

1 If I *knew* (know) her number *I 'd call* (call) her …
2 I _____ (help) you if I _____ (have) time …
3 If she _____ (speak) English she _____ (get) a good job …
4 We _____ (go) to the party if it _____ (be) on Saturday …
5 If I _____ (be) younger I _____ (learn) to play the violin …

c Match the ending to the right sentence.

☐ … but we're working on Friday.
1 … but I don't know it.
☐ … but I'm much too old now.
☐ … but I can't. I'm too busy.
☐ … but she's never tried to learn.

PRONUNCIATION

Sentence stress

a ○10○ Listen and write the six sentences.
1 *What* would you *do* if …?

b Underline the stressed words. Listen again and check.

2 ►◄ What would you do …?
A *p.122* B *p.125*

3 *Talk about … your dreams*

Tell a partner. Ask *Why?*
If I had more free time, I'd learn to play the saxophone.

you have more free time

you can be a famous person

you aren't here today

you can fly

you have a servant

you can choose any job

you are very, very rich

you can live anywhere in the world

you are 100 years old

you can speak English perfectly

Communication

Student A

1 B Lifestyles 🄺

a Ask **B** your questions.
How often do you have a shower?

?

How often …?
have a shower
go to the theatre
drink tea
do exercise

What kind of …?
food / like
films / watch

What time …?
wake up
start work / school
have lunch
get home at night

When …?
listen to music
read the newspaper
study English

b Answer **B**'s questions. Ask *What about you?*

2 A Have you ever …? 🄺

Take turns to ask and answer.
Ask **B** your questions.
Have you ever been to a fortune-teller?
If **B** answers *Yes, I have.*, ask another question.

Have you (ever) …?
- (be) to a fortune teller?
- (miss) a plane?
- (work) in a shop, bar, or restaurant?
- (smoke)?
- (speak) in English on the phone?
- (sleep) on a beach?
- (win) a prize or lottery?
- (move) house?
- (fail) an important exam?
- (meet) a famous person?

2 D Crossword 🄺

a Ask **B** for the definitions of your missing words.
What's 1 down ? What's 12 across?
Guess the words and complete your crossword.

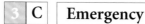

b Give definitions of the words **B** asks for.
It's a place where …

3 C Emergency 🄺

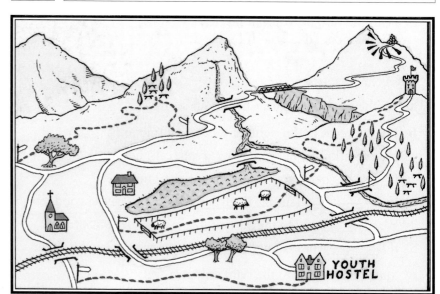

a You go for a long walk, starting from the Youth Hostel. Draw your route on the map.

b Talk to **B** on your radio. Describe your route for **B** to draw.

c Listen to **B**'s route. Draw it in a different colour.

4 🔍 Find the differences

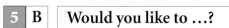

a You and **B** have a similar picture, but there are ten differences. Describe your picture to **B** in as much detail as you can.
What's different?

b Listen to **B** describe the picture. What's different in your picture?

5 B Would you like to …? Ⓐ

Take turns to ask and answer.
Ask **B** your questions. Ask *Why (not)?*
Answer **B**'s questions. Ask *What about you?*

Would you like to …

- change your job / course?
- have five children?
- learn to do a new sport?
- buy a new car?
- be very, very rich?
- be very famous?
- write a novel?
- meet the president of your country?
- live abroad?

5 D 20th century quiz Ⓐ

a In your group, make the six questions.

1 Alfred Hitchcock directed *Psycho* in 1960. (Who?)
2 Germany won the World Cup in 1954, 1974, and 1990. (Which country?)
3 Michael Jackson made the record *Thriller* in 1988. (Who?)
4 The Vietnam war ended in 1975. (When?)
5 The Channel Tunnel opened between France and England in 1994. (What?)
6 Salvador Dali died in 1988. (Which Spanish painter?)

b Take turns to ask the questions to groups **B** and **C**.

6 B Jerry and Anna Ⓐ

a Read the description of Jerry.

Jerry Dowles I'm 34 years old, and I'm quite tall (1m 85). I've got long hair, and brown eyes. I'm an architect. I've got a flat in west London, and I drive a Fiat Uno. I smoke a little, about five cigarettes a day. My favourite actress is Isabella Rossellini, and my favourite actor is Mel Gibson. At the weekend I like going out and listening to jazz. I'm Taurus, and I think I'm open and generous.

b Answer **B**'s questions.

c Turn back to *p.81*. Ask **B** questions and fill in the chart for Anna.

7 A Have they done it yet? Ⓐ and Ⓑ

a The Jacksons are going on holiday on Saturday. Look at the picture of their house for one minute.

b Turn to *p.124*.

7 C What should I do? Ⓐ

a Read and memorize your problems. Then tell **B** and **C**. They'll give you advice. Which is the best idea?

Your problems

1 My friend wants to share a flat with me, but I prefer living alone. What should I say to him / her?
2 I want to go abroad for the first time this year, somewhere cheap and interesting. Where should I go?

b Listen to **B** and **C**'s problems and give some advice.
You should … / Why don't you …? / What about …?

7 📖 On the phone   **A**

a You're on holiday in Turkey. Phone Turkish Airlines to confirm your flight home. Check what time you have to be at the airport.

> **Flight no.** TA019   **To** (your capital city)
> **Departure** 06.15

b You're Maria's friend. She isn't there now. Ask if **B** would like to her leave a message.

c You're in Britain. Phone the International Operator to make a reverse charge call to your family at home.

7 ◁▷ I'm sorry, I don't agree   **A**

Take turns. Read your sentences to **B**. **B** agrees / disagrees and says why. Then say what you think. Then listen to **B**.

I think …

- people shouldn't get married until they're 30.
- women should do military service.
- people shouldn't have more than one child.
- public transport should be free.
- children should have to stay at school until they're 18.
- museums should give back antiques to their country of origin.
- a family shouldn't have more than one car.

8 C Where are they made?   **A**

a Make complete questions. Ask **B**.
Where are pears grown?

Questions

1 Where / pears (grow)?
2 Where / Hyundai cars (make)?
3 Where / coffee (grow)?
4 Where / the best whisky (produce)?
5 Where / a third of the world's uranium (produce)?

b Answer **B**'s questions using your information.

- **Rice is grown mainly in the USA, India, and China, but also in Italy and Spain.**
- **Bananas are grown in India, Africa, Israel, South America, and the Canary Islands.**
- **Sake is an alcoholic drink made from rice. It's made in Japan.**
- **Pineapples are grown in Hawaii, Africa, and South America, but the biggest producer is Thailand.**
- **The top two petrol-producing countries in the world are first Saudi Arabia, and second Venezuela.**

8 ◁▷ What have you got in common?   **A**

a Write down:

- a kind of food you like
- something you can do very well
- a film you've seen recently
- a foreign country you've been to
- a place you'd like to visit
- something nice you did last week
- something you're going to do this weekend

b Take turns. Tell **B** about what you've written.
I like … / I can …

Then listen to **B**. Agree / disagree.

I don't like pop music.

   → *Don't you? I do. Why don't you like it?*

   OR

   ↘ *Neither do I. I never listen to it. I prefer …*

9 C What would you do …?   **A**

a Make questions. Ask **B**.

1 What would you do if you (win) first prize in the national lottery?
2 What would you do if you (fall) in love with your best friend's partner?
3 If you (can) choose to be a man or a woman, which would you choose?
4 If you (have) a time machine, would you travel to the past or the future?
5 If you (can) be an animal, which animal would you be?

b Answer **B**'s questions. Ask *What about you?*

Student B

1 B Lifestyles Ⓑ

a Answer **A**'s questions. Ask *What about you?*

?
How often …?
go to the cinema
drink alcohol
eat chocolate
have a bath
What time …?
get up
finish work / school
have dinner
go to bed
What kind of …?
music / listen to
books / read
When …?
relax
go out in the evening
drink coffee

b Ask **A** your questions.
How often do you go to the cinema?

2 A Have you ever …? Ⓑ

Take turns to ask and answer.
Ask **A** your questions.
Have you ever done yoga?
If **A** answers *Yes, I have.*, ask another question.

Have you (ever) …?
- (do) yoga?
- (be) in the papers or on TV?
- (find) any money in the street?
- (smoke) a cigar?
- (write) a poem?
- (walk) in your sleep?
- (lose) your passport / identity card?
- (say) 'I love you' to somebody in a foreign language?
- (have) a terrible holiday?
- (see) a film in English?

2 D Crossword Ⓑ

a Look at your crossword. Answer **A**'s questions. Don't say the word, but give a definition, e.g. *It's a thing which …*

 across ↓ down

b Ask **A** for definitions of your missing words.
What's 2 down ? What's 4 across?
Guess the words and complete your crossword.

3 C Emergency Ⓑ

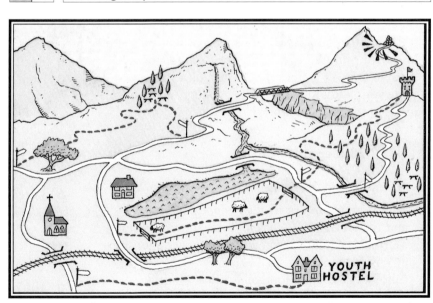

a You go for a long walk, starting from the Youth Hostel. Draw your route on the map.

b Listen to **A** describe his / her route. Draw it in a different colour.

c Now talk to **A** on your radio. Describe your route for **A** to draw.

4 🔍 Find the differences **Ⓑ**

left | right

a You and **A** have a similar picture, but there are ten differences. Listen to **A** describe the picture. What's different in your picture?

b Describe the picture to **A** in as much detail as you can. What's different?

5 B Would you like to …? **Ⓑ**

Take turns to ask and answer.
Answer **A**'s questions. Ask *What about you?*
Ask **A** your questions. Ask *Why (not)?*

Would you like to …

- speak another language?
- know your future?
- learn to fly?
- write your autobiography?
- move to the town / country?
- retire when you're 45?
- be a politician?
- be a film star?
- conduct an orchestra?

5 D 20th century quiz **Ⓑ**

a In your group, make the six questions.

1 Tom Hanks won Oscars for *Philadelphia* in 1994 and *Forrest Gump* in 1995. (Which American actor?)
2 Martina Navratilova won nine tennis championships at Wimbledon. (Where?)
3 Julio Iglesias played football for Real Madrid. (Which famous singer?)
4 Nelson Mandela became president after 25 years in prison. (Who?)
5 Neil Armstrong walked on the moon in July 1969. (When?)
6 George Orwell wrote the books *Animal Farm* and *1984*. (Which British writer?)

b Take turns to ask the questions to groups **A** and **C**.

124

6 B Jerry and Anna **Ⓑ**

a Read the description of Anna.

Anna Malik I'm 26 years old. I'm 1m 71 tall. I've got long, dark hair, and brown eyes. I'm a doctor, and I'm training to be a heart specialist. I've got a small house in north London, and a 1959 Mercedes. I don't smoke. My favourite actress is Isabella Rossellini and my favourite actor is Jeremy Irons. At the weekend I like eating out and going to the theatre. I'm Gemini, and I think I'm intelligent and quite extrovert.

b Turn back to *p.81*. Ask **A** questions and fill in the chart for Jerry.

c Answer **A**'s questions.

7 A Have they done it yet? **Ⓐ** and **Ⓑ**

Things to do

wash the car	cut the grass
put the bikes in the garage	water the plants
repair the garage door	iron the clothes
close the windows	go to the supermarket

Look at the list of jobs. In pairs, take turns to ask and answer about the list.

A *Have they washed the car yet?*
B *No, not yet. / Yes, they have. / I can't remember.*

7 C What should I do? **Ⓑ**

a Read and memorize your problems. Then tell **A** and **C**. They'll give you advice. Which is the best idea?

Your problems

1 I'm a secretary. I'm bored with my job. I want to do something new and exciting. What should I do?
2 I want to get fit. What should I do?

b Listen to **A** and **C**'s problems and give some advice. *You should … / Why don't you …? / What about …?*

7 ☎ On the phone **Ⓑ**

a You're the Reservations clerk at Turkish Airlines. Confirm **A**'s flight. **A** has to be at the airport two hours before the flight leaves.

b Phone your friend Maria. She's out. Leave a message.

c You're the International Operator. **A** wants to make a reverse charge call. Ask what number **A** wants. Ask for **A**'s name and how to spell it. Then phone the number and put **A** through.

7 ◁▷ I'm sorry, I don't agree   Ⓑ

Take turns. Read your sentences to **A**. **A** agrees / disagrees and says why. Then say what you think. Then listen to **A**.

I think …

- boxing and Formula 1 should be illegal.
- governments should pay parents to look after children.
- every country should speak the same language.
- people shouldn't smoke in restaurants or night clubs.
- all films on TV should be in the original language, with subtitles.
- everybody should go to university.
- people shouldn't eat meat.

8 C Where are they made?   Ⓑ

a Answer **A**'s questions using your information.

- **Coffee is grown mainly in South America, but also in Kenya, Indonesia, and Jamaica.**
- **Hyundai cars are made in South Korea.**
- **The best whisky is malt whisky, which is produced in the Highlands of Scotland.**
- **Pears are grown all over Europe and South America, but the world's biggest producer is China.**
- **A third of the world's uranium is produced in Canada.**

b Make complete questions. Ask **A**.
Where are pineapples grown?

Questions

1 Where / pineapples (grow)?
2 Where in Europe / rice (grow)?
3 What is sake, and where (make)?
4 In which two countries / most petrol (produce)?
5 Where / bananas (grow)?

8 ◁▷ What have you got in common?   Ⓑ

a Write down:

– a kind of music you don't like
– a famous book you haven't read
– something you can't do very well
– something important you didn't do last week
– something you aren't going to do tonight
– a country you wouldn't like to go to

b Take turns. Listen to **A**. Agree / disagree.

I like hamburgers.
    ↗ *Do you? I don't. I'm a vegetarian.*
    OR
    ↘ *So do I. With lots of cheese.*

Then tell **A** about what you've written.
I don't like … / I haven't read …

9 C What would you do?   Ⓑ

a Answer **A**'s questions. Ask *What about you?*

b Make questions and ask **A**.

1 If you (be) a local politician, what's the first thing you would do?
2 What would you do if you (find) your friend's personal diary open on the table?
3 If you (can) play any musical instrument, which would you choose?
4 If you (live) alone on a Pacific island, what luxury would you most like to have?
5 If you (can) meet anybody, dead or alive, who would it be?

Student C

5 D 20th century quiz   Ⓒ

a In your group, make the six questions.

1 Greta Garbo said 'I want to be alone'. (Which Swedish actress?)
2 Brazil won the World Cup in the USA in 1994. (Where?)
3 The Beatles made their first record in 1962. (When?)
4 Mikhail Gorbachev won the Nobel Peace prize in 1990. (Which president?)
5 America built the world's first computer in 1946. (Which country?)
6 Agatha Christie wrote *Murder on the Orient Express*. (Who?)

b Take turns to ask the questions to groups **A** and **B**.

7 C What should I do?   Ⓒ

a Read and memorize your problems. Then tell **A** and **B**. They'll give you advice. Which is the best idea?

Your problems

1 I want to have a romantic evening with my partner, just the two of us. What should I do?
2 It's my best friend's birthday next week and I want to get a special present. What should I buy?

b Listen to **A** and **B**'s problems and give some advice.
You should … / Why don't you …? / What about …?

125

Listening

1 Introduction · 4 ·

1 A Good morning. Can I help you?
   B Yes, can you give me the name of a good hotel?
   A The Majestic is good. It's very central.
   B Can you spell that please?
   A Yes, it's M-A-J-E-S-T-I-C.
   B Sorry, could you repeat that?
   A M-A-J-E-S-T-I-C.
   B Where exactly is it?

2 A Can I have your address please, madam?
   B Yes, it's 59 Greyfield Road.
   A Can you spell 'Greyfield', please?
   B Yes, it's G-R-E-Y-F-I-E-L-D.
   A Thank you.

3 A So where do you live?
   B In a small town called Burford.
   A What? Birdfoot?
   B No, Burford. That's B-U-R-F-O-R-D.
   A B-U-R-F-O-R-T?
   B No, -O-R-D. D for dog.
   A Oh sorry.

1 A · 7 ·

S And now it's time for the lunchtime European weather check for November 7th. First to London. What's the weather like there, Tony?
T Well, it's cold and grey, and surprise surprise, it's raining. 7° here, a horrible day, Stephanie.
S Thanks, Tony. Over to Moscow, now. Come in, Natasha.
N It's freezing here today, Stephanie. Minus 2° and it's snowing.
S Over now to Gabor in Budapest. What's the weather like there, Gabor?
G Not very nice at all here today, Stephanie, 10°, cold, and cloudy.
S And now to Alessandra in Milan. Buon giorno, Alessandra.
A It's very foggy here, Stephanie. I can't see anything. The temperature is only 13°.
S Thank you, Alessandra. And now to Costas in Athens. Is it good weather in Greece today, Costas?
C Yes, Stephanie, it's quite warm here. 17°, but it's very, very windy!
S Well that's it for the European weather check, and now back to the news room.

1 C · 10 ·

I So where did you go, Bruce?
B Well, I wanted a relaxing holiday because I was very stressed. So I went to the Caribbean.
I Did you have a good time?
B No, I didn't. It was terrible!
I Oh dear. Well, tell me all about it. When did you go there?
B About two years ago.
I Who did you go with?
B Nobody. I wanted to be alone. I really needed to relax.
I And how did you get there?
B By plane to Barbados, then I got a small boat to the island.
I Where did you stay?
B In a small hotel on the beach.
I That sounds nice. What was the weather like?
B Terrible. It was too hot. It was 45° every day.

I Wow, that's hot! What was the food like?
B It was awful. I couldn't eat it.
I Really?
B Yes. It was always cold and badly-cooked.
I What did you do?
B Nothing. I stayed in the hotel. It was too hot to go out in the day and at night it was too dangerous. I just stayed in the hotel all the time.
I So how long did you stay?
B Only for three days.
I You went to the Caribbean for three days?
B Yes, on the third night I decided to go home. That was the end of my relaxing holiday. Only three days and it cost me a fortune!
I Oh dear.

1 🧳 · 19 ·

This is a special announcement for passengers on flight BA 617 to London. Due to technical problems the flight is delayed. Boarding time is now 12.15 at Gate number 21. I repeat. Flight BA 617 to London. New boarding time is 12.15 at Gate number 21. British Airways would like to apologize for …

1 🧳 · 20 ·

A Can I see your passport, please? Thank you. Are you here on holiday?
B No, I'm on business.
A That's fine. Enjoy your stay.

B Excuse me. Where are the trolleys?
C They're over there.
B Could you change this for me, please? I need a coin for a trolley.
C Yes, here you are.
B Thanks a lot.

1 🧳 · 21 ·

P Excuse me. One of my cases hasn't arrived.
W Can I see your ticket, please? You've come from Jakarta on flight BA 617 and you've got three pieces of luggage.
P Yes.
W Right. I'm going to take the details. What colour is your suitcase?
P It's black.
W What's it like?
P It's big, and it's got my name and address on it.
W What's in it?
P My clothes, and some important documents.
W Fine. OK. What's your name?
P Pieter Okker. That's P-I-E-T-E-R.
W And how do you spell your surname?
P O-double K-E-R.
W And your home address?
P 29 Beethoven Straat, Amsterdam. That's Beethoven – B double E-T-H-O-V-E-N, and Straat – S-T-R double A-T.
W Thanks. And where are you staying in London?
P At the Hilton Hotel.
W Do you know the phone number?
P Yes, it's 0171 689 5022.
W And how long are you going to be there?
P For two weeks. Until October 5th.
W Right. Thank you. Don't worry. When it arrives, we'll phone you at your hotel.
P Thank you.

2 A · 2 ·

I Have you ever lost your passport?
J Yes I have. Once.
I What happened?
J Well, I was on holiday in Barcelona in 1978. At the end of my holiday, I went to the port to get the ferry to Italy. I was saying goodbye to my sister at the port, when I suddenly discovered that I didn't have my passport – only half an hour before the ferry left!
I So what did you do?
J I went to the police station at the port and asked them if they'd found a British passport. They looked at me and said, 'Well, we've found a British passport, but it isn't yours.' So I said, 'What's the name on the passport?' and they looked and they said 'Jan Latham-Koenig.' So I said, 'That's me, it *is* my passport!' But they looked at the photo and then they looked at me again and said, 'No, this passport isn't yours.' The problem was that my passport photo was from 1968, ten years before. In the photo I had very long hair, like a typical hippie. But then, in 1978, I looked completely different. I had very short hair. And I was wearing a jacket and tie.
I So, what happened?
J Well, luckily I had my driving licence in my wallet with my name on it. After a lot of talking they decided to give me my passport. Thank God!
I And did you catch the ferry?
J Yes, just!

2 B · 6 ·

B So here we are again with *Guess my job*. And on this week's panel are Jane Usher and Nick Kenton. Welcome to you both, Jane and Nick.
J Thanks, Brian.
N Nice to be here, Brian.
B Well, before we start, let me tell you the rules again. The panel can ask our mystery guest ten questions. He or she can only answer 'Yes', 'No', or 'Sometimes'. After the tenth question the panel have to guess the job. If they get it right, they win £1,000 for charity. If they get it wrong, our mystery guest takes home £500. And now please welcome tonight's first guest, Martin. Hello Martin, welcome to the show.
M Thanks, Brian.
B Right. Let's have the first question.

2 B · 7 ·

B Right. Let's have the first question.
N Do you have to get up early?
M No. No, I don't.
J Do you have to work at weekends?
M Sometimes.
N Do you have to work at night?
M Yes, I do.
J Do you have to wear a uniform?
M Yes, I do. Well, a kind of uniform.
B Now remember Martin, you can only answer 'Yes', 'No', or 'Sometimes'.
M Sorry Brian.
N Do you have to have special qualifications?
M No.
J Do you have to work outside?
M No, I don't.
N Do you have to travel?

M No.

J Do you have to speak other languages?

M No, I don't. Well, some French words sometimes. Oops, sorry Brian!

N Is your job well-paid?

M No, it isn't. Not really.

B And now for the last question, Jane.

J Is it tiring?

M Yes it is. Very tiring.

B Right. Now panel. You've got 30 seconds to decide …

2 D · 12 ·

A OK, this is how you play the game. I have a card with six words on it. Now, I have to define the words to you. But I can't say any of the words on the card. You have to guess all six words in one minute. OK?

B Yes, I think so.

A Good. Are you ready?

2 D · 13 ·

A Are you ready?

B Yes.

A Right. Here's the first word. It's a person, a person who works for the government.

B Is it a politician?

A No, it isn't. It's a person who works in places like government offices.

B I know. A …

A OK. The second word. It's a place. It's a shop. It's a shop where you can buy medicine, aspirins, and things like that.

B It's a …

A Good. Number three. Oh, this is easy. It's a thing which tells you the time.

B A clock?

A No, not a clock. It's smaller. You wear it.

B Oh. A …

A Great. Number four. It's an animal which lives in Africa I think and –

B An elephant?

A No, it's black and white, and like a horse.

B A …

A That's right. Now the fifth word. It's a place where people go on Sundays.

B A …

A Brilliant. Now the last one. It's a person who drives fast –

B A racing driver? Michael Schumacher?

A No, no. He works in a city. He takes people from one place to another.

B A …

A Yes, well done. Only 59 seconds. Now it's my turn to guess.

2 🧳 · 14 ·

1 The British Airways flight to Milan is now boarding at Gate 15.

2 Excuse me. How much are the tickets for the Mozart concert?
   They're sixty dollars each.

3 What's your seat number, madam?
   It's 17G.

4 How often are the trains to the city centre?
   Every forty minutes.

5 A cheese sandwich and a coke, please.
   Right. That's £2.90, please.

2 🧳 · 16 ·

A Hello. The centre of London, please.

B All trains go to Victoria station. Single or return?

A Single, please. How much is that?

B £9.80, please.

A Sorry? How much?

B £9.80.

A Thanks. What time's the next train?

B At 11.20, so, in ten minutes. Platform 7.

A And how long does it take?

B About half an hour.

2 ◁▷ · 19 ·

1 **A** Yes, madam. Can I help you?

   B Yes, er, have you got a … – er, I'm sorry, I don't know the word – it's a thing which you use to open bottles of wine?

   A A corkscrew? Yes, of course. This one?

   B How much is it?

   A It's £2.99.

   B OK, fine. I'll have it.

2 **A** Now, have you worked in a pub before?

   B Well, I haven't worked in a pub, but I've worked in a restaurant.

   A Ah, good, and when was that?

   B Three years ago.

   A And what did you do, exactly?

   B I worked as a waiter.

3 **A** A table for two, please.

   B Er, I'm afraid that's not possible, sir.

   A Why not? There are a lot of empty tables.

   B I'm sorry, sir, but you aren't wearing a tie.

   A What do you mean?

   B I'm afraid all men have to wear a tie. And you can't wear jeans. You have to wear trousers.

   A Come on Maggie, let's go somewhere else. What a ridiculous rule!

2 🔍 · 21 ·

And now the main points again. A <u>plane</u> has <u>crashed</u> in <u>South Korea</u>, <u>killing</u> all <u>180 passengers</u>. The <u>plane</u>, which was a <u>Boeing 747</u> flying from <u>London</u> to <u>Seoul</u>, <u>crashed</u> as the <u>pilot</u> tried to <u>land</u> in the <u>fog</u>. Among the <u>dead</u> were <u>ten Europeans</u>, including <u>two British tourists</u>.

The <u>pound</u> has <u>fallen</u> against the <u>dollar</u> for the <u>second</u> consecutive <u>day</u> and <u>closed</u> today at <u>1 dollar 70 cents</u>.

The <u>German racing driver</u> Michael <u>Schumacher</u> <u>won</u> the <u>British</u> Grand <u>Prix</u> at <u>Silverstone</u> yesterday. <u>Schumacher</u>, driving a <u>Ferrari</u>, finished <u>ten seconds ahead</u> of the <u>Italian</u> Jean <u>Alesi</u>, who came <u>second</u>.

The <u>weather today</u> is going to be <u>dry</u> and <u>sunny</u> in <u>all</u> parts of the <u>country</u>. <u>Temperatures</u> are expected to reach <u>28°</u> <u>centigrade</u>.

2 🔍 · 22 ·

A Did you read that story in the paper today about the man who wanted to commit suicide?

B No. What happened?

A Well, he was very depressed because he lost his job last year. So he drove to the centre of town and parked his car. Then he went up to the top of a very high department store – I think it was the tenth floor – and he was going to jump off.

B But he didn't?

A No, the police arrived and they talked to him for about an hour, and finally they persuaded him not to jump. So they told him to go home and he went back to his car – and that's when he discovered that the police had given him a parking ticket!

2 🔍 · 23 ·

1 This is a recorded announcement. British Airways main office is open from 9.00 a.m. to 5.30 p.m. from Monday to Friday and from 9.00 a.m. to 1.00 p.m. on Saturdays. The office is closed all day Sunday. For urgent flight information, please phone the British Airways flight information desk at Heathrow or Gatwick airport.

2 The 9.32 train to Brighton, calling at East Croydon, Gatwick airport and Brighton only, is now standing at platform 16. A buffet car is available on this train.

3 **A** OK Bill, that's great. Where are we going to meet?

   B Let's meet outside the British Museum. Do you know where it is?

   A Not exactly, but I'll find it. At about six o clock, then?

   B Fine. Don't worry if I'm a bit late.

4 **A** Sheraton Hotel. Can I help you?

   B Good morning. I'd like to know the price of a double room for one night.

   A During the week it's £85 a night, but there's a special weekend offer of £66 for Friday and Saturday nights. When do you want to stay?

3 A · 1 ·

Right, ladies and gentlemen, if you are ready? The next seven items all belonged to famous rock stars. First we have a pair of round metal glasses which belonged to John Lennon. Then we have a classical Gibson guitar which was Elvis Presley's. This typical black hat from the 1940s was Michael Jackson's. Here we have a stylish pair of Elton John's high-heeled shoes. Next we have an original striped jacket which belonged to Keith Richard. This pair of high-heeled boots was Prince's, and finally, we have David Bowie's watch. The first item is John Lennon's glasses. Do I hear £1,000? £1,000. £2,000 to my right. £3,000. £4,000. £5,000 to my left. Any advance on £5,000 …

3 B · 5 ·

T Hi. This is Tim Hurst's answerphone. Sorry I'm not here to take your call. Please leave your name and message after the tone. Thanks.

D Hello, Tim? It's me, Debbie. Hope you're OK. I sent you a postcard but I don't know if it's arrived. Listen. I'm going to a conference at Budapest University. I'm flying to Budapest next Sunday, and I'm staying for a week. Listen, I'm leaving …

3 B · 6 ·

D Hi Tim, it's Debbie again. Sorry I didn't finish my message. As I was saying, I'm going next Sunday, Sunday March 14th. I'm arriving in Budapest at half past ten your time. I'm flying with Malev Airlines – flight number MA 209 – MA 209. I'm staying at the Danube Hotel – that's D-A-N-U-B-E. Listen Tim, I really hope we can meet in Budapest. Call me at home. My number's 0161 855 907 – 0161 855 907. OK? Bye!

3 C · 12 ·

Hello. Hello. Can you hear me? It's Jim here. I've found the French girl and she's OK, but she can't walk. I think her leg's broken. I'm going to tell you how to get to us. Have you got the map in front of you? OK, first go down the path, past the lake. Have you got that? OK, then go along the path for about three hundred metres. Go across the field on your left. OK? Good, then go through the forest and then down into the valley. All right? Then go over the bridge and up the hill. We're on the other side. Have you got all that? Be as quick as you can.

3 🗎 ° 16 °

1 A Reception. Can I help you?
  E Yes, could I have a coke and a cheese sandwich for room 149, please?
  A Certainly, sir. Would you like anything else?
  E No, thanks.
  A Room service.
  E Thank you. Can you put it on my bill, please?
  A Yes, of course.
2 A Good afternoon.
  B Hello, is that Reception?
  A Yes, madam. Can I help you?
  B Yes, the TV in my room doesn't work. Could you repair it, please?
  A Yes, of course. I'll do it immediately. What's your room number?
  B Room 301.
3 A Reception.
  D Hello, this is Mr Simpson from room 637. There aren't any towels in my room. Could you bring me one, please?
  A I'm very sorry, sir. I'll bring you one right away.
  D Thanks.
4 A Reception, can I help you?
  C Yes, this is room 418. Could you wake me at 6.45 tomorrow morning?
  A 6.45, room 418. Yes, of course, sir. That's fine.
  C Thank you very much.

3 ◁▷ ° 17 °

1 A What are you doing tonight?
  B I've got tickets for *Hamlet*.
  A Where?
  B At the National. The Royal Shakespeare Company.
  A Fantastic.
2 A Are we doing anything this evening?
  B Yes, my mother's invited us for dinner.
  A Oh no! Do we have to go?
  B Yes, sorry, we do.
3 B Hello.
  A Hi. This is Sarah. Listen. Would you like to see a film tonight?
  B OK. What film?
  A I can't remember the name. It's French.
  B With subtitles?
  A Yes.
  B Good. Because my French is terrible.
4 A What time are you going?
  B I'm leaving at about 6.00.
  A How are you getting there? By train?
  B No, I'm flying.
  A You're so lucky. I love Berlin.
5 A Did you get the tickets?
  B Yes, they were really expensive.
  A How much?
  B £40 each.
  A Wow!
  B But it's going to be a good game. Liverpool and Manchester United.

3 ◁▷ ° 18 °

Well, it was a Monday, I think, about half past nine in the evening and I was having dinner at my home here in Barcelona when the phone rang. It was a Scottish policeman and he spoke to me in English. At first, I didn't know what he was talking about. He said, 'We've found your bag, sir.' I said, 'Bag? What bag?' I just couldn't believe it after all this time! I never thought I'd see it again. The policeman said they'd send me my bag as soon as possible. In fact it took a month to arrive from Scotland. I was very excited when it arrived. I opened it, and I was amazed! Everything was in perfect condition, even the money – 47,000 pesetas. But the most incredible thing is that after fourteen years my pen still writes!'

4 A ° 2 °

The Americans watch much more TV than the English, although most of it isn't as good. They worry much more about their health. Every supermarket sells thousands of vitamins and diet foods. In fact, I think the Americans probably live more healthily because they do a lot more outdoor activities like camping and sailing. But apart from sport there's less for young people to do. Because they can't drink until they're 21, young Americans can't go to nightclubs or bars. Young people in England have a much better social life.
I think English people dress more stylishly than the Americans. In the States everyone wears jeans and trainers. In general, young Americans have less freedom and are more dependent on their families. In England, it's more normal for young people to leave home when they finish school.

4 C ° 7 °

Z Hello, Julie. How are you feeling?
J A bit better, thanks.
Z Did you go to the doctor's yesterday?
J No, I didn't. I didn't go anywhere. I just stayed in bed all day, and took aspirins.
Z Did you? That's good. … I phoned you yesterday to see how you were feeling. Nobody answered.
J I was probably sleeping.
Z What did you think of the match, Julie?
J Match? What match?
Z You weren't sleeping, Julie. Somebody saw you at the tennis match yesterday – at Wimbledon.
J But I – Who saw me?
Z My husband. He's a great tennis fan. He goes to all the matches at Wimbledon. He was sitting behind you.
J But he – but –
Z Come into my office, Julie. You and I need to have a talk. A serious talk.

4 🗎 ° 13 °

P Good evening. Do you speak English?
W Yes, sir. How many people?
P A table for three, please.
W Come this way.

P Have you got a menu in English?
W Here you are, sir.
P This looks good. What are you going to have?

W Are you ready to order?
P What do you recommend?
W The pepper steak's very good.
P Hmm! What are you having, Benni?

B I'll have the pepper steak, and the soup to start.
W How would you like your steak, sir? Rare, medium, or well-done?
B Well-done.
P What about you, Hana?
H The roast chicken for me, please. And to start, I'd like the salad.
W And you, sir?
P I'd like the salmon and the roast chicken.
W So that's two salmons and one salad, is that right?
B No, one salmon, one soup, and one salad.
W And two roast chickens and a steak.
B That's it. Thanks.
W What would you like to drink?
P A bottle of red wine.
H I'd like some mineral water too, please.

W Here are your starters. Enjoy your meal!

4 🗎 ° 14 °

1 B Excuse me, please. This soup's cold.
  W I'm very sorry. I'll get you another one.
2 B Excuse me, please! This steak is rare. I asked for well-done.
  W I'm sorry, sir. I thought you said rare.
3 H Waiter. Sorry, but this glass is dirty.
  W I'm sorry, I'll bring you another one.
4 H Excuse me, I haven't got a fork.
  W Really. Oh dear. Here you are, madam.
5 H I'm afraid I didn't order this. I asked for roast chicken.
  W I'm sorry, madam. I'll change it for you at once.

4 ◁▷ ° 16 °

… Thank you. Yes, I can promise you that if we win the elections, we'll create 800,000 new jobs. I repeat, 800,000 jobs. Everybody will have a job. And not just a job, but a home too, because if we win, we'll build more houses and flats. There won't be any more people living on the street. Yes, there'll be no more homeless people if you vote for the New Democrats. And you'll have the money to buy a house, because if we win, you'll pay less tax. Yes, we'll cut taxes by 10%. Thank you. And don't think we've forgotten our children or our older people. We'll spend more money on education. Classes will be smaller and teachers will be better. And finally, if you vote for us in the next elections, pensions will go up by 20%. Yes, 20% more for all our pensioners. Believe me, you're safer with us. So remember, on May 25th, vote for the New Democrats, for a better future TODAY!

5 A ° 3 °

I Could you tell us about your favourite things, Natalia?
N My favourite things? Well, at the moment, one of them is my new car. It's a BMW. I've always wanted one, and I finally bought it when I was in Madrid in August, so I've only had it for a few weeks!
I What else?
N Well, most of the things that I like are important to me for the memories they bring. For example, I've got a yellow T-shirt which I've had since 1980.
I Why is that so important?
N I got it at the Moscow Olympics. I wore it when I carried the Olympic torch through Rostov. I was only 14 years old, and it was very exciting.
I How long have you had this cup?

N Since 1986. It's my most important trophy. It was my first world championship in Amsterdam, and I was the best junior player. And this is the first Olympic medal I won. I've had it for about ten years now, since the Seoul Olympics.
I Which is your most important possession?
N Well, I've got two. This gold bracelet which my husband gave me for my birthday, last January. And the most important is this photo of my parents.
I How long have you had that?
N They gave it to me when I left Russia in 1991. I never go anywhere without it.

5 B ·5·

I How old are you, Charles?
C I'm 85.
I Do you feel your age?
C No, not at all. I still feel quite young and I've got a lot of energy. I think you're only as old as you feel.
I Where were you born?
C I was born in France. My mother was French and my father was from Liverpool. I moved to England when I was 14.
I What did you want to be when you were young?
C That's easy. I always wanted to be a professional footballer.
I What did you do before you retired?
C I was an architect. I worked for the local government in Coventry. I retired when I was sixty-five.
I How long have you lived in Coventry?
C A long time. Let me see. I've lived here since 1953.
I What do you do in your free time?
C Well, my wife died five years ago and so I live alone now. My children are all married. So I like being busy. I like cooking and photography. I'm studying French at university. I'm also trying to learn Spanish. I like travelling. I couldn't travel very much when my wife was alive because she didn't like flying, but now I travel a lot. This year I've been to Spain and France. I also like listening to music.
I What kind of music do you like?
C I like classical music of course but I also listen to pop music. I'm a big fan of Annie Lennox and Queen.
I What are your plans for the future?
C I've got lots of plans. I want to speak Spanish well. My French is very good but I'm only a beginner at Spanish. I'd also like to travel more. I'm hoping to go to New York next winter. I've never been there, and I've always wanted to.

5 ·10·

P Excuse me, could you tell me how to get to …?
A Sorry. What did you say?
P Can you tell me the way to …?
A Yes, of course.
P Can you show me on the map?
A Yes, sure. OK. It's not far. We're here at the Bowling Green. Go up this street, Broadway, for about 400 metres. Take the first turning on the right. Then go straight on until you get to Exchange Place. Turn left into Nassau Street, then take the next turning on the right. That's Wall Street. There's a subway station there. Go along Wall Street for about 200 metres, and it's on the left. You can't miss it.

P Thanks very much.
A You're welcome.

5 ·12·

P Excuse me. Do you know this area?
A Yes.
P Am I near the Metropolitan Museum of Art?
A No.
P Is it far? I mean, can I walk there from here?
A No way. It's about 100 blocks away. You'll have to get a bus.
P What number bus?
A Several buses go there. Get a number 4, 5, or 6 from that stop over there, and get off at 86th Street. It's about ten stops.
P Thanks very much.
A You're welcome.

P Excuse me. Does this bus go to 86th Street?
B No, this is the wrong direction. You need to go back the other way. Get off at the next stop, cross the street, and go back in the other direction.
P Oh no …

P Excuse me, is this the right stop for the Metropolitan Museum?
C Yes, it is.

P Excuse me! Could you tell me the way to the Metropolitan Museum?
D Sorry. No speak English.
P Oh, I'm sorry!

P Excuse me! I'm a bit lost. Do you know the way to the Metropolitan Museum?
E I'm sorry. I don't know. I'm a tourist. I'm lost too. Can I have a look at your map?

P Excuse me!
F Yes?
P Can you tell me the way to the Metropolitan Museum?
F Yes, it's right here in Central Park. Go straight on, through the park, round the lake, and past the fountain. Take the first turning on the left, and it's on your right. OK?
P Past the fountain then the first turning on the right?
F No, on the left, then it's on your right.
P OK. Thanks a lot.
F That's OK.

P Excuse me! Is that the Metropolitan Museum?
G Yes, it is. But it's closed. It never opens on Mondays. It's open again tomorrow from 9.30 until 5.15.
P Oh no! I don't believe it!

6 A ·1·

1 I don't think I'm a typical housewife. I love shopping but I don't really like anything else. I don't like cleaning, and I absolutely hate washing-up.
2 My wife works so I have to do a lot of housework. I like cooking, especially at the weekend, and I don't mind vacuuming. What I really hate is ironing.
3 I like shopping and I don't mind ironing. I find it very relaxing. What don't I like? I don't like cleaning.
4 I have to say I don't do very much in the house. I usually wash up every evening and I go shopping on Saturdays. I don't mind washing-up but I hate shopping. Especially in the supermarket. It's so boring.
5 I'm a perfectionist, so my house is always really clean. In fact I enjoy cleaning and I love cooking. I make all my own bread and cakes.

6 B ·6·

I So Jerry, how was your evening? How did you get on?
J Well, Anna's very extrovert and very talkative. She talked a lot! All evening, in fact. I think she's probably a generous person, too. She didn't let me pay for our meal. We had a nice evening together and we laughed a lot. So I think we got on quite well.
I Are you going to meet again?
J Well, I'd like to, but I don't know when. She's very hard-working and likes her job. She doesn't have a lot of free time.
I Do you think she'd like to see you again?
J Yes, I think so.

I So, Anna, how was your evening with Jerry?
A It was good. We had a really good time.
I What did you think of Jerry?
A Well, he's very friendly and he made me laugh a lot. So that was good. He's got a nice smile. At first he was shy but in fact when you get to know him he's very talkative. Perhaps that was the problem for me. I think he likes talking much more than listening, especially about himself. And I think perhaps he's a bit mean. When I offered to pay he accepted immediately. I didn't like that.
I Would you like to meet him again?
A No, not really. He's not my type.

6 D ·9·

I Do you like living in Fanlac, Jean François?
J I like it a lot. That's why I live there! It is a very small village with only about ten houses, so it's very quiet. The houses are old and beautiful and the village is surrounded by lovely fields and forests.
I It sounds great.
J Yes, it is. We live very close to nature. We grow a lot of our own food. It's a very friendly place too. Everybody knows everybody, and we help each other all the time.
I What don't you like?
J The only real problem is that it's twenty kilometres to the nearest big town. There aren't any shops or bars and so we have to go a long way every time we need something, even a newspaper. We're very cut off from the outside world. And there's no cinema, of course – I miss that. The other thing I don't like is that it's difficult to have a private life. There are no secrets in Fanlac. Everybody knows everything that you do!

6 ·11·

P Have you got those jeans in my size?
A Which ones?
P The black ones.
A What size are you?
P I'm 32.
A Let's see. Here you are.
P Can I try them on?
A Yes, there's a changing room over there.

P They're a bit too small. Have you got a bigger size?
A These ones are 34.
P Yes, these are fine. OK, I'll take them.
A Would you like anything else?
P No, thanks. How much are they?
A They're $49.95.

6 ⊞ ° 12 °

1 A Excuse me, the zip's broken on these jeans. Can I change them?
  B Sure, just take another pair.
2 A Excuse me. I bought this radio yesterday and when I got home I found that the volume control doesn't work. I'd like my money back.
  B Have you got the receipt?
  A Yes, here you are.
  B That's fine. OK. Could you please write your name and address here?
3 A Excuse me, there's a button missing on this shirt. Have you got another one?
  B I'm terribly sorry. I'll just go and look.

6 ◁▷ ° 13 °

Professional sportspeople can earn a lot of money, but their lifestyles aren't easy. The Spanish tennis player Arantxa Sanchez-Vicario has been one of the top players in women's tennis since she was seventeen.
She spends about nine months a year travelling round the world playing tennis, so she's away from home, living in hotels, most of the time. She wakes up at about eight o'clock, and she trains six days a week, every day except Sunday. She trains on the tennis court for four and a half hours every day and she also spends one and a half hours in the gym. She goes to bed at ten o'clock every night.
Her diet is quite strict. She eats a lot of pasta and salads. She doesn't eat many sweet things although she occasionally eats a little chocolate. She doesn't smoke and she never drinks coffee. And she never drinks alcohol, except for a glass of champagne when she wins a championship.

7 A ° 1 °

L Andy, this is Louise. Can you hear me?
A Are you on the mobile?
L Yes, I'm on my way to London. But there's a lot of traffic. Listen, don't forget to book my hotel in Lisbon for tomorrow.
A I've already done it. I booked it yesterday.
L Great. Have you picked up my tickets yet?
A No, I haven't been to the travel agent's yet. I'm going this afternoon. But I've confirmed the flight times with the travel agent. You're leaving at 8.30.
L Have you rented a car for me?
A Yes, I have. You pick it up at the airport.
L What about the fax to Brazil?
A I've finished it but I haven't sent it yet.
L And the report? Have you written it yet?
A Yes, it's on your desk. Don't forget to sign it before you leave.
L Great. Oh, I nearly forgot! The most important thing of all! Have you found my passport?
A Yes, luckily! It was in your drawer under some documents.
L Brilliant. That's it then. See you later. Bye.
A Bye.

7 B ° 5 °

I John, why did the BBC invite you onto their programme *Hearts of Gold*?
J To give me an award. The award was a medal – a 'heart of gold' in fact. It was for my work in Romania, in Negru Voda. The programme heard about it and decided to give me the award. It was a great surprise.

I You first went to Negru Voda in 1991, is that right?
J Yes, and when I saw the terrible conditions there I knew I had to help. I went straight back to Britain to get money and medicine to send them.
I What did you have to do first?
J Well, the first thing we had to do was to rebuild the orphanage. Luckily, I'm a builder. I gave up my job in England to work there full time. Then we realized that we needed more people, and I persuaded my wife and some friends to come out too.
I Why did you need more people?
J To work with the children in the orphanage. There were so many children, and not enough helpers, because they really all needed individual attention, which they'd hardly ever had.
I How long did it take to rebuild the orphanage?
J It took about five years altogether. The mayor of Negru Voda opened it last year.
I How did you feel on that day?
J Wonderful. When we looked at the children's faces, smiling and laughing, children who, five years before, never spoke and never smiled, we knew we'd done the right thing.

7 C ° 10 °

M And who's our next caller?
S Hello. My name's Sarah.
M Hello, Sarah. And what's your problem?
S Well, I've been married for five years now, and until now we've been really happy together. But about six months ago, my husband bought a dog.
M What's wrong with that?
S Well, since he's had the dog, he's been obsessed with it. He spends hours taking it for walks.
M Why don't you go with him?
S I did at first, but now he meets up with other dog owners, and when they're together, they only talk about dogs. He never talks to me. And I think the dog hates me too.
M What about buying another dog for you?
S We can't. Our flat's too small for two dogs. And my husband's dog's an Alsatian! The worst thing of all is that I think my husband loves the dog more than he loves me.
M Well, Sarah, I think you should talk to your husband and explain how you feel. Perhaps he doesn't know you feel lonely and …

7 D ° 11 °

One morning an old lady called the Gas Company to tell them her gas fire didn't work. Two men arrived at midday to repair it. They started work and she went upstairs to clean the bedrooms. They quickly repaired the fire and turned on the gas to see if it was working, but they forgot to turn it off. Then they went into the garden to have a cigarette. When they came back in, the living-room was full of gas. So they turned the gas off and opened the windows, but then they saw the old lady's canary. It was dead on the floor of its cage. They were very embarrassed! So they picked it up and put it back on the perch. Just then the old lady came downstairs. When she came into the living-room and saw the canary, she screamed. 'What's the matter?' the men asked …

7 ⊞ ° 14 °

Call 1
A Pois não? Em que posso ajuda-lo?
P Hello. Er, do you speak English? Is that Varig Airlines?
A Yes, can I help you?
P Yes, can I have Reservations, please?
A Just a moment, I'll put you through … Sorry, it's engaged. Can you hold?
P Yes, OK.
B Hello, Reservations.
P Yes, my name's Pieter Okker, and I'd like to confirm my flight to Bangkok.

Call 2
A Hello.
P Hello, can I speak to Ronald, please?
A I'm sorry but he isn't here at the moment. Who's calling?
P This is Pieter, Pieter Okker. I'm an old friend of Ronald's from Holland. What time will he be back?
A I'm not sure. He's working late tonight. I'm Anna, his wife.
P Can I leave a message?
A Yes, sure.
P Can you tell him I called? I'll call back later.
A Fine. I'll tell him.
P Thanks very much. Bye.
A Goodbye.

Call 3
O International Operator.
P Good morning. I'd like to make a reverse charge call to Holland, please.
O What number do you want?
P The number is 251034470.
O Could I have your name and number?
P Yes, it's Pieter Okker O-double K-E-R, and my number is 780780.
O Hold the line, please caller … Go ahead, caller. You're through now.
P Thanks. Hello? Hello? Is that Simone?
S Hi, Pieter.
P Hello, darling. Are you OK?
S Pieter, do you know what time it is? It's three o'clock in the morning. I was asleep …

7 ⊞ ° 15 °

R This is 453981. Sorry there's nobody here to take your call. Please leave a message after the beep and we'll call you back.
P Hi, Ronald. This is Pieter. Pieter Okker from Amsterdam. It's 6.30. I phoned earlier but you were out. I'm here in Rio on business. I'll be here until Tuesday, then I'm going to Bangkok. I'd like to see you. I'm staying at the Copacabana Hotel. My room number is 307 and the phone number is … 780780. I'll be in the hotel between 8.00 and 9.00 p.m. Can you call me back then? Hope to see you soon. Bye.

8 C ° 7 °

I Caroline, when did you start the society?
C In 1990.
I Why?
C Well, I thought that there must be other people like me and that it would be nice to meet from time to time.
I Your members are all chocolate addicts, is that right?
C Well, not serious addicts, just people who love chocolate. In fact psychologists say that chocolate is not really addictive.
I What kind of people belong to Chocoholics Unanimous?

C All kinds of people, but there are more women than men.

I And how often does the society meet?

C We meet several times a year and we always have dinner. Of course, chocolate is included in every course. For example, at our last dinner we had roast beef with chocolate sauce, potatoes cooked in white chocolate –

I Ugh!

C Delicious!

I And how much chocolate do members eat?

C Well, that depends. Most of us eat some every day. But I know that one of our members eats at least a half-kilo box of chocolates every evening.

I Do your members worry about being chocolate addicts?

C No, not at all.

I Have you ever tried to give it up, or eat less?

C No. Why? I don't smoke or drink much, and I do regular exercise, so why shouldn't I enjoy the pleasure of eating chocolate?

8 D · 10 ·

G Can you all hear me? Don't worry, I'm going to speak slowly.

Ts Yes. / Fine. / No problem.

G Good. The Tower we are in now is called the Bloody Tower. Do you know what 'blood' is? Good. Well, the Tower has a very special connection with Anne Boleyn. Anne Boleyn was the second wife of Henry VIII – you know, the king who had six wives. Henry divorced his first wife, Catherine, and he married Anne because he wanted a son. But Anne couldn't give him a son, only a daughter. So Henry decided to marry again. But first Anne Boleyn had to die. Come with me.
It all happened very quickly. One day Anne was the Queen of England and the next day, on 2nd May 1536 she was arrested and brought here to the Bloody Tower. She was kept in this room for 18 days. She slept in that bed there. Then, on 19th May, she was taken from here and executed. Her head was cut off, like this. But since then, the ghost of Anne Boleyn has been seen and heard many times here in the Tower of London. Sometimes she sits in a dark corner of the room, just over there. She wears a long, grey dress, and a white hat. Sometimes she's seen with her head, sometimes without it, and sometimes she's carrying her head under her arm. Other people have seen the ghost of Anne Boleyn walking in the Bloody Tower. And some people have heard it crying, saying 'I am innocent. I am innocent.' Perhaps one of you will see the ghost of Anne Boleyn today!

8 · 11 ·

R Good morning, Mr Okker. It's 8.00.

P Thank you. … Oh, I feel awful …

P Hello, Reception. I don't feel very well …

8 · 12 ·

P I need to see a doctor.

R1 Just a moment. The doctor for this hotel is Doctor Kriangsak. That's K-R-I-A-N-G-S-A-K. I'll give you her number. It's 7649763. You have to make an appointment.

P Does she speak English?

R1 Yes, very well.

P Thanks.

P Hello. Do you speak English?

R2 Yes, a little.

P Could I make an appointment to see the doctor as soon as possible, please. I'm a tourist.

R2 Yes, could I have your name, please?

P Pieter – P-I-E-T-E-R – Okker – O-double K-E-R.

R2 What nationality are you?

P I'm Dutch.

R2 Have you got any medical insurance?

P Yes, I have.

R2 Is half past nine this morning OK?

P Nine thirty. Yes, that's fine.

R2 Don't forget to bring your passport and insurance documents.

P All right. What's the address?

R2 In Rama Road, that's R-A-M-A, number 428.

P R-A-M-A, Rama, number 428, is that it?

R2 That's right.

P Thank you. Goodbye.

8 · 13 ·

D Good morning. Mr Okker, isn't it?

P Yes, that's right.

D Please sit down. Now, what's the matter?

P I've got a really bad stomachache and a headache. I feel terrible.

D What did you have for dinner last night?

P I had fish, some vegetables, and I had a few glasses of wine …

D Well, Mr Okker, I think you've got a stomach virus. It's very common at the moment. You must rest for a few days.

P Does that mean I can't go out?

D Well, you can go out if you like, but don't try to do too much.

P I won't. I'll take it easy.

D The most important thing is your diet. You mustn't eat any fried food or drink any alcohol.

P Don't worry, I won't.

D Here's a prescription for some medicine. There is a pharmacy on the corner of this street. Read the instructions in the box. How long are you staying in Bangkok?

P Only for another two days.

D Well, if you don't feel better, come back and see me tomorrow.

P Thank you very much.

8 · 14 ·

1 **A** Listen to this! It says in the paper that a tiger escaped from the zoo last night.

  B Did it? Not near here I hope? Was it London Zoo?

  A No, it wasn't. It was in Bristol.

  B Oh no. My parents live in Bristol, next to Bristol Zoo!

2 **A** I've got some great news.

  B Have you? So have I. What's your news?

  A I've just got two tickets for us for Saturday. It'll be a brilliant match.

  B For this Saturday? Liverpool and Chelsea?

  A Yes, of course. Why, what's the matter?

  B I've just got two tickets as well.

  A Oh no!

3 **W** Are you ready to order?

  A Yes, please. I'll have the chicken in lemon sauce.

  J Andrew! I thought I knew that voice.

  A James, I don't believe it. What are you doing here?

  J Having dinner, like you!

  A What a coincidence! After all these years! How are you?

4 **A** Right. What would you like to drink?

  B No, you paid last time. I'll get these. What do you two want?

  A / C A pint of lager.

  B Right. Two pints of lager and a coke.

9 A · 7 ·

Part 7

One morning George and the consul were talking on the patio when someone knocked loudly on the door of the British Consulate. A servant opened it. A woman came in. She was clean, cool, and fresh. When George saw her he turned white with terror.
'Hello, George, I was so afraid that I'd missed you again,' she said.
'Er, hello Mabel,' he said. He didn't know what else to say.
She smiled at him. 'You haven't changed at all', she said. 'I was afraid that perhaps after seven years you would be old and fat and bald. I've been so nervous. Imagine how terrible it would be if after all these years I didn't want to marry you!' She turned to George's friend. 'Are you the Consul?'
'Yes, I am.'
'That's good. I'm ready to marry him as soon as I've had a bath.'
And she did.

9 · 9 ·

P Hello. Could I have my bill, please?

R Certainly, sir. Here you are.

P What's this 2,000 for?

R That's for your phone calls.

P Oh, right. Do you take American Express?

R Yes, that's fine.

P Could you call me a taxi to the airport?

R Certainly, sir.

A Good afternoon. Your tickets and passport, please.

P Just a moment. Oh no!

A What's the matter?

P I've left my passport at the hotel.

A What time's your flight?

P At ten to eight.

A It's only seven o'clock. If you get a taxi and ask the driver to hurry, you'll just make it.

A Your tickets and passport, please.

P Here you are.

A Do you have any hand luggage?

P Only this bag.

A That's fine. Would you like smoking or non-smoking?

Travel phrasebook

Translate, or complete and translate.

1 📦 *Getting there*   **Your language**

Do you have any hand-luggage?
_____

Would you like smoking or non-smoking?
_____

Can / Could I have a window seat, please?
_____

Board at *12.50* at gate number *11*.
_____

Sorry? Could you repeat that?
_____

The flight is delayed.
_____

I'm here on business / holiday.
_____

Thanks a lot.
_____

You're welcome.
_____

Excuse me, one of my cases hasn't arrived.
_____

2 📦 **From the airport to the hotel**

Can I change *$100*, please.
_____

What's the exchange rate?
_____

How do I get to *the station*?
_____

How often are the trains to *the city centre*?
_____

Single or return?
_____

What time's the next *train*?
_____

How long does it take?
_____

(It takes) about *half an hour*.
_____

(Can you take me to) *the Hilton Hotel*, please.
_____

How much is that?
_____

3 📦 *At the hotel*

I've got _____ reservation.
_____

A single / double room _____ a bath / bathroom.
_____

May _____ see your passport, please?
_____

Could you _____ in this form, please?
_____

It's on the *first* floor.
_____

The *TV* in my room doesn't _____.
_____

Could you wake _____ up at 7.15 tomorrow?
_____

There aren't _____ *towels* in my room.
_____

Could I have a *sandwich* for _____ 109, please?
_____

Can you put it on my bill, please?
_____

4 📦 *At the restaurant*

A table for *three*, please.
_____

Have you got a menu in English?
_____

What do you recommend?
_____

I'll have the *soup* to start, and then the *steak*.
_____

Rare, medium, or well-done?
_____

I'd like some *mineral water*, please.
_____

Excuse me, I didn't order this. I asked for
  the *chicken*.
_____

Just a *black coffee* for me.
_____

Could I have the bill, please? We're in a hurry.
_____

I'm sorry, but I think the bill is wrong.
_____

5   Asking the way

Could you _____ me how to _____ to the *bank*? _____

_____ you tell me the _____ to the *bank*? _____

_____ you know where the *bank* is, please? _____

Can you _____ me _____ the map? _____

Take _____ first turning on the right / left. _____

Go straight on until you get _____ *the traffic lights*. _____

Turn left / right into *Wall Street*. _____

Is _____ a *post office* near here? _____

_____ it far? _____

_____ this bus go to *86th Street*? _____

Is this the right stop for the *art gallery*? _____

6   Shopping

Can I have some of that *cheese*, please? _____

Which one? _____

This one or that one? _____

How much are these / those? _____

What size are you? _____

Can I try them on? _____

They're a bit too *big*. Have you got a *smaller* size? _____

These are fine. I'll take them. _____

Can I change these *jeans*, please? _____

The *zip*'s broken. _____

I'd like my money back, please. _____

Have you got another one? _____

7   On the phone

Is that *Varig Airlines*? _____

Can I have *Reservations*, please? _____

I'd like to confirm my flight to *Bangkok*. _____

This is Pieter. Can I speak to *Ronald*, please? _____

Who's calling? _____

What time will he be back? _____

Can I leave a message? _____

Can you tell him I called? _____

I'll call back later. _____

I'd like to make a reverse charge call to *Holland*, please. _____

8   At the doctor's

What's _____ matter? _____

I've got _____ *stomachache*. _____

I don't feel very well. _____

I need _____ see a doctor. _____

Could I make an appointment to see the doctor? _____

As soon _____ possible, please. _____

Have you _____ any medical insurance? _____

9   Going home

Could I have my bill, please? _____

Do you take *American Express*? _____

Could you call me a taxi to *the airport*? _____

I've left my *passport* at the hotel. _____

1 Activities

A Daily routine

Match the verbs and pictures.

- [ ] get dressed
- [ ] get home
- [ ] get to work / school / university
- [ ] get up

- [ ] have a shower / bath
- [ ] have breakfast / lunch / dinner
- [ ] start / finish work / school / university
- [1] wake up

- [ ] go to bed
- [ ] go home
- [ ] go to work / school / university

B Free time

Match the verbs and pictures.

- [ ] go cycling /ˈsaɪklɪŋ/
- [ ] go dancing
- [ ] go jogging
- [ ] go shopping
- [ ] go sightseeing /ˈsaɪtsiːɪŋ/
- [ ] go swimming

- [ ] go out
- [ ] go to the cinema / theatre
- [ ] go for a walk

- [A] go away *for the weekend*
- [ ] go on holiday

C Housework

Match the verbs and pictures.

- [ ] clean *the floor*
- [ ] cook
- [ ] do the washing
- [ ] do the washing-up
- [12] iron /ˈaɪən/
- [ ] tidy *my room*

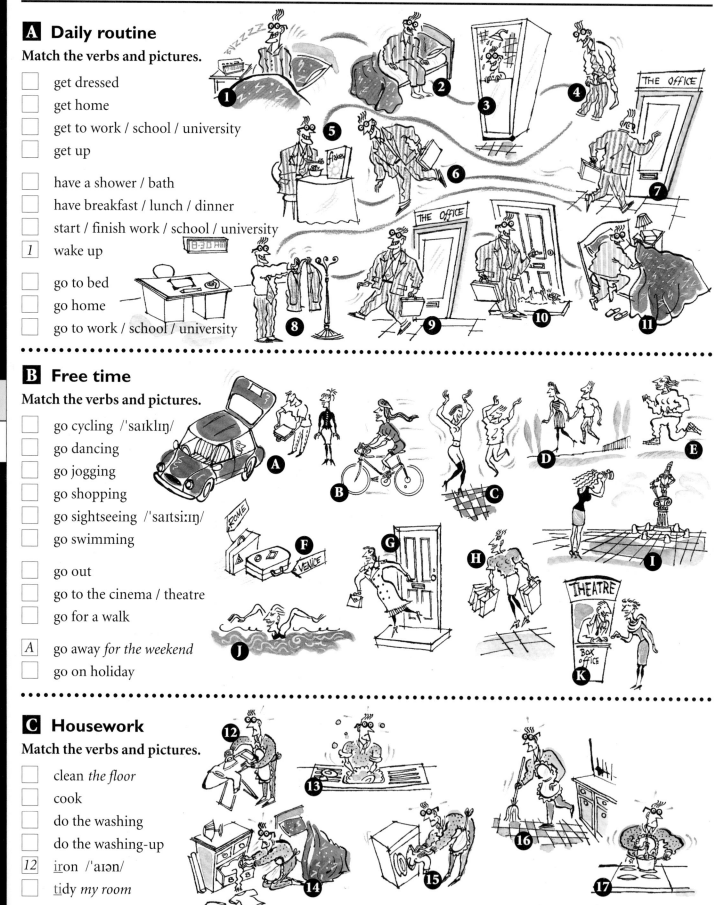

2 Prepositions

A Prepositions of place
Match the prepositions and pictures.

2	behind /bɪˈhaɪnd/
	between
	in front of
	inside
	near
	next to (= beside / by)
	opposite
	outside
	under

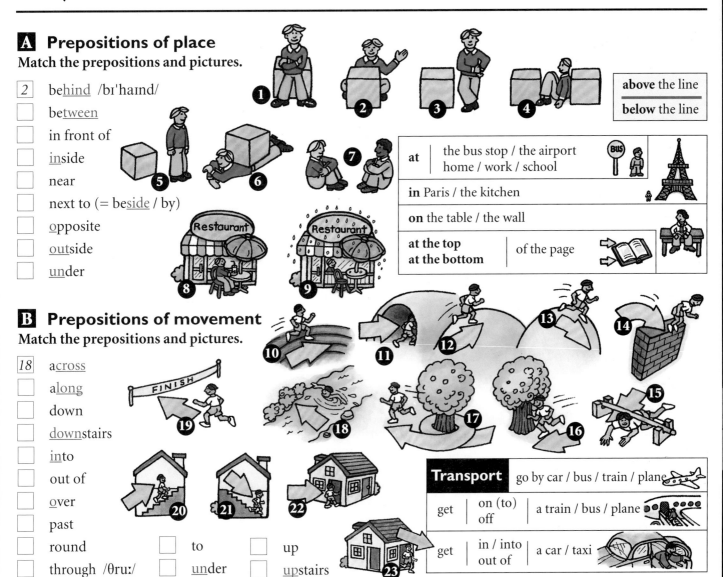

above the line
below the line

at	the bus stop / the airport home / work / school
in Paris / the kitchen	
on the table / the wall	
at the top **at the bottom**	of the page

B Prepositions of movement
Match the prepositions and pictures.

18	across
	along
	down
	downstairs
	into
	out of
	over
	past
	round			to			up
	through /θruː/		under			upstairs

Transport	go by car / bus / train / plane
get	on (to) off	a train / bus / plane
get	in / into out of	a car / taxi

3 High numbers

Complete the numbers.

102	a / one hundred and two
200	_____ hundred
310	three hundred _____ _____
421	four _____ _____ twenty-one
533	five hundred _____ _____ - _____
644	_____ _____ _____ _____ - _____
1,000	a / one thousand
7013	_____ _____ _____ _____
11,800	_____ thousand _____ _____

_____	twelve thousand five hundred and fifty-five
14,000	_____ _____
66,779	_____ - _____ _____ _____ _____ _____ _____ - _____
100,000	a / one hundred _____
1,000,000	a / one _____
_____	eight million, seven hundred and fifty thousand, three hundred and eighty-two

135

4 The body

A Appearance, clothes, and colours
Match the words and pictures.

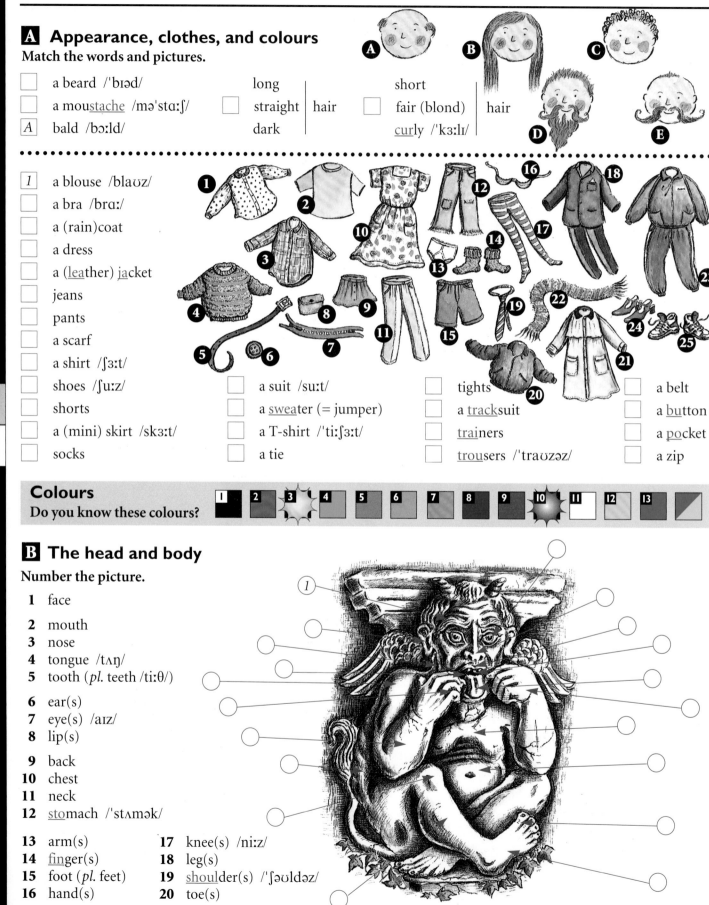

- [ ] a beard /ˈbɪəd/
- [ ] a moustache /məˈstɑːʃ/
- [A] bald /bɔːld/

long
- [ ] straight
dark

hair

short
- [ ] fair (blond)
curly /ˈkɜːlɪ/

hair

- [1] a blouse /blaʊz/
- [ ] a bra /brɑː/
- [ ] a (rain)coat
- [ ] a dress
- [ ] a (leather) jacket
- [ ] jeans
- [ ] pants
- [ ] a scarf
- [ ] a shirt /ʃɜːt/
- [ ] shoes /ʃuːz/
- [ ] shorts
- [ ] a (mini) skirt /skɜːt/
- [ ] socks

- [ ] a suit /suːt/
- [ ] a sweater (= jumper)
- [ ] a T-shirt /ˈtiːʃɜːt/
- [ ] a tie

- [ ] tights
- [ ] a tracksuit
- [ ] trainers
- [ ] trousers /ˈtraʊzəz/

- [ ] a belt
- [ ] a button
- [ ] a pocket
- [ ] a zip

Colours
Do you know these colours?

| 1 | 2 | 3 | 4 | 5 | 6 | 7 | 8 | 9 | 10 | 11 | 12 | 13 | |

B The head and body
Number the picture.

1 face

2 mouth
3 nose
4 tongue /tʌŋ/
5 tooth (pl. teeth /tiːθ/)

6 ear(s)
7 eye(s) /aɪz/
8 lip(s)

9 back
10 chest
11 neck
12 stomach /ˈstʌmək/

13 arm(s)
14 finger(s)
15 foot (pl. feet)
16 hand(s)

17 knee(s) /niːz/
18 leg(s)
19 shoulder(s) /ˈʃəʊldəz/
20 toe(s)

5 Food

A Meat, fish, fruit, and vegetables
Label groups 1 to 4. Match the words and photos.

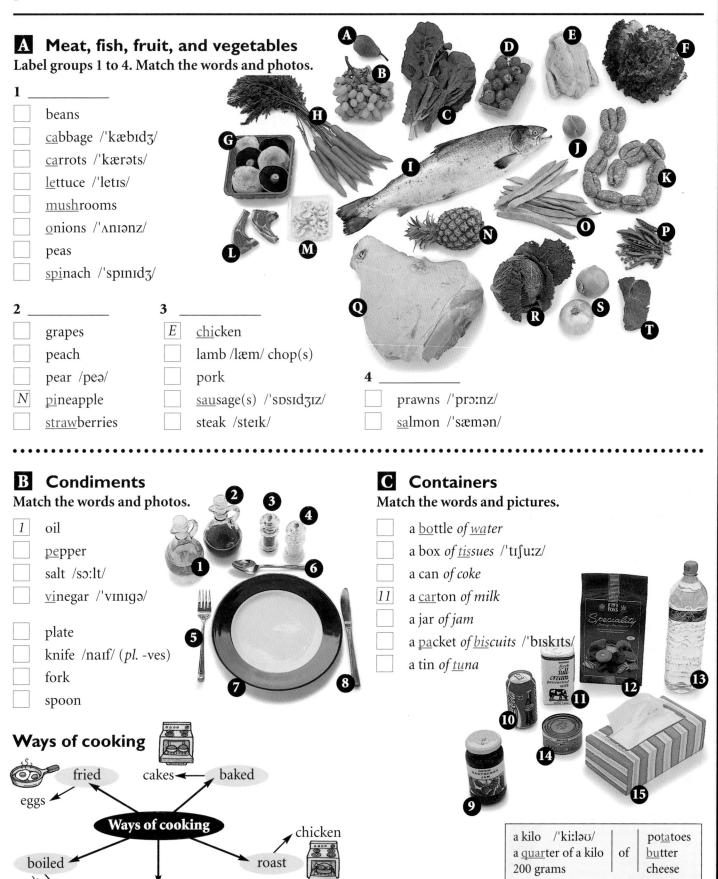

1 _____

- [ ] beans
- [ ] cabbage /'kæbɪdʒ/
- [ ] carrots /'kærəts/
- [ ] lettuce /'letɪs/
- [ ] mushrooms
- [ ] onions /'ʌnɪənz/
- [ ] peas
- [ ] spinach /'spɪnɪdʒ/

2 _____

- [ ] grapes
- [ ] peach
- [ ] pear /peə/
- [N] pineapple
- [ ] strawberries

3 _____

- [E] chicken
- [ ] lamb /læm/ chop(s)
- [ ] pork
- [ ] sausage(s) /'sɒsɪdʒɪz/
- [ ] steak /steɪk/

4 _____

- [ ] prawns /'prɔːnz/
- [ ] salmon /'sæmən/

B Condiments
Match the words and photos.

- [1] oil
- [ ] pepper
- [ ] salt /sɔːlt/
- [ ] vinegar /'vɪnɪgə/

- [ ] plate
- [ ] knife /naɪf/ (pl. -ves)
- [ ] fork
- [ ] spoon

Ways of cooking

- fried
- eggs
- cakes → baked
- **Ways of cooking**
- boiled
- rice
- grilled → fish
- roast → chicken

C Containers
Match the words and pictures.

- [ ] a bottle of water
- [ ] a box of tissues /'tɪʃuːz/
- [ ] a can of coke
- [11] a carton of milk
- [ ] a jar of jam
- [ ] a packet of biscuits /'bɪskɪts/
- [ ] a tin of tuna

a kilo /'kiːləʊ/ a quarter of a kilo 200 grams	of	potatoes butter cheese
half a litre /'liːtə/	of	milk

137

6 Adjectives

A Places

Match the adjectives and pictures. Write the opposites.

		Opposites
6	ex<u>ci</u>ting	*boring*
	<u>dir</u>ty	_____
	<u>da</u>ngerous	_____
	<u>crow</u>ded	_____
	high	_____
5	small	_____
	<u>mo</u>dern	_____
	<u>na</u>rrow	_____
	<u>noi</u>sy	_____
	<u>com</u>fortable	_____

<s>boring</s>
low
<u>em</u>pty
large (= big)
clean
old
<u>qui</u>et
safe
un<u>com</u>fortable
wide

....

B Personality

Match the words and definitions. Write the opposites.

		Opposites
	<u>frien</u>dly	*unfriendly*
	<u>ge</u>nerous	_____
	in<u>te</u>lligent	_____
	<u>la</u>zy	_____
1	<u>sel</u>fish	_____
	shy	_____
	<u>tal</u>kative	_____

1 a person who only thinks about him / herself

2 a person who likes giving things to other people

3 a person who doesn't like working

4 a person who talks a lot

5 a person who finds it difficult to talk to new people

6 a person who is open and makes friends easily

7 a person who learns and understands well

<u>ex</u>trovert
hard-<u>wor</u>king
mean
<u>qui</u>et
<u>stu</u>pid
<s>un<u>frien</u>dly</s>
un<u>sel</u>fish

....

C Feelings

Match the words and pictures.

	a<u>nnoy</u>ed (= <u>an</u>gry)
	bored
7	de<u>pressed</u>
	em<u>ba</u>rrassed
	ex<u>ci</u>ted
	<u>frigh</u>tened (= a<u>fraid</u>)
	<u>in</u>terested
	pleased (= <u>ha</u>ppy)
	stressed
	sur<u>prised</u>
4	<u>wo</u>rried

NEWS

7 Verbs

A Confusing verbs

Complete the chart with the right pairs of verbs.

carry / wear	watch / look at	say / tell
meet / know	miss / lose	win / earn
borrow / lend		

1

borrow

a book **from** the library
some money **from** a friend

a pen
some money **to** a friend

2

a bag / an umbrella

clothes / glasses

3

the TV
a football match

a painting
some photos

4

a prize / a match

a good salary
£1,000 a month

5

somebody for the first time

somebody for a long time

6

a train / a class

your glasses / your job

7

something / hello

me (etc.) something
a story

B Phrasal verbs

Match the verbs and pictures.

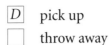

| D | pick up |
| | throw away |

| | put on |
| | take off |

| | turn on |
| | turn off |

| | turn up |
| | turn down |

	look after *someone who's ill*
	look for *something you've lost*
	look up *a word in the dictionary*
	fill in *a form*
	get on with *my parents very well*
1	take / give back *something you've borrowed*
	take out *something from your pocket*
	try on *clothes in a shop*

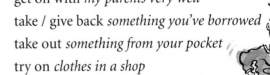

8 Do, Make, Get

A do or make?
Match the expressions and pictures.

3	aerobics
	an exam
	an exercise
	housework
	military service
	your homework

	a cake
	a mistake
	lunch
	the bed

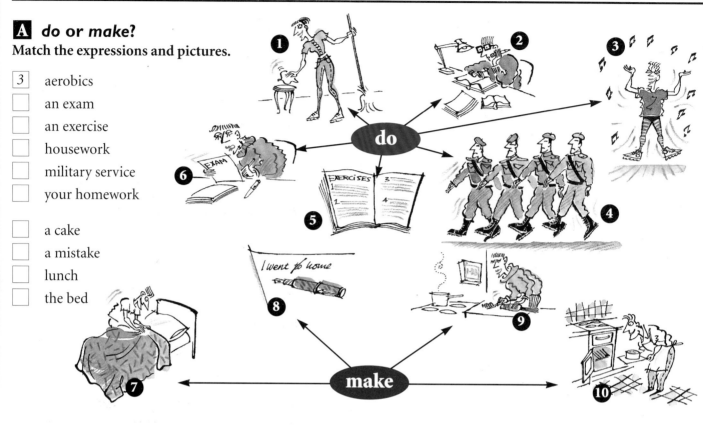

B get
Match the expressions and pictures.

B	wet
	lost
	married / divorced

| | a new car |
| | a job |

| | a taxi |
| | a fax / letter |

| | to work |
| | home |

| | up |

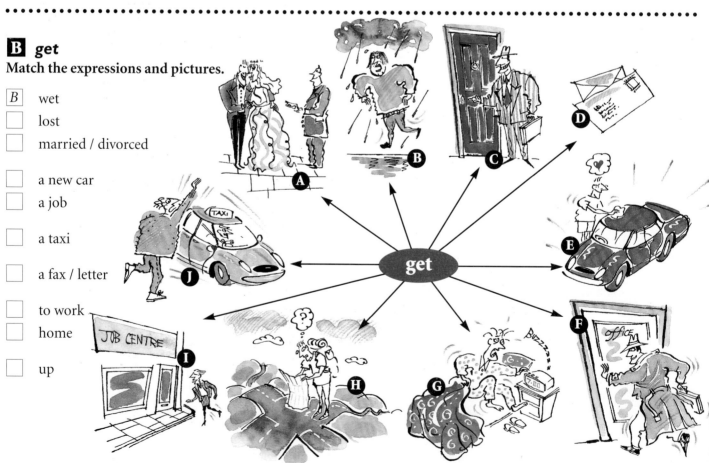

9 Irregular verbs: the top 60

Infinitive	Past simple	Past participle	
be	was / were	_____	/bi:n/
become	became	become	
begin	began	begun	
break	broke	_____	
bring	brought	brought	/brɔ:t/
build	built	_____	/bɪlt/
buy	bought	_____	/bɔ:t/
can	could		
catch	caught	caught	/kɔ:t/
choose	chose	chosen	
come	came	come	
cost	cost	cost	
cut	cut	_____	
do	did	_____	/dʌn/
drink	drank	_____	
drive	drove	_____	/'drɪvn/
eat	ate	_____	
fall	fell	_____	
feel	felt	_____	
find	found	_____	
fly	flew	flown	/fləʊn/
forget	forgot	forgotten	
get	got	got	
give	gave	given	
go	went	_____ (been)	
grow	grew	_____	/grəʊn/
have	had	_____	
hear	heard	_____	/hɜ:d/
keep	kept	_____	
know	knew	_____	/nəʊn/
leave	left	_____	
lend	lent	lent	
let	let	let	
lose	lost	_____	
make	made	_____	
meet	met	_____	
pay	paid	paid	/peɪd/
put	put	_____	
read	read	_____	/red/
ring	rang	rung	
run	ran	run	
say	said	_____	/sed/
see	saw	_____	

sell	sold	sold	/səʊld/
send	sent	_____	
sit	sat	sat	
sleep	slept	_____	
speak	spoke	_____	/'spəʊkən/
spend	spent	spent	
swim	swam	swum	
take	took	_____	
tell	told	told	/təʊld/
think	thought	thought	/θɔ:t/
understand	understood	understood	
wake (up)	woke (up)	woken (up)	
wear	wore	worn	
win	won	_____	/wʌn/
write	wrote	_____	/'rɪtn/

A Put the past participles in the chart.

heard   seen   been   met   read   gone   made   had

B Put the past participles in the chart.

broken   written   driven   said   drunk   done   slept
spoken   fallen   won   lost   left   known   found

C Put the past participles in the chart.

cut   put   felt   taken   bought
grown   eaten   kept   built   sent

Verb + preposition
Remember these verbs with their prepositions.

agree with *somebody*
ask for *a coffee*
fall in love with *somebody*
go to *the cinema*
invite *somebody* to *a party*
listen to *the radio*
look at *a photo*
pay for *a meal*
speak / talk about *something*
speak / talk to *somebody*
spend money on *clothes*
wait for *the bus*
work as *a mechanic*
work for *IBM*
worry about *money*
write to *a friend*

Vowels

Consonants

■ short vowels
⚊ long vowels
▨ diphthongs

■ voiced
▨ unvoiced

Key to vowels

1 fish /fɪʃ/	9 computer /kəmpˈjuːtə/	16 owl /aʊl/
2 tree /triː/		17 boy /bɔɪ/
3 cat /kæt/	10 bird /bɜːd/	18 ear /ɪə/
4 car /kɑː/	11 egg /eg/	19 chair /tʃeə/
5 clock /klɒk/	12 up /ʌp/	20 tourist /ˈtʊərɪst/
6 horse /hɔːs/	13 train /treɪn/	
7 bull /bʊl/	14 phone /fəʊn/	
8 boot /buːt/	15 bike /baɪk/	

Key to consonants

21 parrot /ˈpærət/	30 zebra /ˈzebrə/	38 right /raɪt/
22 bag /bæg/	31 shower /ˈʃaʊə/	39 witch /wɪtʃ/
23 key /kiː/	32 television /ˈtelɪvɪʒn/	40 yacht /jɒt/
24 girl /gɜːl/		41 monkey /ˈmʌŋkɪ/
25 flower /ˈflaʊə/	33 thumb /θʌm/	
26 vase /vɑːz/	34 mother /ˈmʌðə/	42 nose /nəʊz/
27 tie /taɪ/	35 chess /tʃes/	43 singer /ˈsɪŋə/
28 dog /dɒg/	36 jazz /dʒæz/	44 house /haʊs/
29 snake /sneɪk/	37 leg /leg/	

11 Classroom language

A Complete and learn the phrases to help you speak English in class.

Ex<u>cuse</u> *me*!

Can / _____ you help me, please?

How _____ you | say … in <u>Eng</u>lish?
             | spell it?
             | pro<u>nounce</u> it?

Where____ the stress?

Sorry? / Pardon?

_____ / Could you say that a<u>gain</u>, please?

What____ the | <u>di</u>fference between … and …?
         | the <u>o</u>pposite of …?
         | the *past tense* of …?

What _____ this word mean?

I _____ | under<u>stand</u>.
        | know.
        | re<u>mem</u>ber.

Is this right _____ wrong?

Which page _____ it?

I can't _____ *the board.*

_____ you got *a pen,* please?

Can / _____ I have *a <u>copy</u>,* please?

Here you _____.

<u>So</u>rry I_____ late.

Sorry I didn't come _____ class last *Monday.* I was *ill.*

See you _____ *Tuesday*!

_____ a good *week<u>end</u>*!

You _____!

B Translate and learn the phrases to help you speak English together.

Your language

What do you mean? _____

What do we have to do? _____

What did he / she say? _____

Just a <u>mo</u>ment / <u>mi</u>nute, please. _____

We haven't finished (yet). _____

Whose turn is it? _____

It's my / your turn. _____

What do you think? _____

What / How a<u>bout</u> you? _____

Do you a<u>gree</u>? _____

I agree / I don't agree (with you). _____

I'm not sure. _____

Per<u>haps</u>. / <u>May</u>be. _____

It de<u>pends</u>. _____

For e<u>xample</u> … _____

It doesn't <u>ma</u>tter. <u>Ne</u>ver mind. _____

OXFORD
UNIVERSITY PRESS

Great Clarendon Street, Oxford OX2 6DP

Oxford University Press is a department of the University of Oxford. It furthers the University's objective of excellence in research, scholarship, and education by publishing worldwide in

Oxford New York

Auckland Cape Town Dar es Salaam
Hong Kong Karachi Kuala Lumpur Madrid
Melbourne Mexico City Nairobi New Delhi
Shanghai Taipei Toronto

With offices in

Argentina Austria Brazil Chile Czech Republic
France Greece Guatemala Hungary Italy Japan
Poland Portugal Singapore South Korea
Switzerland Thailand Turkey Ukraine Vietnam

OXFORD and OXFORD ENGLISH are registered trade marks of Oxford University Press in the UK and in certain other countries

© Oxford University Press 1997

The moral rights of the author have been asserted

Database right Oxford University Press (maker)

First published 1997

2009 2008 2007 2006

30 29 28 27 26 25 24 23

ISBN-13: 978 0 19 435522 3

ISBN-10: 0 19 435522 5

Printed in China

ACKNOWLEDGEMENTS

The Publisher and Authors would like to thank the following teachers: Sarah Bampton, David Barnes, Cristina Brieba, David Dunn, Bernie Hayden, Tim Herdon, Sue Inkster, Amanda Jeffries, Catherine Kendall, Pam Murphy, Cristina Nogueira, Roy Pearse, Cristina Rajagopalan, Jacqui Robinson, Lynda Ryalls, Jacek Rysiewicz, Agota Tongori for comments on the materials.

Staff and students at the British Council, Valencia, the Friends Centre, Brighton, Portslade Community College, Kingsway College, London, and Eurocentre, Brighton for all their help in piloting the course and making valuable suggestions; Svetlana Bogdanova, Charles Bornat, Jan Latham-Koenig, Natalia Morskova, Sinead O'Connor, and Julie Willis for agreeing to be interviewed; Joseph Brennan (for the Sinead O'Connor interview), Michael O'Brien (for *Love me tender*), Robert Knibbs (for information about Mexico City), Carmen Dolz (for input on the pronunciation charts), Angela O'Leary (for help with quotes), Sarah Chrisp (for the American photos), John Heslop (for information about New York), Gill Hamilton (for several photocopiable activities), and Bernie Hayden for help with the Workbook.

Special thanks to Cristina Mayo, Ma Angeles Rodriguez, and Carmen Dolz for all their support, and to Joaquin, Marco, and Krysia who were always in mind.

The Publisher and Authors would like to thank the following for their kind permission to use articles, extracts, or adaptations from copyright material: A life in the day of Sir Anthony Hopkins, adapted from an article by Garth Pearce, reproduced from the Sunday Times Magazine 26 December 1993 with permission © Times Newspapers Limited, 1993. *Best of times, worst of times,* adapted from an article by Rosanna Greenstreet, reproduced from The Observer 1992 with permission © The Observer. Extracts adapted from *The Amish* by Carys Bowen-Jones reproduced from Marie Claire magazine November 1991 by permission © Robert Harding Syndication. Extracts reproduced from Gatwick Express information leaflet by kind permission of Gatwick Express. Extract *Never stop on the motorway* taken from Twelve Red Herrings by Jeffrey Archer reproduced by permission of Harper Collins Publishers Limited. Extracts taken from *Under loch and key* in The Daily Mail by permission © Daily Mail / Solo Syndications. Adapted from article *First Person: Jack Charlton* reproduced by permission © Margaret Rooke and Ruby Millington, 1994 – this article was first published in The Telegraph Magazine. Extracts adapted from *Henry VIII and his Six Wives* by Janet Hardy-Gould, *Sherlock Holmes Short Stories* by Sir A. Conan Doyle, *Rainforests* by Rowena Akinyemi © Oxford University Press. *Just not their day: Mrs Moira Poor* article reproduced by permission of the Big Issue. Extracts adapted from *Man of the Month* by Deborah Holder reproduced from Marie Claire magazine by permission © Robert Harding Syndication. Adapted from *The Throw-away Society* taken from Dossier: The Green World reproduced by permission of International Book Distributors Ltd. Extracts: *The Original Levi Store* and *Zabar's* reproduced by permission © Time Out New York Guide. *A day in the life of Arantxa Sanchez-Vicario* adapted from an article by Nigel Bowden from The Sunday Times Magazine 20 June 1993 with permission © Times Newspapers Limited, 1993. *Heart of Gold* printed courtesy of BBC Television. Extracts adapted from *The dead budgie* from Urban Myths by Phil Healey and Rick Glanvill published by Virgin Books by permission. Extracts adapted from *Take me home,* The Book of Heroic Failures © Stephen Pile, 1979 reproduced by permission of the author c/o Rogers, Coleridge & White Ltd., 20 Powis Mews, London W11 1JN. Extracts taken from *Message in a bottle* in The Daily Mail by permission © Daily Mail / Solo Syndications. Extract *Cyrano de Bergerac* taken from Elliot's Guide to Films on Video published by Boxtree March 1993. Adapted from article *Beryl keeps hers under the bed* by Fiona Hunter, Good Housekeeping Magazine reproduced by permission from Good Housekeeping Magazine / @ National Magazine Company. Extract reproduced from *Death by Chocolate* by Helge Rubenstein, The Chocolate Book published by Penguin. Extracts adapted from *10 Lincoln / Kennedy Coincidences* taken from The People's Almanack Presents The Book of Lists 3, by Amy Wallace, David Wallechinsky, Irving Wallace published by Bantam Books USA / Canada with permission. Extract adapted from *Mabel* taken from Collected Short Stories by W. Somerset Maugham, published by Heinemann, reproduced by permission from Reed Books and A. P. Watt on behalf of The Royal Literary Fund.

Every breath you take written and composed by Gordon M Sumner © 1983, used by permission Magnetic Publishing Limited. *You don't have to say you love me* music by Pino Donaggio and words by Vito Pallavicini, sub-authors Simon Napier-Bell and Vicki Wickham © 1965, Edizioni Musicali Accordo, USA, reproduced by permission of B Feldman and Co Ltd / EMI United Partnership Ltd, London WC2H 0EA. *Love me tender* words and music by Elvis Presley and Vera Matson © Elvis Presley Music, USA Carlin Music Corporation, Iron Bridge House, 3 Bridge Approach, London NW1, used by permission of Music Sales Limited, all rights reserved, international copyright secured. *Don't you want me* (EMI – 66.6% ownership)

words and music by Philip Oakley, Adrian Wright and Jo Callis © 1981, reproduced by permission of EMI Virgin Music Ltd, London WC2H 0EA; (IMP – 33.34% ownership) © 1981 Warner / Chappell Music Ltd, London W1Y 3FA, reproduced by permission of International Music Publications Ltd. *Another day in Paradise* © 1989 Philip Collins Ltd / Hit & Run Music (Publishing) Ltd, international copyright secured, all rights reserved, used by permission. *I want to break free* words and music by John Deacon © 1984, reproduced by permission of Queen Music Ltd / EMI Music Publishing Ltd, London WC2H 0EA. *Message in a bottle* written and composed by Gordon M Sumner © 1979, used by permission Magnetic Publishing Ltd. *Imagine* words and music by John Lennon Copyright 1971 Lenono Music Ltd, all rights administered by BMG Music Publishing Ltd, used by permission, all rights reserved. *Nothing compares to you* © 1986 Controversy Music, Warner / Chappell Music Ltd, London W1Y 3FA, reproduced by permission of International Music Publications Ltd.

Although every effort has been made to trace and contact copyright holders before publication, this has not been possible in these cases: extract about Fogg's Hotel taken from Sovereign Scanscape; *Bath time; Who's bin done,* Rolling Stone Magazine. We apologize for any apparent infringement of copyright, and if notified, the publisher will be pleased to rectify any errors or omissions at the earliest opportunity.

Illustrations by: Rowan Barnes Murphy, Rupert Besley, Mark Edwards, Neil Gower, Paul Hess, Ed McLachlan, Belle Mellor, Mark Oldroyd, Anne Stanley, Gill Tyler, Bob Wilson.

Location photography by: Julie Fisher; p.83 by Susie Barker / Harley Evans.

Studio photography by: Mark Mason.

The publishers would like to thank the following for permission to reproduce photographs or logos: Allsport / Clive Brunskill, Mike Powell, Stephen Munday; Antony Blake Photo Library / Milk Marque; Assignments Photographers; Catherine Blackie; Alex Bornat; BBC Photographic Library; Bridgeman Art Library; British Airways / Wace Creative Imaging; Paul Burgess; Camera Press / Brian McCreeth, BG Silberstein, Gavin Smith, Strenbreth; Christies Images; Collections / Brian Shuel; Colorsport; EMI (courtesy Kobal); Foggs Hotel, Stockholm, Sweden (p. 46); Format Partners / Pamela Alassmann, Brenda Prince; Geoff Franklin; The Ronald Grant Archive; Hammer / United Artists (courtesy Kobal); Greenpeace; Robert Harding Picture Library / Robert Francis, Simon Harris, Steve Myerson, Walter Rawlings; Historic Royal Palaces; Hulton Getty; Hutchison Library / Crispin Hughes; IBM; Image Bank / David De Lossy, Brett Froome, Marc Romanelli, Martin Taolienn; LucasfilmLtd / Paramount (courtesy Kobal); Médecins sans Frontières; National Portrait Gallery; NHPA / John B Free, Stephen Krasemann; Paramount (courtesy Kobal); Popperfoto; Rex Features / Alain Pele, Sipa; Paul Seligson; Quadrant / Auto Express; Quadrant / Phil Talbot; Scope Features; Frank Spooner / A Bercy, Husain, Benainous Soorcelletti; Still Pictures; Still Moving Picture Company / Doug Corrance, Derek Laird, Rondeau, Paul Tomkins; Sygma / Delafosse, Gianni Giansanti, Goldberg, P Habans, Maureen Lambray, Ross Marino, F Meylan, Gino Sprio; UNICEF; Warner Brothers (courtesy Kobal); Claire Oliver Williams; Woodmansterne; Zefa Picture Library; Zoetrope / Columbia Tri-Star (courtesy Kobal). The Red Cross emblem is a symbol of protection during armed conflicts and its use is restricted by law – the emblem is reproduced on p.93 with kind permission of the British Red Cross. The photograph on p.108 of The Princes Edward and Richard in the Tower is by Sir John Everett Millais (1829–96) Royal Holloway & Bedford College, Surrey / Bridgeman Art Library.

Thanks to Paul Seligson and Carmen Dolz for the English Sounds Chart, p.142.